tear here

Motivational Tips
25 Great Ways to Motivate People

1. Listen!

2. Be sincere.

3. Use incentives.

4. Be a coach.

5. Promote camaraderie.

6. Encourage ideas and discussion.

7. Set clear goals.

8. Get rid of routines.

9. Develop a purpose.

10. Discipline fairly.

11. Be a mentor.

12. Be a confidante.

13. Keep secrets.

14. Recognize achievements.

15. Award achievements.

16. Create security.

17. Inspire!

18. Offer a challenge.

19. Make work fun.

20. Encourage!

21. Recognize what's important to your team.

22. Be friendly.

23. Invest people in the cause.

24. Be optimistic.

25. Create satisfaction.

alpha
books

Motivational Traps
25 Sure-Fire Motivation Busters

1. Assume you have control.
2. Take control without earning it.
3. Be pessimistic.
4. Hoard incentives.
5. Complain loudly.
6. Complain often.
7. Stifle creativity.
8. Encourage the status quo.
9. Discourage camaraderie.
10. Never deviate from routines.
11. Don't set goals.
12. Ignore the big picture.
13. Tell secrets.
14. Don't take time to listen.
15. Be uninterested.
16. Be insincere.
17. Discipline unfairly.
18. Never discipline.
19. Take your team for granted.
20. Pass the buck.
21. Ignore the wishes of your team.
22. Don't communicate.
23. Assume you're right— all the time.
24. Discourage high achievers.
25. Create busy work.

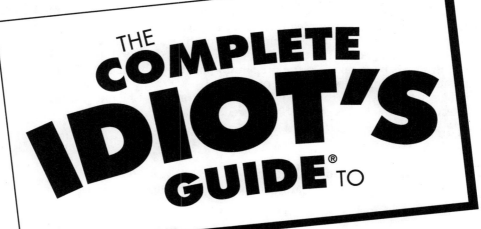

THE COMPLETE IDIOT'S GUIDE® TO

Motivating People

by Michael Ramundo
with Susan Shelly

alpha
books

Macmillan USA, Inc.
201 West 103rd Street
Indianapolis, IN 46290

A Pearson Education Company

International Standard Book Number: 0-02-863200-1
Library of Congress Catalog Card Number: Available upon request.

02 01 00   8 7 6 5 4 3 2 1

Interpretation of the printing code: The rightmost number of the first series of numbers is the year of the book's printing; the rightmost number of the second series of numbers is the number of the book's printing. For example, a printing code of 00-1 shows that the first printing occurred in 2000.

Printed in the United States of America

Note: This publication contains the opinions and ideas of its author. It is intended to provide helpful and informative material on the subject matter covered. It is sold with the understanding that the author and publisher are not engaged in rendering professional services in the book. If the reader requires personal assistance or advice, a competent professional should be consulted.

Contents at a Glance

Appendixes

Contents

Appendixes

Foreword

Anyone in a position of leadership must have the ability to motivate and inspire.

From the president of the United States to the manager of the neighborhood McDonald's, people interested in leading others must have the ability to inspire them to follow.

Fifty years of international leadership experience gives me broad awareness of the relationship between leadership and motivation. Global experience has taught me that the ability to motivate is as vital for the first-grade teacher in a rural school as it is for the supervisor in a downtown office building or the all-powerful world leader.

Does your goal require a team? Motivation is that requisite glue that enables your team to do what needs to be done. It is the fuel that incites your team to strive to the highest possible level of performance. Your ability to motivate is at the heart of your success.

I've observed that far too many people never address, or even consider, the issue of motivation, thinking that people only work for money, or that the goal is so important and well-defined that the team is intrinsically motivated. Or, they are task oriented and assume the whole issue of motivation is simply a personal matter.

In fact, though, everyone leading others needs the ability to motivate. Parents need to motivate their children. Teachers must motivate and inspire their students. Coaches must motivate the team to win. The General must inspire the troops. The conductor must mold the musicians into a resounding symphony and, yes, the shop floor foreman must motivate his or her assembly line workers to perform at peak levels and stand proud of the products they produce.

During my 25-year international career with Milacron, I continually observed how the ability, or lack of ability, to motivate others was a key factor in the effectiveness and success of our managers. Those managers who knew how to motivate met their goals, produced the profits, and moved through the ranks. The successful leaders were always those buoyed by the successes of the workers they had inspired. Those who couldn't motivate others stayed behind.

This book will serve as your valuable resource and is helpful to anyone leading others. Written in a simple, straightforward and user-friendly manner, it's suitable for any team leader. The many real-life stories provide you with practical examples and advice on how to, or how not to, handle situations that impact the motivation of your team. You'll benefit from the experiences of others, and learn from their mistakes.

When you finish reading this book, you'll know what it means to motivate others, and the best methods for doing so. You'll understand on a very practical level the best ways to relate to the members of your team, and to make them want to do what's best—for them, your organization, and, ultimately, for you.

—Donald G. Shively

Donald G. Shively is currently consulting for various international corporations, the World Bank, and the United Nations. He retired from Milacron, a billion-dollar capital equipment manufacturer, in 1986 as Executive Vice President, Operations.

Introduction

Anyone who is a leader, or hopes to be a leader, must be able to motivate people to do what he or she wants them to do. Leadership and the ability to motivate others are so intricately entwined that it's nearly impossible to have one without the other.

There are many different approaches to motivation, and a lot of people make their livings as "motivational" speakers, or by designing and presenting workshops and seminars dealing with the topic. Every one of these folks may tell you that he or she knows the secret of motivation, and is willing to pass it along to you if you sign up for his or her talk or seminar.

When it comes right down to it, however, you don't need a two-day seminar on how to motivate the members of your team, because your team members already are motivated. Everybody who gets up in the morning and gets to work on time is motivated to some degree. People have always been motivated to do more and live better. It's that motivation that's moved us from the cave to the condo, and from the ox and cart to the automobile. It's enabled us to evolve into the society that we are today.

Your job, as a leader, is to channel the motivation that your team members already possess, so that it enhances the greater good of the team. You need to get your people motivated to do what you want them to do, and when you want them to do it.

If you can do that, your role as a leader will be clearly defined, and you and your team will be headed for great things. In this book, you'll get lots of ideas and tips that can help you motivate your team to do what you want them to do. So, look over the information carefully, and consider the practical advice that it contains.

There's no magic formula for motivating people to do what you want to. Motivating your team requires a level of trust between you and your team members, a desire to be a good and effective leader, and a fair amount of common sense. Let's get started.

What You'll Find in This Book

The Complete Idiot's Guide to Motivating People is divided into five parts.

Part 1, "Getting It in Gear," takes a close look at this thing called motivation. It tells why motivation is so important, and why, as a leader, you need to be able to motivate other people.

It examines the sources of motivation and how you can make the members of your team happy that they work for you and within your organization.

Once you've got the basics down, you'll be ready to move on to **Part 2, "Where, Why, What, Who, and When: The Biggest Motivators."** This section deals with each of these motivators and tells you why each one is so significant.

Just in case you think that these big motivators are the only ones, however, there's **Part 3, "The Other Motivators,"** to set you straight.

This part of the book deals with the up-close and personal stuff, like problems your workers might be experiencing and how to discipline fairly when it's necessary. You'll learn the importance of being sincere and how to build security among your team.

Now that you're a sensitive and sincere leader, you're ready to move to **Part 4, "Your Role in Motivation."** This section deals with the role of a leader and how important it is to have the proper motivational skills and knowledge.

You'll find out what kinds of things are really important to your workers, and which things are guaranteed to be turn-offs.

Part 5, "Putting It All into Motion," tells you how to keep motivation running high once you've got it pretty well in place. It also deals with motivating high performers (which every leader wants) and problem employees (which every leader sooner or later gets).

Because you'll be practically a motivation expert by now, this section also deals with some challenges such as layoffs, plant closings, and salary cuts. If you know how to do it, you can keep your team motivated, even in the worst of times.

When you finish this book, you'll have an overview of how to motivate people and how to keep your team happy and working toward its goals. You'll understand the importance of being an effective leader and how leadership and the ability to motivate are so closely interwoven. In short, you'll be a person who knows how to motivate people.

Extras

In addition to the information contained within the chapters, you'll find lots of bits and pieces of wisdom and information throughout this book.

These snippets, known as sidebars, make the book not only more readable, but more personal and relevant, as well. Here's what to look for:

Defining Moments

These are the author's take on different concepts, terms, and ideas, as they apply to motivating a team.

Backfire

These are warnings, aimed at preventing you from making big mistakes that could demotivate your team.

Rally the Troops

These are tips or bits of upbeat information to help you be able to better motivate your team.

Here's How It Works

These little-known pieces of information are presented for your entertainment and use.

Acknowledgements

Without Bert Holtje and Susan Shelly, this book would never have been born.

A very special thank you to Gary Krebs, Al McDermid, and the many other good folks on the development team at Macmillan.

Another special thank you to Donald G. Shively who writes the forward to this, my third book. Donald, I've been lucky to have you as a great mentor throughout my career. Thank you for all the advice and helping me see through all the fog that tough career choices create for all of us.

To Beverly Thomas, my lover, wife, best friend, and partner. You're always there for enjoyment of the uptimes, and close by with a helping hand during the downtimes. Every day I'm more happy I married you.

To my lovely Tara and Jonathan. I do this work to make tomorrow better for both of you. You and all others of the future are the inspiration that motivates me, and others like me, to act. Make this imperfect world a better place for those who follow you. I am aware of only a few of my far-too-numerous imperfections, and my brain provides me only scanty skill for learning. Still, though, I will try ever harder to be the best father I can be. I love you both. Go forward with tranquility.

Trademarks

All terms mentioned in this book that are known to be or are suspected of being trademarks or service marks have been appropriately capitalized. Alpha Books and Macmillan USA, Inc. cannot attest to the accuracy of this information. Use of a term in this book should not be regarded as affecting the validity of any trademark or service mark.

Part 1
Getting It in Gear

To be a good motivator, you've got to understand where motivation comes from and what, exactly, it is.

In Part 1, we start at the very beginning. You'll learn why it's important to be able to motivate others, especially the members of your team. Nearly everybody has reason to motivate someone else—whether it's an employee, a spouse, a child, or a friend.

You'll learn the sources of motivation, and how you can cultivate it among your workers. And, importantly, you'll also learn how to avoid and overcome obstacles in the workplace that, if not dealt with properly, might demotivate your team.

So, get ready to begin learning the fine art of motivation, and being more successful as a leader.

Chapter 1

Who Needs This Motivation Stuff, Anyway?

In This Chapter

➤ Everyone needs to be able to motivate

➤ Motivation makes the world go 'round, and sets people apart from other living things

➤ Motivation is what persuades someone to do what you want him to do

➤ Good leaders anticipate conflict and take steps to avoid it

➤ Many bosses would benefit from better coaching skills

➤ The need for motivation increases as workers acquire more choices

---

Lots of people think that understanding the art of motivation is important only if you're a big-shot executive or someone in charge of an operation that requires great efficiency and speed.

Most of us, they feel, don't need to be bothered learning about how motivation works, and the many ways it affects our jobs, our families, and our lives.

In reality, motivation is a topic that everybody should be concerned about. If you answer yes to any of the questions below, then you need to know and understand how motivation works, and how to inspire it in others.

➤ Do you ever try to get your kid to clean his room?

➤ Do you ever need to get some help from your neighbor?

➤ Do you need to find and organize a team of people who are willing to help with a community project?

➤ Have you ever needed somebody in the shipping department to help you locate an order that's been lost?

➤ Would you like the people who answer to you to improve the quality of their work?

➤ Would you like to talk your spouse into joining you for a vacation at your favorite resort?

If you nodded your head to any of these, it means you're leading a cause and you're trying to get others to follow.

As a leader, you'll need to understand all about motivation and how it works. Why? Because when you know how motivation works, you'll be able to get people to motivate themselves to do what you want them to do.

Rally the Troops

Humans are always motivated to do something. The question is: Are they motivated to do what you want them to do?

Motivation—An Eternal Engine

Motivation is our engine. It's the reason that our houses are warm in winter and cool in summer. It's the reason our highways are paved and our drinking water is clean. It's the reason we change the status quo, and it drives us to do what we do.

Motivation is one of the things that sets us apart from all those other creatures out there.

Consider Gimli, my wife's five-pound-furry thing that she calls a dog. Gimli hangs on Beverly's arm at every opportunity, day and night. If Gimli's hungry, he jumps around and follows Beverly until he's been fed. Once that need has been met, the dog is content to once again settle onto Beverly's arm. When Bev's had enough, Gimli will reluctantly head for his bed. The dog's motivations are limited. He cares only to seek food (chocolate, or any other junk food) and the comfort of Bev's arm. Gimli's world is very small, and that's the only world he will ever perceive.

On the other hand, consider Vivian. Vivian, or Vivs, as she's called, is the bouncy two-year-old who lives across the street. Vivs is a joy to have around, especially because I get to enjoy all the fun playtime, then toss her back to her mom when she gets cranky—or needs to have her diaper changed.

Vivs is a lot different than that five-pound furry thing my wife calls a dog. Vivs, like Gimli, loves food, and I keep her interested in me by giving her anything she will eat. When she's eaten as much as her little stomach can hold, I have to get a bit more creative in order to keep her with me. Usually, some stories, toys, silly whispers, and tussling will keep her on the couch with me. When I run out of ideas, or energy, and want to sit quietly for a little while, Vivs quickly loses interest.

When that happens, she's down off my lap, scurrying about and looking for something to do. She'll search and explore, crawling under a table to see what's there, or climbing onto the sofa to look at a painting on the wall. She's constantly moving—searching, exploring, and learning. Vivs is extremely motivated to learn about the world and to stimulate herself.

Obviously, there's a big difference between Gimli and Vivs. Gimli is content to eat a bowl of his favorite dog food, then stretch out for a good, long nap. When he wakes up, he starts the same routine again.

Defining Moments

Motivation is an eternal engine. Perception and imagination are its fuel.

You, me, and Vivs, on the other hand, are always motivated to do things. We have an innate desire to change things. We move things, study them, enjoy them, smash them, build them back up, and so on. There's no way that we—or most of us, anyway—are content to sit by passively, waiting only to eat and go back to sleep. We've got to keep moving and doing because we're motivated to. Our eternal engines never shut down.

What fuels these eternal engines? Perception and imagination. The question we have to look at, then, is not whether or not people are motivated. We've already answered that question. The question at hand is whether or not people are motivated to do what we want them to do and when we want them to do it.

When Are You Motivating?

You might not realize it, but you're motivating people all the time. Take a look at a few examples of situations in which you'd be motivating someone:

➤ Anytime you're persuading, selling, convincing, or cajoling

➤ Anytime you're trying to get somebody focused on a goal

➤ When you're trying to get an employee to fill an order correctly

➤ When you're convincing your kid to take out the trash or the painter to touch up the ceiling

Rally the Troops

We use our ability to communicate to get others to create what we think should be created. We're all pushing and shoving as we all mold the world into what we believe it should be.

➤ When you're convincing your significant other to take you to the movies

➤ When you're trying to get your kid to leave you alone so you can finish the last few pages of that great book

Anytime you work to persuade others to do something, you're trying to motivate. We all do it. We have wants, needs, beliefs, ideas, and goals to accomplish. Unlike animals, we have the ability to perceive that things can be different and the desire to make them different.

In order to do that, we need help from others. In order to get that help, we try to convince people to help us create what we think should be created, or change things in other ways. We try to motivate them.

Competing for Attention, Time, and Energy

So, now we've got a whole lot of people who are all motivated and trying to motivate others. If you think about that for a minute, it gets a little scary, doesn't it? Doesn't it bring to mind visions of a bunch of motivated, intense people, all scurrying around, trying to convince others to become motivated in order to help them achieve their goals?

Rally the Troops

People naturally do what they want to do, and not necessarily what we want them to do. We must compete for the attention, time, and energy we need from others.

A high degree of motivation among many people can be a problem because we're not all motivated to do the same things at the same time. We must constantly compete with everyone around us for attention, time, and energy that we need from others.

The Story of Bill, Joe, and the Misplaced Order

Bill, who works over in shipping, is at work one Saturday, going through his normal half-day routine. He's picking orders, boxing them up, labeling them, and stacking the boxes on shipping pallets, all the while looking forward to the end of his shift.

Everything is moving along just fine. Bill likes the organized routine of his job, and he's counting down the last hour before noon, when he can get home to his family and that cookout they've been planning. It's a great spring day, and he's thinking they might even catch a baseball game.

Meanwhile, Joe is over at his desk in the sales department, spending a few hours cleaning up some paperwork that hadn't gotten done during the week. The phone rings, and even though Joe has a feeling he shouldn't—he answers it. Ms. VIP Customer is calling.

Ms. VIP needs her big shipment. It was supposed to get to her yesterday, but didn't. She's about beside herself because her big sale starts tomorrow, and what's she supposed to sell? If she doesn't get that shipment, it will be a terrible blow to her business, and she certainly won't be very anxious to deal with this company again.

As Joe listens to her drone on, he realizes that the world has suddenly changed. His laid-back Saturday morning is no longer laid-back. It's turned into a fire-fighting day.

Rats! Joe heads over to shipping, where he sees Bill. By now, Bill is very close to the end of his shift. Joe tells him about the problem, and says he'll need a hand finding the misplaced order. As you might imagine, Bill's response is less enthusiastic than Joe would have liked.

Backfire

Be careful whenever you interrupt what someone is doing or thinking. Always begin by acknowledging that you're interrupting, and apologize for doing so. Say something like, "Gee, I'm sorry to bother you, but…"

All Joe has to do is look at Bill's face to know he's irritated with Joe, the company, Ms. VIP Customer, and the world in general. Bill starts, very slowly and reluctantly, searching for Ms. VIP's misplaced order.

By this time, Joe is getting a little annoyed. He can't believe Bill's lousy attitude! Doesn't Bill even care about helping an important customer? Obviously, Bill has no clue how the system works around here, or that it's the customer from whom all paychecks come. Man, what kind of idiots are they hiring in shipping nowadays?

In Bill's Defense

Let's be fair. Does Bill really have a lousy attitude, or is he just frustrated because a new and important force is now conflicting with his plans and competing for his time, attention, and energy?

Bill had his day all planned. He had defined important goals, and his perception was focused elsewhere. He was thinking about his family, his cookout, and the baseball game.

It's not that Bill is lazy or a bad employee. It's just that he was motivated to finish his work and get on with his other goals for that day.

Joe's request changed Bill's plans, big time. He had to readjust his thinking and accept a completely different reality. Bill's attention was invested in his day and his family, and now Joe's telling him that he needs it. He's resentful toward Joe because Joe's the one who Bill sees as disrupting his plans. Joe is asking Bill to give the task of finding the misplaced order the energy Bill had designated for other things. Joe has disrupted Bill, and it's causing conflict.

Defining Moments

Conflict is an emotional disturbance that results from a clash of opposing goals, or from an inability to reconcile those goals. If I want to move toward a goal and you want me to move toward a different goal, I am likely to experience conflict and anxiety. I might become frustrated or even angry over the conflict. Good leaders avoid conflict, are sensitive to others, and work around situations where conflict is possible.

Most people's time, attention, and energy are always occupied and focused toward something. Asking someone to move in a different direction always carries the potential for conflict.

Gaining Control

Competent leaders don't wait until conflict occurs to try to manage it. They are constantly alert to potential conflict and maneuver around it before it occurs. They do this by listening to people's needs, explaining things, apologizing for being disruptive, and adjusting the incentives when necessary. In short, they motivate. They're in control of the situation.

Don't Assume You Already Have Control

Leadership means being proactive. It means taking the time to gain positive control so others can follow. Effective leaders don't assume they have control, and they don't simply seize control when it becomes necessary.

Good leaders earn the right to control, and they use control only when it's necessary. They evaluate the environment, watch the flow, and study the current motivators. By doing these things, they earn the right to lead.

Consider our sales friend, Joe. Joe made an assumption that the attitudes of all employees are similar to his. He assumed that everyone would instantly recognize the importance of Ms. VIP Customer and would be happy to work late on a Saturday to find her order.

Rally the Troops

Good leaders do more than just manage conflict well. Good leaders are proactive, and take time to win the right to control. They use their control to steer around conflict—before it occurs.

While many employees probably do have the kind of attitude that Joe assumes, not all do. Joe asked Bill for some important help in order to achieve a worthwhile goal. But by the way he asked, he seized control.

Joe didn't earn the right to control; he simply took the control. In doing so, he created ill will, anxiety, and a communication barrier between himself and Bill.

Control Is Something That Has to Be Earned

When Joe came into the shipping department and told Bill he needed help, Bill blamed Joe for the disruption to his plans. It was not Ms. VIP Customer who threw the monkey wrench into Bill's well-oiled plans for his day. It was Joe. Bill's reaction to the situation might have been completely different if he'd taken Ms. VIP's call, rather than Joe.

Joe could have done much better with Bill if he had understood how to assess the situation and taken time to choose the right words when asking Bill for help. He took control, all right, but Bill resented it because Joe hadn't earned the right to take control.

Backfire

Watch your words carefully. A few words probably are not enough to destroy or build a relationship. But words build upon each other and help us form attitudes, both good and bad. Once uttered, whatever we say is something we'll have to deal with in the future. Good words strengthen a future relationship, while bad words serve to weaken it.

The need to proactively control situations such as the one between Joe and Bill is at the heart of all this motivation stuff, and the reason for this book. It's really rather easy, as long as you're willing to earn the right to control instead of simply seizing it.

You begin to earn control when you take time to think before you act, listen to the people around you, and always remember that motivation is a process to follow and not simply a single act.

You Can't Own Your Employees

Being the boss doesn't mean that you own your employees. We have been fighting against slavery for centuries. Nobody owns anybody, even if you're paying them for their time.

Many years ago, when I was younger and far more naive, I was planning a presentation about motivation for a group of senior-level executives. There were somewhere between 100 and 150 of these executive types in the audience. Some older, and seemingly wiser, educators had advised me to challenge the thinking of these executives with some provocative statements concerning the roles of bosses and workers. "Go for the jugular," they told me. "Shake things up, a little," they said.

Heeding their advice, I opened with a line that was something like this, "Ladies and gentlemen, if customer satisfaction is important to your future profitability, then the future of your organization is in the hands of your front-line customer service people."

The executives were immediately threatened and defensive, thinking I was recommending that they pass the reins of power to the customer service folks. Needless to say, the presentation went downhill from there. One executive even wrote me a letter

Rally the Troops

Being the boss means you are ultimately accountable and responsible. It does not mean you are ultimately in control. The right to control is something that must be earned.

saying in part: " …(Ramundo) is totally wrong, corporate America will never relinquish responsibility and control to the front line."

I learned my lesson from that episode, and have since redefined "provocative" for all senior-level presentations.

Still, way too many of the upper-level types I encounter in my workshops continue to wildly overestimate their power simply because of the titles they carry. They believe that being the boss means being in control.

Performance Isn't the Same as Motivation

Too often, managers overreach and, as a result, end up getting mediocre, or even poor, performance from the workers they supervise. These managers and supervisors are not discussing ideas or building teams. They're simply tossing out instructions and demanding that the troops fall into line.

Effectively, these supervisors are telling workers that they—not the workers—are ultimately responsible for the work. They insist that the work be done the way the supervisor wants it, and that workers are being paid to follow instructions and do what they're told to do.

Under this sort of management, the troops do fall into line and perform for their money. But that's all they'll do.

They perform and act out the job, but they're not motivated to perform and live the job. The difference between those two stances is immeasurable.

Rally the Troops

Motivated people want to do their jobs. Leadership is not telling others to work; it is causing others to want to work.

Unmotivated workers are like actors, who perform while the audience watches but drop their roles the second the curtain falls.

Motivated people, however, are not actors performing roles. They're living real life, and they're invested in the outcome. They're not doing a job just because they're being paid for it; they're doing a job because they want to do it. To motivated people, a job is an important part of their lives, and it spills over and inspires other parts of their lives. They live their jobs, just as they live other parts of their lives. Their jobs make motivated people whole.

Bosses Should Be More Like Coaches

Coaches, not bosses, inspire their teams to live their roles, rather than play their roles.

Coaches don't demand performance, they earn performance. They don't demand work from their teams, they work with their teams. They don't observe games and correct their teams, they get right into the games with their teams.

Coaches don't allow their teams to fail, they fail along with them. Ultimately, coaches only can win when their teams win.

Leaders are coaches first. Coaches:

> ➤ Don't own, or try to own, their teams

> ➤ Understand that their teams ultimately control the games

> ➤ Are distant, listening and watching, but still very much in the game with their teams

> ➤ Don't ask the team to perform, but inspire the team's performance

> ➤ Position their players so that their strengths are maximized

> ➤ Draw as much as possible from their players

> ➤ Orchestrate the action

Defining Moments

To **orchestrate** means to arrange, or put something together. It means to organize something, or a group, so as to achieve a desired or effective result. The best orchestra conductor never needs to touch the instruments. They touch the hearts of their musicians.

Just a Job Isn't Enough

Our jobs give us money. The money we earn gives us food, shelter, and clothing.

Forty or 50 generations ago, that was good enough. Workers didn't ask for much more than to be given the means to stay alive for another day.

That system resulted in serfs and the feudal servitude systems of the time. One family served as the economic means for an entire town. Everyone in the town worked for the family and, in exchange, were allowed to grow food and build shelters on the family's land.

We've Moved Beyond Basic Needs

That system may have worked once, but not any more. Our economy is more advanced and has now gone global. Due primarily to our emerging capacity to communicate globally, the world economy is expected to double by about 2025 from its 2000 level.

World population by 2050 is expected to level off at around ten billion, twice its 2000 level.

These expectations hold the promise of a higher standard of living for everyone. An increased standard of living promises more choices for the people it affects. It promises to offer them more than their most basic needs.

Conditions Are Predicted to Keep Getting Better

In about 1950, nearly 60 percent of the world's population lived below absolute poverty. That deplorable state of affairs has improved, although there's still a lot of room for improvement. At year 2000, the percentage of global population living below absolute poverty is down to 30 percent. While still not great, conditions have improved.

These improved conditions, in the forms of less starvation and better education, mean that the number of choices available is increasing for many people.

As more people have access to more choices, greater leadership skills will be required in order to accomplish objectives, and motivation will become more important than ever.

As a leader, you've got tough competition when it comes to attracting and keeping the best people on your team. You're competing with other companies, other managers within your own company, and with other forces in society.

Here's How It Works

Every group of managers that I talk with says it's getting harder and harder to find bright, talented workers, because the demand for them is so high. When you do find one, you'd better be able to motivate him or her to want to be part of your team.

Offer an Experience, Not Just a Job

If you offer someone a job, he's likely to perform that job for as long as it's the best job he can get. The job you offer, however, is in competition with all the other jobs for which that employee might be qualified. When a better job comes along, you can kiss that employee goodbye.

If you offer an experience, however, that includes much more than a job, you'll motivate and challenge your employees. They'll reach for new heights in an effort to be part of the experience. An example of a company that provides a work experience, rather than just jobs, is Microsoft.

Microsoft is known as a fairly low-paying company, although full-timers do get significant benefits, including stock options. This helps create a highly motivated team. Microsoft fell behind on the first wave of the Internet explosion largely because the idea of the Internet didn't get Chairman Bill Gates all that excited.

When Gates realized his mistake, and started pushing the Internet in every aspect of Microsoft's broad product development effort, his employees dug into the challenge. They had good reason to spend all night at their desks rewriting millions of lines of code. Many stock analysts had moved the stock from a recommended "buy" to a recommended "hold." Gates and all his followers were positioned to lose real money. Bill Gates didn't turn things around for Microsoft, the motivated employees who spent their nights working on Microsoft's Internet products did.

As the leader, Gates was smart enough to build an environment in which employees were motivated to rise to new challenges. He has successfully created the Microsoft experience, not just jobs.

How This Book Will Help You

As you read this book, you'll learn how to create and build an experience for people who work for you. Chapter by chapter, step by step, you'll learn the entire, simple process of creating motivation. When you finish, you'll know how to create an inspired, motivated team of workers.

Getting people to do what you want them to, when you want them to do it, might currently seem impossible to you. You may even feel a little discouraged, and be wondering why you bothered to buy this book.

Take heart. This book will provide the basic tools that you'll need to be able to motivate folks to do your bidding. Sure, it will take some practice, but once you catch on, you won't have any problems.

This book will teach you about providing incentives, and which ones work the best. You'll learn how environment plays a big role in motivation, and how the five "W" questions—who, what, when, where, and why—lie at the heart of the issue.

You'll learn how to get employees to trust you, and how to be a good and sympathetic listener.

Rally the Troops

The most important thing to remember is that everyone is motivated to act all the time. When we talk about motivation in this book, what we're really talking about is getting others to do what you want done at a particular time.

A sound management style goes a long way in creating motivation. These are just a few of the many topics that will be covered in the five sections of this book. So, settle in, and get motivated to learn how to motivate. It's what this book is all about.

The Least You Need to Know

➤ Anyone who ever tries to get someone to help him, or to do something for him, needs to know how to motivate other people.

➤ While animals are contented with the most basic status quo, humans are motivated to do whatever they can to keep things moving and changing.

➤ Motivation is the force that causes a person to do what you want him to, and when you want him to do it.

➤ Effective leaders don't wait for conflict to occur and then use heavy-handed techniques to quell it. They take steps to avoid conflict.

➤ Being a boss or supervisor doesn't mean you're in control of your workers. Being in control has nothing to do with a title.

➤ Managers are competing with more and more forces for employees, and must learn to motivate their employees by offering more than a job in order to keep them.

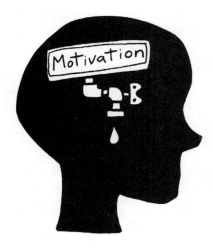

Chapter 2

Sources of Motivation

In This Chapter

➤ Thinking about what makes an environment motivating

➤ Physical and psychological environments

➤ Connecting satisfaction and dissatisfaction

➤ Linking attitude and behavior

➤ Encouraging workers to be their best

➤ Different types of power

In the first chapter, we talked about motivation as an engine that keeps us running and allows us to accomplish what we set out to do. We called it an eternal engine because it never stops.

In order for us to keep active and doing things, we must have a constant supply of motivation. Without it, we wouldn't get out of bed in the morning, much less get to work and be able to motivate others, as well. Our motivation is like a spring. It flows constantly, providing a continuous source of energy and power.

In this chapter, we're going to talk about what fuels the eternal engine that is motivation. What keeps our engines running? Why is it that we feel motivated to get up in the morning, get through the day successfully, and get back in bed at night?

We'll look at how we can increase our sources of motivation and make ourselves more powerful and effective. And we'll see how our attitudes affect our environments, and how our environments affect our attitudes, too.

So, let's get started and take a look at how and where our motivation originates.

The Internal Engine

Just as motivation is an eternal engine, it's also an internal engine. We do what we want to do—that's the bottom line.

You can't will things to happen within your company and expect to sit back and watch them unfold. That's not a realistic expectation.

Neither can you communicate with a few at the top and expect that things will work effectively throughout the organization. Messages need to be repeated over and over to everyone, and the environment you create should be one that encourages people to interact with each other, to listen and exchange ideas and concerns.

The best leaders understand how to create an environment that encourages motivation. Once the right environment is established, these leaders rarely have to tell people what to do.

Here's How It Works

Anyone who's ever been a manager surely can relate to how nice it would be to have workers who are motivated to do what they need to and who foster motivation in each other through effective communication. Creating an environment that encourages communication and motivation is worth the effort a hundred times over because it makes your job, and your life, so much easier.

Rather, these effective leaders create environments where people are comfortable, and happy to be. They're motivated to take care of the environment, and they'll work together to do so.

When this happens, you've got a great situation because people are working together as a team for the good of the organization. Isn't that what every leader hopes for?

Defining the Environment

To achieve an environment that encourages motivation, you've got to pay attention to it. You've got to make sure that people are comfortable within it.

Some years ago, I worked with Gary—a man in a hurry.

Gary spent most of his day running around, oblivious to those around him. I remember watching him one day and being amazed at how oblivious he was to the environment he shared with other people in the office.

Backfire

Motivation decreases with discouragement. If something within an environment is causing people to be discouraged, their motivation will suffer.

Marilyn, the office secretary, was sitting behind her desk one day, but turned to the side because she was typing (on a typewriter—I told you this was a while ago!). She wasn't working with anything on her desk at the time, but it was clear that the desk belonged to her and was her personal workspace.

As is common, Marilyn kept some office supplies on the top of her desk. You know, stuff like staplers, tape, paper clips, and so forth. These were kept toward the front edge of the desk, so that anybody walking by could borrow them when necessary.

Well, along comes Gary, storming around the office the way he always did. He grabbed Marilyn's stapler, stapled some papers together, and set the stapler down in the center of her desk.

Gary never said a word to Marilyn. He didn't ask if he could use the stapler, didn't thank her, didn't even give her a nod. He simply grabbed the stapler from its home position, dropped it back onto the center of the desk, and rushed off.

Marilyn's spontaneous reaction was one of irritation. She stopped typing, picked up the stapler, and slammed it down back where it had been on her desk. She then resumed typing.

Gary, on the other hand, didn't have a clue as to how he had impacted her environment. For that matter, Gary never noticed how he impacted anyone's environment. He never understood how disruptive he was, or how he affected the other people in the office. He never worked as part of a team. He was only motivated to look after himself and his needs.

Eventually, the boss was able to get rid of Gary, and the environment improved because of it.

Everything within an environment must be considered. Think about the elements in your environment.

➤ Is it a desirable place to work?

➤ Is it safe?

➤ Is it clean?

➤ Is it well-lighted?

➤ Is it comfortable?

➤ Is the temperature about right?

➤ Is it "user-friendly"?

A user-friendly environment is physically comfortable for employees. It has computers and other office equipment that work (well, usually), and good chairs. Things that workers need are accessible.

Owning an Environment

A good environment encourages ownership. People should be encouraged to personalize their spaces. Take a look around your company sometime.

You'll see that motivated workers on the main shop floor will have personalized their workspaces, or toolboxes, or whatever. In the office, motivated people will have made their desks their own with pictures of their families, maybe a special bowl in which to keep paper clips, a vase with a few flowers, or something like that. You might even see some pictures of that record-breaking marlin caught during last year's fishing contest.

Effective leaders recognize the importance of these subtle personal touches. They encourage a family environment.

Backfire

Cliques within a workplace are common, but they're dangerous. A worker who feels left out and isolated won't be motivated to do her job, much less her best job. Keep an eye out for cliques and try to break them up early.

The Psychological Environment

Although the physical environment of a workplace is important, you also have to be concerned with the psychological environment. Be observant. Watch how people work together. Are they working as a team, or are there cliques?

Try to find methods of keeping people close to others. Assigning special projects so that people must work in team situations might do this.

Let's have a true-story look at how an effective leader can improve a bad situation by changing the psychological environment of an office.

Sue Jones was asked to take over the customer service operation at a company owned by one of my clients. It was a miserable department that had been poorly managed for years.

The department had about 35 people, but never the same ones. The entire workforce turned over every year.

Morale was terrible. People within the department really hated each other. Resources were short, and everyone was overworked.

There was never was enough time to train the endless flood of new people, and the workload was so incredible that Sue couldn't even call a staff meeting, let alone get ahead of the issues.

One day, Sue, who was an effective leader, had an inspired idea.

"Look," she said to all in her department who could hear and cared to listen, "this Thursday I am going to be here at 7:30 a.m., one half-hour before starting time. I can't shut down the phones, and we have to be back at it at 8 a.m. I can't force anyone to come in at 7:30, and I don't have any budget to pay for the half hour of overtime. Anyone who wants to come in early is welcome. I'll buy donuts. Those of us who show up will start looking for better ways to get things done."

Backfire

Any improvement, no matter how slight, is likely to help the troops become motivated. On the other hand, if you have the power and resources to make a major improvement, but you make only a small improvement, your efforts will be viewed as hypocrisy, and result in anger and resentment.

A few workers showed up on Thursday. A few more came the next week. And so it went. Within a year, Sue's half-hour Thursday morning meeting had evolved into one of the most important meetings in the company. She was attracting everyone in her department.

The Thursday morning meeting also attracted the attention of the company president and that of all key managers. Everybody started working together to reverse the slide and resolve the issues that the customer service department was uncovering.

Sue had changed the environment. She had come up with something positive, and her workers responded.

When Sue first organized the meetings, she didn't have the means to make them very attractive to employees. All she could offer were donuts and a chance to improve a bad situation. But the workers responded to that opportunity, and the meetings became desirable, simply for that reason.

It's important to remember that you don't need to create a perfect environment in order to help people motivate themselves. You only need to create a better environment. People generally are pretty tolerant and forgiving. If someone makes an effort to help, most people will respond favorably. Little things can go a long way when it comes to motivation.

Here's How It Works

Jack Welch, chairman of General Electric, is generally considered to be one of the great leaders of our time. He keeps informed, and uses every opportunity to make his presence known. Anyone may receive a handwritten note from Welch, from those who report directly to him on down to hourly workers. The notes have impact because they are intimate and spontaneous.

The psychological environment is a little more difficult to change than the physical one. You can't just look through a catalogue and order a better place. It takes some time and effort, but the results of a healthy psychological environment are well worth it.

Satisfaction vs. Dissatisfaction

The best environments are focused on keeping workers satisfied. You have to understand, though, that high satisfaction is not the reciprocal of dissatisfaction. An example will clarify this premise.

Let's say you have an employee named Joe. Joe believes that he's underpaid for the work he does. As a result, Joe is quite dissatisfied. His primary motivation will be to ask for more pay, or to look for another job if your company won't, or can't, pay him what he thinks he's worth.

A natural assumption to make is that if an underpaid employee is dissatisfied, then an employee who feels he's being paid competitively would be satisfied. This, however, is shaky reasoning. If Joe feels that he's paid competitively, he probably won't be dissatisfied. But he won't necessarily be satisfied, either.

Motivation guru Frederick Herzberg asserted some years ago that the things that make us satisfied with work and life are not the same as those things that make us dissatisfied. Hunger—or lack of food—makes us dissatisfied. The mere availability of food, however, does not satisfy us.

To increase our satisfaction, we eat our food in restaurants, where it's served by tuxedoed waiters. We enjoy good wine and enticing presentations. We need the whole environment to feel satisfied—not just the food. And we're willing to pay far more than the food is worth to achieve the satisfaction.

The satisfaction/dissatisfaction theory applies to all areas of life, including work.

John, Judy, and all your employees are going to be most satisfied, and therefore most motivated, when they are challenged with specific responsibilities. They want and need to be responsible members of the total family.

They want to be treated as responsible, contributing adults, involved with the direction in which your organization is moving. Your employees will have a sense of appreciation for jobs that are done well.

Consider Jane, who was asked to take over a department. The person who had been in the job had been shoved aside—demoted by upper management. Jane had about 40 people in her department. Morale was next to nothing. Turnover was high. No one trusted management to do anything, and Jane was considered part of management.

Rally the Troops

One sure way to rally the troops is to offer some sort of gain sharing. More than 2,000 major U.S. organizations offer gain sharing for all employees. Ford Motor Company offers profit sharing to its members of the United Auto Workers union. Delta has built gain-sharing systems for baggage handlers. Organizations such as Starbucks and Wal-Mart even have gain-sharing systems for first-level employees.

Jane sensed the feelings of the employees. She knew they had no confidence in her, or anyone else in management. At least it wasn't personal. The workers hated their environment, not Jane. They just hated what they perceived she stood for.

Over a six-month period Jane tried to get close to some of the employees. She tried to speak with them, develop relationships, and create a sense of team. She tried to send the message that she was a caring leader who could be trusted.

The employees, however, didn't respond to Jane's efforts. The poor leadership legacy had stung the troops badly, and they couldn't trust Jane or the company. Scars were deep.

Creating positive environments is hard work. Turning deep dissatisfaction into satisfaction always takes time.

Jane, however, was determined.

She made a deal with her employees. "Everyone needs to be heard, and be a part of the system," Jane announced during a department meeting. Her plan was to give each employee 15 minutes of her time, once a month.

During that 15 minutes, the employee could discuss anything he or she wanted to. It was their time—not Jane's or the company's. The time was a gift that Jane was giving her employees.

It was the responsibility of the employees to develop the agenda. They could discuss anything they wanted to—either personal issues or those that were work-related. But the deal was that Jane wouldn't introduce the topics about which they'd talk. That was up to the employees.

Rally the Troops

You can offer your employees opportunities to get themselves motivated, but you can't force them. Motivation requires patience. You have to be willing to implement systems, then give those systems time to work. Don't expect immediate results.

Nobody said much of anything about Jane's plan at first, but Jane wasn't deterred. She prepared and posted a schedule showing each person's 15-minute slot. Most still didn't trust her, but Jane moved ahead and implemented the meetings.

You can guess what happened.

"This is your time, John," Jane would say. "Is there anything you'd like to discuss?"

"No."

"Well, okay then. Perhaps next month."

"Hi Judy, this is your time slot. Is there anything you want to discuss?"

"No."

"Well, okay. But it is your slot, and I'm available. Please spread the word to others. Maybe there will be something you'll want to talk about next month."

And so it went. Leadership is an effort. Building trust takes time; rebuilding trust takes an even longer time. Constructing positive environments where people can motivate themselves is an important leadership task.

Backfire

Jane told what she had done during a training program I led at the University of Wisconsin. The others in the program were terribly impressed, calling her an exceptional manager, remarkable, and so forth. This was surprising and disturbing to me. What Jane did should not have been astounding to other professional, experienced managers. I was bothered that, apparently, they may not have done the same type of thing.

It's extremely difficult to undo all the negatives that history creates. Jane's predecessor had hurt people, and Jane was stuck with the damage. She had to get through all the layers, like peeling an onion. She had to totally rebuild the environment.

Jane acted like effective leaders who for thousands of years have been undoing negative layers created by history. She was persistent and determined, and finally started to make some progress.

Jane was working to create trusting, open communications, but the first noticeable result of her efforts was a decline in the turnover rate. Well, that was something, at least.

She kept working to rebuild the environment, and eventually, productivity improved. Open communications, real involvement, and real problem solving took longer. It was more than a year until employees were really talking to Jane; but finally, it happened.

Jane had motivated, or caused her employees to motivate themselves. They were working together as a motivated team. The ship was no longer sinking. It was again heading in a direction. Jane's team was at least in the race.

The job of leadership is to work on ways to improve the team, and Jane was a fine example of that.

She worked hard to improve communications, the environment, the comfort zones of her employees, trust, risk-taking, competence, and decision-making accuracy.

The job of leadership should not be to work on schedules, technical problem solving, materials shortages, or to design reports. It should not be to check or confirm quality, meet with customers, develop new procedures, develop new policies, or evaluate systems.

These are all jobs for the motivated team. The job of leadership is to prepare the team to perform these highly complex and critical process tasks.

Attitude Controls Behavior, and Vice Versa

Attitudes are personal and confidential. They are contained within the individual.

Behavior is something individuals do, but it is always observable. It is the manifestation of an attitude that controls the behavior.

Effective motivators understand that they cannot control attitude. They can, however, control behavior. A worker can believe that he's Santa Claus if he wants to. It's your job, however, to make sure that he doesn't wear a red suit.

By controlling behavior, good motivators also know they are controlling attitude. Attitude follows behavior, just as behavior follows attitude. Here's an example.

Susan believes that she can't succeed. She's convinced she will fail. That attitude causes her to never try to do anything. She feels that to try to do something will surely result in failure.

Her attitude, therefore, guarantees failure because it prevents her from trying to do anything. That's a classic example of failure.

As her leader, my challenge is not to tell her she has a bad attitude and will never succeed at anything until she changes it. This will certainly make her defensive, and make her attitude even worse.

Susan's perception is her reality, and she will resist and reject any input that contradicts it. She's convinced that she's unable to do what I ask her to, and I'm only setting her up to fail by giving her an assignment at all.

Defining Moments

Behavior is the result of **attitude**, and it's what can be observed. It's the outward result of attitude, which is an internal thing.

Rally the Troops

Many leaders fail because they lack the patience necessary to accomplish attitude adjustments in their workers. We tend to feel that the attitudes of others should mirror our own, and it's difficult to work slowly and subtly to get somebody to change their attitude. Be prepared to take your time, and watch for small, slow steps.

To motivate Susan, I need to ignore her attitude and focus on her behavior. She needs immediate and continuous success over a long period of time—a very long period of time.

Attitudes build over time, and they're difficult to change. Not impossible, mind you, but difficult.

Here's how you have to do it. It's not hard, but you've got to be consistent.

Ask Susan to do something simple, which she has already done successfully. When she accomplishes the task, give her lots of praise. Then, ask her to do it again. Give lots of praise again. Repeat this over and over.

After you've done that for a while, slowly add something else to Susan's routine. Give her a new task, but with only a modest increase in complexity. Add a small step, perhaps.

When she accomplishes that task, continue praising her, and repeat the procedure several times. Recruit others to join you in praising Susan, and keep it up. Soon you'll be able to assign another task.

Is this a slow process? Yes.

Is it laborious and time-consuming? Yes.

Shouldn't Susan simply be able to see the light and realize she's not some kind of failure who can't do anything? Well, maybe she should, but obviously she can't. If she were capable of seeing the light, you wouldn't have this troublesome attitude problem in the first place.

The job of leadership is to create motivated workers. Effective leaders never accept poor or mediocre performance from their workers. They'll do whatever is necessary to improve performance.

Gaining the Power to Motivate

You need power to make things happen. Whether you realize it or not, you have that power. Leaders, as well as everyone else, have all the power they need, but they have to cultivate and develop it.

However, not all forms of power are equal. Some forms of power are much more effective than others. Let's have a look.

Formal Power

Formal power comes through ownership or fiduciary responsibility. For example, if you own your house, then you, not your neighbor, get to decide what color you want it to be.

A supervisor has fiduciary responsibility. He is ultimately answerable to those who own the company—the stockholders. As a leader, you can order what you think should be done, and your team probably will do it.

They're obeying, however, because they have to, not because they want to. The best leaders understand that fiduciary power is very limited, and they use it sparingly.

Acceptance Power

Acceptance power is derived through the strength of your personality. This power will take you as far as those who are following will let you go.

The President of the United States, for instance, can lead as long as the people of the United States allow him to (or he runs out of terms). If he can convince the people to re-elect him, then he buys himself some more power.

The amount of power you accumulate is based upon your ability to sell, to persuade, and to create advantages for others if they follow your leadership.

Rally the Troops

It's very important to understand the difference between formal power, acceptance power, contract power, and knowledge power. Members of your team will respond differently to each type of power, and each one has qualities that make it more valuable than the others in specific circumstances.

Contract Power

Contract power lies in your ability to define a problem that is important to others. The ability you have to motivate others depends on how important they perceive a particular problem to be.

If the problem is perceived as extremely important, and you have the ability to address it or do something about it, you've got a lot of power, and you've got a lot of opportunity to motivate.

Knowledge Power

Knowledge power lies in your ability to assimilate knowledge about important issues. The doctor, for example, has been seen as a leader in the village ever since we first started organizing ourselves into a society.

That's because the doctor holds the most valuable knowledge there is. She knows what to do to keep us alive. A person who's regarded as an expert on any topic commands respect and attains a degree of power.

Think about college professors, scientists, researchers, and so forth. These people all have knowledge power.

Whatever kind of power you have, it will enable you to motivate people if you use it properly. It doesn't matter where the power comes from, as long as you know how to channel it.

The Least You Need to Know

➤ There are many factors that affect motivation within any given environment.

➤ Paying attention to your company's environment can help workers to increase their motivation.

➤ The psychological environment is just as important as the physical one when you're looking to get people motivated.

➤ Because someone is not dissatisfied does not necessarily mean she is satisfied.

➤ Attitude is what's inside a person, while behavior is the outward result of attitude.

➤ Motivating workers to do more than they thought they could is a slow and tedious process, but carries significant results.

➤ There are various kinds of power, but all can be used to motivate.

Chapter 3

Incentives—
The Heart of
Motivation

In This Chapter

➤ Inspiring your team with incentives

➤ Making sure the incentives are authentic

➤ Using negative incentives

➤ Using positive incentives

➤ Offering incentives in an effective manner

➤ Understanding which incentives work best

If you want your team to perform at its peak level, you've got to inspire it to do so. One of the most valuable tools for inspiring your team is an incentive system.

Incentives, which are simply ways in which we recognize and reward performance, are powerful things. Incentives cause people to do all kinds of things that they might not do otherwise. Think about some incentives that you've been offered and what they've inspired you to do.

Here's How It Works

Even when we're kids, we're offered incentives. Maybe you got some money for every "A" on your high school report card. Or were told you could use your dad's car only after you'd finished mowing the grass.

Incentives are powerful motivators, to be sure. But you've got to understand the different kinds of incentives and know how to use them.

Your goal, as a leader, should be to motivate your team to break out of the day-to-day routine and look for ways to improve the future. To do this, you create incentives that make that prospect exciting and fun. You make your team want to push itself to achieve. And you lead your team by example.

You need boundless energy to develop high achievement in others. Your followers need to be inspired not just by your words, but by your actions. Dive in first, and be the last to leave the pool. Be inspired, and sweat with the rest of your team. Act like you believe your team will perform, and it will perform.

Always focus on the excellent things around you.

High achievement from your team is a precious thing, and it should be largely recognized. Incentives can help you do that.

Incentives should be focused on specific accomplishments, not general goodness. Although general goodness is important to the overall performance of your team, it does little to clear new territory, or plow virgin fields. Look for specific excellence, and find and reward those workplace heroes that demonstrate exceptional behavior. Set up a "what did you accomplish?" program.

You should offer incentives that reward those individuals who identify and positively resolve incidents with speed, commitment, and dedication.

The best type of incentive system will:

➤ Have authenticity. The incentives will be genuine recognition of work well done, not a patronizing display of false approval.

➤ Be random, frequent, and focused only on recognizing specific and tangible achievements—not general goodness.

➤ Include significant recognition, such as the sharing of some sort of gain (money, greater authority or responsibility, perk assignments, special projects, and so on), or some other form of high-value, formal recognition.

Positive Incentives

Some people will not want to be publicly recognized for excellence, and you should honor their wishes. In general, however, most of us *appreciate* public recognition for our accomplishments, as long as it's the behavior that's stressed—not the individual.

The key to a successful recognition system, however, is the sincerity that you build into it.

Authenticity—Dying for a Ribbon

If your kid brings home artwork every week from school and you tell him that each picture he shows you is the most beautiful thing you've ever seen in your life, he'll soon catch on to your insincerity.

Defining Moments

If something is **authentic,** it conforms to the facts that we believe about it. For a table to be an authentic antique, it has to *be* old, not just painted in a manner that makes it *look* old. Something authentic must be worthy of our trust, reliance, or belief.

Let's face it. Some pictures are better than others. Some work is better than others as well. When someone is rewarded for something, they need to know that the reward is genuine, that it's sincere.

To offer someone meaningless recognition is insulting. The recognition must be authentic or it's worthless. Let's have a look at what exactly authenticity is and why it's so valuable.

We live in a world filled with false authenticity. We buy "distressed" furniture, which is new but made to look old and weathered. We purchase goods based on the slick advertisements we see, regardless of whether or not we can be sure those ads are true. We eat potato chips made with fake fat, and ice cream made with fake sugar.

Authenticity, the characteristic that means someone or something is genuine and of undisputed origin, often seems to be a precious commodity in our fast-paced, everchanging world.

To an incentive program, however, authenticity is extremely important and necessary. It's probably the most important criteria for a program.

Workers must believe in the incentives program or the program is meaningless. If you tell your team that the best workers will get an perk assignment, for instance, but the perk assignments end up being given to employees who are your friends but not the best workers, your program is meaningless.

The whole team has to work to win a Super Bowl ring. There are specific rules that must be followed in order to achieve specific goals—namely, first getting to, and then winning the Super Bowl and the accompanying ring, and being hailed as the greatest football team in the world.

Here's How It Works

My wife, Beverly, was on an airplane and happened to be seated next to the father of a football player whose team had won the Super Bowl. The father was proudly wearing his son's ring, and he shared with Beverly all his proud stories of his son's accomplishments. The ring was a recognized and authentic symbol of recognition.

All these things—the recognition, the value, and the status—are necessary to build authenticity in the cause. Authenticity doesn't just apply to games, either.

Militaries have always understood the importance of authenticity with their recognition systems. They've mastered authenticity so well, in fact, that soldiers and leaders risk their lives for military ribbons. These ribbons are perhaps worth no more than a buck or two in monetary value—but they're highly prized as symbols of achievement.

Any honorable military person will defend the ribbons of honor handed out for deeds of bravery or great accomplishment. They are held sacred by most members of our society.

No Chairman of the Joint Chiefs of Staff would ever consider testifying in front of the United States Congress, without first assuring that each of his hard-earned military ribbons was properly polished and perfectly displayed on his dress uniform. These ribbons, after all, are symbols of his many achievements as a soldier and/or officer.

The U.S. military is charged with fighting for our nation's cause and principles. It's given the task of defending our families and our way of life against opposing views. People who buy into the cause strongly enough will be motivated by the military's incentive system and therefore willing to die for the ribbons that represent that cause.

Backfire

Part of the anti-war upheaval in this country during the 1960s and 1970s was due to the trashing of authenticity. Anti-war protestors shredded and burned American flags, decorated and wore military clothing, and made mockery of military ribbons and honors. All this caused a terrible clash between what different groups believed to be authentic and good, and severely strained our country.

The Private Sector's Version of Ribbons

In the private economy, things are not always as clear-cut as they are in the military. Because of that, inspired leadership is even more critical to building and maintaining authenticity.

Inequities within the private economy can make it very difficult to inspire your team. If your workers perceive that they're being treated unfairly, especially when it comes to their paychecks, it can be extremely difficult for you to motivate them. Still, if you want to badly enough, it can be done.

You can actually build a pocket of fairness, or a micro-society, inside the larger, more unfair organization. Build authenticity and justice in your own private little corner of the world, and you'll be surprised at the results.

People are flexible. They'll understand, and they'll follow if you can demonstrate that you're trying to build some kind of justice in the larger, unfair world. To keep themselves motivated and inspired, your people need to know that you are continuing the good fight on your and their behalf.

Rally the Troops

Adversity within an organization can result in motivation within a specific group that is affected by the adversity. The group might feel motivated, particularly if it's inspired by a strong leader, to work against the adversity or injustice to overcome it. Be aware of this possibility, and take advantage of it, where possible.

My experience suggests that this is mostly what effective motivators do. Most managers who build highly motivated teams do so in spite of the injustice they find all around. They build authentic reward systems on a smaller scale, sometimes even working around unjust rules, in order to make things better for their own people.

One foreman I know—let's call him Bill—built a motivated team inside a hard-core, tough, unionized auto plant. The work environment was extremely hostile due to dirt, grime, poor quality, and inefficiency. Union members hated management, and management reciprocated the feelings. Relationships were poor, and quality and productivity suffered. There was a lot of waste and rework due to a high rejection rate of the finished units. As you can see, it was a really bad, ugly situation. Except for within Bill's group.

Bill paid attention to his workers and the quality of what they produced. He was perfectly willing to bend the rules of the system and offer incentives, such as time off, if his workers managed to work ahead, get their jobs done, and maintain quality standards. Bill simply would look the other way when his workers left early, and make sure that their time cards were punched at the proper quitting time.

Bill broke the rules, to be sure. I'm not advocating you follow his behavior. But I'm not advocating the hostile work environment caused by the animosity between union and management, either.

Bill needed to feed his family, and he needed to work within the environment as it was, not as it should have been. He had to choose to either build an inspired team within that hostile environment or to accept the norm of poor quality and morale.

Bill's willingness to ignore the rules may have been a serious concern. His team, however, always met its productivity measurements and had the necessary quality

Rally the Troops

Some companies have plaques or trophies that are passed around to the highest-producing teams within a certain period. These recognitions have no material value to workers, but because they're recognized and accepted by everyone within the companies, they achieve value.

requirements. Furthermore, Bill had a very low rate of employee problems. The results he achieved must be considered seriously as well. All constructive developments come from someone willing to take a risk and do something different in order to make something better for tomorrow.

Bill used time off work as an incentive. Many different types of tokens, including those with no material value, can be used to reinforce positive behavior, as long as an authentic commitment to the reward and its meaning exists within the culture.

Nonmaterial rewards have more significance when combined with significant gain-sharing rewards. Bill's use of time off was a form of gain sharing. He couldn't share more money with his team, so he gave them time. Effectively, he allowed them to earn the same pay for fewer hours, provided the fewer hours were properly invested. Normally, I wouldn't recommend using time off as an incentive. Your people will love it, to be sure, but it sends a mixed message. The whole nature of incentives is to reward employees for doing a job well. Giving them time off doesn't make a lot of sense to me. I mean, the coach of the St. Louis Cardinals doesn't give all-star Mark McGwire a couple of games off for slamming in some home runs in the previous game. To the contrary, that coach wants McGwire on the field for every game.

Steps for Creating Effective Incentive Programs

Nearly anything can be used as a reward. Teachers have long known the value of simple gold stars or an "I got caught being good" sticker.

I've seen dozens of items that my clients have used as incentives and rewards, including

- ➤ Puffy stars
- ➤ Ribbons
- ➤ Letters of commendation
- ➤ Certificates
- ➤ Articles in newsletters
- ➤ Recognizing a person or accomplishment in front of a group
- ➤ Testimonials
- ➤ Trips
- ➤ Special projects
- ➤ Money

The key to the success of incentives is not the material value, but the perceived authenticity of the incentive. That's not to say that money isn't important. Money has all kinds of implications, which we'll discuss in detail in Chapter 14, "We've Gotta Talk Money, but How Far Will Your Dollar Go?" For the purposes of this chapter, however, monetary value takes a secondary role.

To create the necessary authenticity, the reward, whatever it is, must be directly related to behavior that is

➤ Specific

➤ Tangible

➤ Observable

➤ Measurable

Backfire

You can easily sabotage your incentive program by setting standards that are too low. Low standards lead workers to expect rewards for average, nonexemplary work, which is a dangerous attitude that should be avoided. Make sure everyone understands that in order to receive rewards, performance must be out of the ordinary. Status quo should not be rewarded, lest it become the goal.

These criteria minimize the possibility of subjectivity, bias, and favoritism occurring.

When setting up an incentive program, think like the military. The behavior to be rewarded must be way beyond what is ordinary or expected. It must be exemplary, have a component of uniqueness, and demonstrate a clear and visible step toward a positive or desirable goal.

Keep these steps in mind when setting up an incentive program:

➤ Develop a reward system.

➤ Clearly describe the type of behavior that will be rewarded.

➤ Set up some sort of review board that determines if someone recommended for the incentive or reward actually deserves it.

➤ Be certain that an awards ceremony, if that's what you decide to do, is suitable for the occasion.

Management of the Triad Corporation, a computer and software company with 1,500 employees worldwide, somehow finds time and money to hold an annual awards banquet to recognize high achievement throughout the company.

In an attempt to shorten the banquet (when I attended it was still running about four hours), company officials don't give out the awards during the banquet, traditionally held in a nice hotel. Instead, they distribute much of the $40,000 in cash, innumerable plaques, and other mementos to the hotel rooms of the award winners following the main ceremony. Many people stay up late that night, anticipating the possibility of recognition. All told, there are about 700 different awards that the 1,500 employees compete for.

Rally the Troops

It's not important that the actual award be scarce or valuable. The key to giving the award value is to make sure the behavior that earned it was scarce and valuable. And, make sure it's behavior that can be repeated. Rewarding Superman for flying, for instance, does little to inspire people who can't fly.

Many awards have multiple winners, and it's not unusual for an employee to receive 10 or 15 different recognitions. There are awards for nearly every category imaginable, including "outstanding achievement," "special recognition," "president's club," "personal development," "sales goal attainment," and so forth. There are also "we care" awards, "the nose to the grindstone" award, and "the innovator" award. My personal favorite, however, is the "bustin' the boundaries" recognition, given to those who work to crash through the artificial departmental and divisional boundaries that always crop up in organizations.

Triad has about 12,000 customers. With $150 million in annual sales, the company has lost only one customer in its 20-year history.

I wouldn't say that astounding record is due to this awards ceremony I've described, but that certainly helps to maintain the motivation of Triad employees, and to keep corporate morale high.

Reward systems don't necessarily have to be related to the organizational hierarchy, although supervisors should obviously generate rewards for subordinates.

Don't be afraid to go outside of your department to reward somebody who's contributed to your team. Or to recognize another department with a memo to the group. Employees, too, can reward colleagues, either within their own departments or in other departments, who help them accomplish tough tasks. Employees can recognize their supervisors, as well. It doesn't matter how the system is set up, just remember that authenticity is the key.

These reward systems don't have to be perfect, but they do have to be fair. If somebody screws up and neglects to reward deserving behavior, don't take it too seriously. Your system will maintain its integrity as long as those in the culture believe in it. Individuals must feel that the excellence that went unnoticed will be rewarded at another time.

All reward and incentive systems that discriminate or show favoritism eventually fail. These flagrantly unfair systems actually produce negative motivation. Unfair systems produce cynicism, poor quality, poor productivity, and poor employees. Only the weakest employees, who have little chance of being hired elsewhere, will stay. The better employees will seek greener pastures.

Types of Incentives

We tend to think of incentives as positive things, but there are negative incentives as well. Both positive and negative reinforcement tools can be used as effective methods of producing the behavior you desire.

When I explain this positive/negative concept, you'll realize it's something you already know about. We all know about it, because we've all lived with it our entire lives.

When we do something for which we're rewarded, or for which we receive positive reinforcement, we're likely to repeat whatever the action was. We want more of the satisfaction that results from the reward, or the positive reinforcement.

This covers an incredibly wide range, from giving the kid $1 for an "A" on the report card to awarding frequent flier miles for credit card purchases.

Here's How It Works

Even animals respond to this positive and negative reinforcement. Show a dog a rolled-up newspaper after he's been whacked once or twice, and you'll see the power of negative reinforcement.

On the other hand, we tend to avoid responses that are accompanied or closely followed by any sort of negative reinforcer. That's because negative reinforcers result in discomfort or punishment—things we want to avoid.

There are thousands of examples of negative reinforcers. They range from scolding a child to handing out traffic tickets to speeders to killing convicted murderers by lethal injection or the electric chair.

Positive and negative reinforcement each can be used to strengthen behavior. Punishment, on the other hand, which we'll discuss at length in Chapter 13, "Fair Discipline—Or How to Spank Nicely," always diminishes behavior. Let's look at the different ways in which negative and positive incentives can be used.

Negative Incentives

A negative incentive or reinforcement means that the leader withdraws or withholds an undesirable consequence, if and when a certain desirable behavior is performed. Huh? Read on.

Sue, the head honcho, notices a gab session going on a bit too long over by the copy machine. Being a mindful boss, she gathers a few sheets of paper, leaves her desk, and walks over to the machine.

Defining Moments

Negative incentives are tools used to manipulate behavior. They result in discomfort or punishment for certain specific behavior or actions, and it's generally desirable to avoid them.

She says nothing to those gathered there. Her only actions are to acknowledge the group with a sort of half smile, glance at her watch, and run off the copies she "needs." Then, she walks back to her desk.

The gab session quickly ends, and everyone goes back to work.

This is a classic example of how experienced leaders use negative reinforcement to produce positive behavior.

Sue is interested in providing positive incentives for her people, so she prefers not to rant and rave about the gab session. Instead, she very effectively expresses her displeasure at what's going on without ever saying a word or embarrassing anyone.

By sending a message that was subtle, but very readable, she was able to convey a message to her team and allow them to correct their behavior. Good work, Sue!

Negative incentives can be used correctly and effectively, even if you, like most good leaders, prefer to focus on positive incentives. Sue, produced a positive result—getting her team back to work—by simply letting it know that she was aware of, and not happy with, its behavior. Her quick glance at her watch said everything that needed to be said.

The employees themselves produced the positive change. Sensing Sue's irritation, they quickly went back to work to minimize the chances of being reprimanded. A reprimand, because it's more directly negative, would be considered a punishment. The employees knew that by displaying positive behavior (getting back to work) they were reducing their chances of getting additional negative reinforcement.

Sue could have overreacted. She could have disciplined the group for gabbing too long, or screamed and hollered, or whatever. That, however, would have been high-risk behavior on Sue's part because her workers might have perceived that she was overreacting. That perception could cause her team to lose some of their trust and confidence in Sue. As a skilled leader who knows her people well and commands their trust, Sue accomplished her objective without risking damaged morale.

Positive Incentives

Positive incentives or reinforcers are everything that the group perceives as positive and desirable. Everything perceived to be authentic can be used as positive incentives. A positive token that's linked to a specific behavior strengthens that behavior. Anything, ranging from simple, verbal compliments to cash payouts, can be used as positive incentives.

Supervisor Bob just happens to walk by one day as Judy is doing a great job diffusing a particularly difficult situation created by an overly demanding customer. Bob doesn't say a word—he simply stands by and observes. Several other department members also watch as Judy professionally handles the situation, keeping the customer satisfied while resolving the situation.

During a staff meeting later that afternoon, Bob takes the opportunity to recognize Judy, giving her, and all other staff members, positive incentive to repeat the behavior Judy displayed earlier in the day. Bob says something like this:

"Judy, I wanted to thank you here, with everyone around, for dealing with that aggressive customer this morning. I just happened to walk by as the situation was in progress. Gill and Jane were in the area, and they saw the whole thing.

"For those of you who didn't hear about this, the customer was way off target, complaining loudly about a shipment he claimed was missing. Judy maintained her composure in a very tough spot. She did several things quite well. She expressed great empathy for the customer's position and continued to reflect what we could do for this customer while ignoring the customer's more obvious taunts. The customer was clearly trying to create a volatile situation, and Judy did a great job of diffusing it. Specifically, when the customer threatened legal action concerning the alleged missing shipment, Judy countered showing him the tracking slips and making him see that the shipment wasn't lost.

"Judy, thanks for a great job. We can all learn from her performance. This is exactly the way we all should handle these situations."

Bob, in this classic example, thanks the employee publicly.

This can be very effective, but you have to make sure that the other team members know you're reinforcing specific behavior, and not just patting your favorite employee's back. Be certain you describe the specific behavior that warranted the positive reinforcement, as the example above demonstrates. Further, be certain to describe the behavior that you want other employees to emulate, and to tell them that it's the kind of behavior you want.

Defining Moments

Positive incentives are tools used to manipulate behavior by causing people to want to act in a particular manner or to demonstrate specific behavior. They generally result in some kind of award or recognition.

Rally the Troops

We tend to express ourselves in positives more than negatives. When we go into a restaurant, for instance, we tell the waiter what we want, not what we don't want. If we get something we didn't order and don't want, however, we'll be sure to say so. The same goes with positive and negative incentives and reinforcers.

Positive reinforcers are more powerful than negative reinforcers because they're things that people want. They can be more openly discussed, and the behavior that produces positive incentives can be more clearly and easily defined than that which results in negative incentives.

Negative reinforcers include things that people want to avoid. They're always linked to undesirable behavior, and they have a lot less power than positive reinforcers. One reason for that is because it's harder to tell somebody what you don't want them to do than to tell them what you do want. Typically, you tell somebody what he or she shouldn't do after it's done. It's a lot easier to define what you want than what you don't want.

Therefore, negative reinforcers have far less power. People only know what the negative behavior is after it occurs.

This is why smart leaders are always focused on positive reinforcement and incentives rather than negatives.

It's much more productive to recognize and reward positive behavior than it is to always be on the lookout for, and ready to punish, negative behavior.

Whenever possible, aim for using positive incentive, rather than negative. Don't, however, overlook the usefulness of negative incentives in certain situations.

Three Ways of Offering Incentives

How and when you present incentives might just be as important as the types of incentives you offer. In this section, we'll look at three ways that you can offer incentives.

Fixed Ratio, or "You Give Me Three First"

This method of reinforcement rewards an individual for a certain behavior that's already been exhibited. It's the carrot-on-the-stick method of reinforcement.

There's nothing wrong with this method; in fact, it usually works pretty well. Some examples of this type of reinforcement that I've seen my clients use include:

➤ The shipping department has met the company's safety goals by remaining accident-free for 30 days. The company provides a catered lunch for all members of the department.

➤ It's desirable for employees to be at work by 7:45 in order to be productive by 8:00. When every employee arrives by 7:45, the boss is charged with buying pastries and coffee the following day.

➤ For every consecutive 30 days of zero-defect work, everyone gets a gift certificate for a local restaurant, a framed certificate, or whatever.

Fixed-ratio incentives often are used to reward achievement within a particular time frame. Whatever it is—30 days of accident-free work, 60 days of defect-free production, or whatever—the achievement earns recognition or a reward. These performance-related awards can be granted to individuals or groups, and they're valuable because, by keeping the time period fairly short, a team is constantly reminded of the important goals and objectives.

Fixed Interval, or "You Get It Every Tuesday"

Fixed-interval incentives are those that are always offered at particular times.

They can be employee-of-the-month programs, for which awards are offered on the fourth Wednesday of each month. They can be the star-of-the-week programs, in which an outstanding employee is named every Friday afternoon.

Fixed-interval incentives can be used for the best salesperson of the quarter, the best overall employee for the year, the best customer service rep of the month, or whatever.

What all these incentives have in common is that they're given after a fixed time interval. Everyone knows what the interval is, and that the incentive will be administered after that interval.

Backfire

Be aware that the fixed interval reward system can result in hard feelings. If two people pass their sales goals, but only one gets the reward, the person not rewarded may feel cheated and experience a negative reaction to the process. That reaction could result in poor performance. A new race, however, may even out the playing field and get everyone back on track.

There is always an employee of the month, for instance. The only question is, who wins the award this month.

This type of incentive does a good job of reinforcing the contest concept. Judy and Bill both want to be named sales rep of the year, and who can blame them?

The prize is a trip to Hawaii. To that end, they both push extra hard, and both therefore surpass their assigned sales objectives. Although both exceeded their sales goals—alas—only one gets the Hawaii trip.

A potential problem with fixed-interval incentives is that they can produce irregular behavior responses. There's often a tendency to see relatively weak performance right after the reward is given, and the strongest behavior just before its time to give the reward.

Variable Schedules, or "You Get It Whenever"

Variable-schedule incentives are the most powerful type there is, and really makes more sense than any other method.

It's very difficult to measure specific excellence or particular accomplishment because nobody can predict when it will occur or what the accomplishment should be. It's a very subjective thing.

Rally the Troops

Keep in mind that incentives don't have to be complicated or of any great value. A trip to Hawaii is a great incentive, but a gift certificate to a local restaurant can be just as valuable.

Excellence is always relative to what's happening. An excellent solution to a tough problem, for example, is only excellent because of the problem. If the problem had not occurred, there would be no excellence. Rewards and incentives that are as random and unpredictable as accomplishment and excellence produce the most motivation.

Fixed-ratio and fixed-interval incentives can be made into variable-schedule incentives by varying the time or the type of positive behavior required. Incentive systems that don't have predictable patterns are the most effective.

A great example of variable-schedule incentives occurs at Larry's supermarket in downtown Seattle.

Every supervisor at Larry's has a pocketful of tokens, each about the size of a quarter. Employees can get one or more tokens at any time, for any customer-focused behavior. Picking up a scrap of paper from the floor might get someone a token today, but might not tomorrow. Cleaning up a spill might get a token or two from time to time, but nobody is ever sure what behavior will be rewarded.

Employees might get tokens for helping customers decide which cheeses to buy, carrying sacks of groceries to their cars, or pointing out where they might find the Fig Newtons.

These tokens have become a private currency at Larry's. They can be cashed in for all sorts of good stuff like dinners, movies, or whatever. Larry's has been honing this positive incentive system for more than 20 years with terrific results.

Employees are psyched and always upbeat. They dress up for Halloween, chat constantly with customers, or give away a free sandwich or two. They're doing virtually anything they can to show customers that they care about the store. They have made the place famous.

Shopping at Larry's is hardly routine. Larry's is way more than a place you go for groceries. Larry's is an experience. It's not unusual to pass by Larry's and see a tour bus parked in front of the store. Larry's is a tourist attraction.

As you've learned in this chapter, any type of incentive can produce results. Some types, however, produce better results than others.

The Least You Need to Know

➤ Using incentives is one of the most powerful ways that you can motivate and inspire your team.

➤ Incentives that aren't authentic will never be effective.

➤ Negative incentives have their place, but generally aren't as powerful as positive ones.

➤ Nearly everyone responds well to positive incentives.

➤ The manner in which you offer incentives is nearly as important as the type that you give.

➤ Some incentives work better than others; it's important to understand which ones work best, and why.

Making Your Operation the Place to Be

We're all affected by our environments. Some people are affected less so than others, but everyone is to some extent.

It's important to be comfortable in your environment, whatever it is. Some people are perfectly comfortable working in a closed-in cubicle, while others can't stand the feeling of confinement. Some people love the ease of living in a small apartment, while others feel they need a lot of space and surrounding property.

Making sure that your workers are comfortable within their job environment is an important part of keeping them happy and motivated. In this chapter, we'll look at how you can do that, both physically and emotionally.

This Place Is a Dump!

Generally, our homes tend to be a nicer and more comfortable environment than our workplaces. If you take a worldwide view, that becomes a frightening thought.

In Lahore, Pakistan, I saw many people living in mud huts, with no utilities of any sort.

Those people, though, were motivated to make something better out of what they had, as has been the case with people since the beginning of time.

As I watched the people in Lahore, I was stricken by the intrinsically motivated character that defines human beings. I saw men hauling PVC pipe to a nearby construction site on wooden carts pulled by donkeys. The cart, made from a 5,000-year-old design and loaded down with PVC pipe, created an incongruous scene. Although their method of transportation was primitive, these people were using what they had to make their environments better.

Here's How It Works

Regardless of how bleak or desperate a situation is, people will take steps to improve it. They'll flee a war-torn country and go into unknown situations across borders to improve their environments. It's not in the nature of humans to be satisfied if they think there's a better way.

Here's something important to remember: No matter how bad things are, you can be sure that they'll improve. That's because it's in the nature of humans to make things better. Someone will begin the movement, and she will create a following of people who will help. She'll motivate others, because they'll see that her effort will improve the quality of their lives.

And that's the whole point. If your place is a dump, and you do nothing to make the dump better or nicer, somebody else will.

Leadership has nothing to do with talking about what should be. It has everything to do, however, with making what should be real. Leadership is constantly allowing others to envision a tomorrow that's better than today.

Okay, So Maybe It's Not the Greatest

In the late 1970s, I was promoted to manager of customer and service training at the Cincinnati Milacron, a company that produced computer-driven, metal-cutting machines.

At this particular time, customer training wasn't regarded as very important by most companies, and Milacron was no exception. The company spent little effort, and fewer resources, on its customer service department. To make things even worse, the guy whose position I was taking was a real jerk who'd done nothing to keep the department running smoothly. From what I could tell, his primary functions were complaining about his parking space and browsing through the copies of *Playboy* he kept in his desk drawer.

The customer training operation at this place was out of control. There were some good folks and there were some duffers. All the good ones were overworked, with nobody fighting to get them any relief. The duffers, of course, did nothing, and no one was holding their feet to the fire to get them going.

Backfire

When you interview prospective employees, be careful not to mislead them about working conditions. Don't, for instance, conduct the interview in your office and neglect to show them the rest of the facility. If conditions aren't what you'd like them to be, be honest and up-front about the situation. If you're not, you're likely to end up hiring workers, only to lose them a short time later.

The office was a piece of terrible old manufacturing space, partitioned off from its surroundings with a few pieces of drywall. Staff members wore their coats while they sat at their desks during the winter in a desperate attempt to keep warm.

The customer training department was responsible for training customers to operate and maintain the complex computer-controlled metal-cutting machinery. But there were few pieces of equipment available to the trainers, very few classrooms in which to train, and no written training material. Frankly, the thing was a damned mess.

I knew that I needed to get more equipment, better office and shop space, and I had to hire a bunch of new people. The problem was, how was I supposed to attract decent workers to this swamp?

Months earlier, I had interviewed a guy named C.P. C.P. was finishing up his degree after serving time in the military, and had come to the company during one of our standard open recruiting sessions. When I had first interviewed C.P., neither I nor anyone else had a job for him. We were just doing general recruiting.

Months later, after my promotion, I was rummaging through files looking for potential employees. I didn't remember C.P., but I'd given him high marks in the initial interview. When I called him, his wife told me that C.P. had really wanted to work with us, and had waited for months to hear from us. Unfortunately, when he hadn't heard from us, he'd taken a position with another company. Would he speak with me anyway, I asked.

Well, C.P. called back. He declined to come in for an interview, saying he felt he owed something to his new employer. Could he just come down on a Saturday, I asked, and

Rally the Troops

Try to keep these thoughts in mind when you're facing tough situations:

Don't apologize for the world, and don't make excuses. Don't say you're going to make everything better when you know very well that you can't. These things don't motivate anybody. You've got the lemons that you got, so call them exactly what they are. What you need are people who are capable and willing to make lemonade from those lemons. And that's exactly what you should tell them.

we'd cover all his expenses. I just wanted him to see what we were trying to do. He agreed.

It was a short interview. After spending only a few minutes with him, I remembered why I had ranked him at the top so many months before. He had great spirit. This was a guy who could make things happen. I wanted him on my team.

But how could I possibly get him to join up? I had nothing but trash to offer. He had just taken a good job with another firm. Operating on pure instinct, I said, "Let's go for a walk."

We walked out of our lousy offices and down into the main shop. Things got increasingly more depressing as we moved into the bowels of the operation.

What had been white lines marking the aisles were stained black with soot and grease. Machinery in this area was covered with layers of black metal chips mixed with oil and coolant. We could barely see the controls on the equipment around us, but it didn't matter too much—the filthy machinery wasn't all that noticeable in the pathetic lighting. Air filtration was done only with our noses. Workers in the shop never bothered to even glance up to see who we were. It was awful.

Off to the side, however, was one of our brand-new machines. Crates, pieces of sheet metal, and cables were still sitting about, unattached. This new training machine was sitting in one of the trashiest places of the shop. We stopped.

"You see this?" I asked.

"Yeah," C.P. responded.

"A customer pays $200,000 for a brand-new machine like this," I said. "This is what we think of that customer. This is where we bring him for training. As you can see, I've got a real problem. I need for you to bring customers to this dump and train them to run this thing. Furthermore, the customer has to love you by the time the training is over. I'm not even sure how to go about getting *you* trained to run this thing so that you can train other people. This is where we start, this is the job I have. What do you think?"

C.P. simply replied, "When can I start?"

C.P. came to work and replaced me as manager five years later. He rose to great heights within Milacron before eventually leaving to start his own company.

On that day, C.P. taught me something about how to motivate people when you have nothing but a dump to offer. Don't beat around the bush or try to sugarcoat your situation. Get right into it and tell people like it is, right up front. No matter how painful or bad it is, tell them straight out. Covering it or rounding off the harsh corners only makes things worse. Sugarcoating puts your integrity on the line, and it doesn't motivate anybody to dig in and make things better.

Using Lemons to Make Lemonade

Once you've been completely up-front and you've laid out the dismal situation with which you and your team are faced, you can expect to see some defectors.

Not everyone will be able to cope with what you're asking for. You're going to need your team's creative energy, along with their blood, sweat, and tears. If they can't live with the straight talk and the prospects that lie ahead, then they aren't right for the job. You might as well start looking for someone else.

Laying out the cold, hard truth is exactly what Field Marshal Bernard Law Montgomery did when he assumed command of the demoralized 8th British Army in North Africa in August 1942.

Backfire

Some people, in fact, probably many people, will not have the guts to tackle seemingly insurmountable problems. Other people, however, will be challenged and motivated to figure out solutions. Just don't expect that everyone will react with the energy and enthusiasm that you'd like to see.

By October, his re-energized forces had defeated Field Marshal Erwin Rommel at the Second Battle of El Alamein, turning the tide in North Africa and ultimately leading to the expulsion of Rommel's forces.

Be clear and crisp when explaining your goals. Tell your team exactly how hard you're all going to fight. Montgomery, for example, offered a three-point plan: Hold and reorganize position, prepare attack, and win.

When I started working with C.P. and other high-energy performers to turn around the training operation at Milacron, I didn't even have a three-point plan. But I did have enthusiasm and a conviction about what the operation should be. I also had determination and a willingness to take some risks.

I hired people without having offices in which to put them or phones for them to use. That forced a problem on building engineering, which had to build offices for us.

We scheduled training on equipment we didn't have, which meant we had to borrow the equipment from other departments. The people in those departments started rooting for us to get our own equipment, in hopes that we'd go away and leave them alone.

We ordered equipment without having any place to put it, which meant that the building engineering staff was forced to find space for us. We ordered engineering to clean up and paint the shop areas for our customers, which meant that our bosses needed to pull money from other budgets, or fire all of us. They found the money.

Because we had no designated training space, we had customers all over the shop areas—sometimes more than 100 in a week. That meant we were becoming a pain in the neck for everyone who worked in the shop. It became very obvious that we needed our own training place, and within five or six years, we got it. We finally were recognized as a valuable part of the overall operation. We had, indeed, made lemonade.

Here's How It Works

There's always risk involved when you're trying to improve a really crummy situation. You might not find people to help, or you could fail. But when you think about it, what do you really have to lose? Chances are you'll improve the situation, even if it doesn't work out exactly the way you'd like.

Promote 'Em Right on Outta Here

There is a common refrain in my leadership classes, and it goes something like this:

It's tough to find good people. Once you get ahold of one, you'd better do everything in your power to keep her.

It's true. It *is* tough to find good people. And you should do everything in your power to keep them within your organization. Remember, though, that keeping good people within your organization is not the same as keeping them with your department. One of the best ways to keep the best and brightest people within your organization is to get them promoted right out of your department.

Sound self-defeating? Yeah . . . in a way it does. But when you think about it, it makes sense. If you're interested in recruiting the best people around, one of the greatest tools you can use to attract them is a history of promoting good people to positions of greater responsibility. Think about it.

You're conducting an interview with some very sharp, young person who'll be completing her MBA next month. You know you're competing with several other major firms for the best students coming out of this particular school. How would a statement like this sound to that young MBA student?

"During the past 24 months, we've hired ten people into the position we have for you. We consider this position to be our premium training opportunity for leadership candidates. Eight people were promoted from this entry spot into important leadership positions during the last 12 months."

I'd think that would be enough to attract the attention of this desirable candidate, wouldn't you?

The best workers are the best because they accept responsibility. So give them all they can handle. Getting people promoted motivates the entire team, even those not actively seeking promotion. If you do this, your team will see you as a professional leader—one who is willing to push her people forward into greater responsibility—not selfishly hold them back from the advancement that they've earned and desire.

Rally the Troops

It may come to pass that somebody you promoted someday ends up as your boss. Chances are, if you were fair and encouraging to that person, she'll end up being fair and encouraging to you, too.

Getting people promoted helps your personal position of power and influence within the company, too. Those you promote will not forget how you helped them advance their careers. They'll become your cheerleaders, saying positive things about you to those left behind. This can be a big help to your overall motivation objectives.

Those whom you promote also can help you with ongoing problem solving throughout your career. They become key allies wherever they're positioned. You can be assured, knowing you can still go to them after they've been promoted and ask for their help when necessary.

These former team members also become good eyes and ears for you. No one is perfect. You, like all leaders, will make mistakes. These allies you create will help watch out for your backside. They'll tip you off if somebody is out for you or if there's trouble brewing elsewhere. Maintain these relationships and cultivate them well. Those you help will help you with all the ongoing problems that tend to damage motivation and morale.

Camaraderie

Camaraderie is a very important and yet often overlooked factor when trying to motivate a team. Where there is sharing of goodwill and a lighthearted rapport among employees, you'll always find motivated teams. The teams are healthier and they accomplish more. People work side by side, always looking out for their comrades.

Smart leaders understand the power that a sense of family brings to the workplace, and they'll go out of their way to build camaraderie and community.

Herb Kelleher, co-founder and CEO of Southwest Airlines, works continuously to build and maintain a sense of family within his organization. His efforts have paid off tremendously. Southwest, in 1999, has the best profits and on-time performance record of any airline in America.

Southwest is a unionized operation. At some companies, the union is an anchor. At Southwest, the union is simply part of the leadership team. The union is always involved, with Kelleher making sure that it understands the importance of productivity and accuracy. Unionized employees are part of the company's profit sharing plan.

What is Kelleher's leadership style, you ask. Kelleher doesn't have a particular style. His "style," if you will, is just being himself.

This is the first lesson for building a sense of family: You've got to be authentic.

We covered the topic of authenticity in Chapter 3, "Incentives—The Heart of Motivation," and it applies here, as well. You just can't fake this inspiration stuff.

Here's How It Works

Think about the best jobs you've ever had. Chances are they weren't the ones that paid the most or had the fanciest offices. They were the ones in which you had a sense of camaraderie and belonging. They were the ones in which you felt connected with the other employees and the organization itself.

Kelleher wants a company bound together by love not fear. His favorite slogan is "We smile because we want to, not because we have to."

This all may sound hokey to you, but if it does, don't say so to Southwest's employees. They live with Kelleher's philosophy, and they've built a profitable company, to boot.

There can be no cooperative team if there are so many levels of management that nobody knows who their boss is. Stay away from complex management plans, and avoid layers upon layers of rules. Spend your money instead on training and communicating your mission to your employees.

Train them to use good judgment and to make the correct decisions. Kelleher hates bureaucracy, and he fights it throughout Southwest. He pushes his people to have fun, and he means it. Bureaucracy tears down the sense of family, camaraderie, fun, and ultimately, it destroys the team.

Kelleher actually feels that it's close to a sin not to have fun. Life's too short. This view is reinforced at Southwest, and Kelleher insists that his executive vice presidents spread the same message he does. Employees are encouraged to joke around with the passengers, to have fun with them, and make them feel that they're a part of the Southwest family.

Let your people know exactly what you think of them.

Kelleher, for example, values the employee first, not products or customers. Traditionalists, who mostly put the stockholders first, might argue about Kelleher's priority.

Scholars give customers, stockholders, and employees equal priority, arguing that all three constituencies need equal amounts of executive attention. To the scholars, the most effective leaders maintain a perfect balance among the three.

Rally the Troops

Always be on the lookout for opportunities to boost morale and create camaraderie. If you see people who work particularly well together, then, by all means, let them work together. Be aware of what's happening and open-minded to opportunistic situations.

Kelleher puts the employees first, arguing that if he treats the employees right, they will treat the customers right. If they treat the customers right, customers will keep coming back. Ultimately, with this scenario, the shareholders will be treated right. Kelleher certainly has a point, and he's built a dedicated team.

At Southwest, the super-fast 20-minute turnaround for which the airline has become known was not planned. The tight-knit team, which enabled this strategy to occur, evolved because of extenuating circumstances.

Management gets credit for taking advantage of the opportunities available to it but can't be credited with creating those opportunities.

When Southwest was first formed, it had brutal competition. Competitors did everything possible to run the upstart into the ground before it even got off the ground (no pun intended). Yet, as often happens when people are under attack, the employees responded. Employees hunkered down and fought back even harder than their competitors. Management was shrewd—or maybe desperate—enough to capitalize on this powerful force coming from their employees.

The airline had only four planes in those days, and the war against its competition had consumed all its available cash. The only way to raise more cash was to sell one of the planes, which meant reducing the passenger-carrying capacity by 25 percent.

Slicing the schedule by 25 percent meant certain disaster for the fledgling airline. Such a restricted schedule surely would have pushed Southwest over the precipice. The only alternative was for the company to produce the same schedule with three planes that it used to have with four. This meant one thing, and it was desperately important. Turnaround time at the jetway had to be dramatically reduced—something no one in the airline industry had ever done before.

Kelleher knew that in order to achieve this goal, he had to get his highly committed team to respond to the challenge. It did, and its members worked flawlessly together to build the now 20-minute turnaround, a highly profitable concept that no one in the industry has been able to match.

Here's How It Works

We all know that teamwork is important, but think of some of the situations in which it's life-or-death. Medical emergency personnel have to know exactly what each person is supposed to do at any given time, in any given situation. The same is true with firefighters. How about astronauts conducting experiments in space, or circus performers who rely upon each other during high-wire walks and other acts? Teamwork is not an option in these situations; it's absolutely vital.

Kelleher says that watching the procedure is like watching a ballet. As the plane taxies into the gate, the entire crew moves into action before the plane snugs up to the jetway. Everyone is already in position by the time the plane comes to a full stop. All parts of the team move as a unit, each helping the other.

Some employees call it coordinated chaos, but the 20-minute turnaround is now an art form at Southwest. The airline has maintained the best on-time record, fewest customer complaints, and lowest lost-baggage claims for the time period between 1994 and 1999.

Us vs. Them

Contests, games, and other forms of competition have always been a part of society, and they're great motivators. Just think of the power that organized games have. Professional sports permeate all societies and have the power to keep multitudes glued to the television or sitting in the stadium for hours each week. War also is a powerful motivator, but in a very negative way.

Games and contests are not war, although the lines are not always clear. The entertainment committee that organized the grand opening of the Roman Coliseum planned gaming events that included the slaughter of 5,000 humans and 50,000 animals during its 90-day opening celebration. I suppose that was considered a suitable event for that time and place—sigh....

Games, contests, and wars all can be motivators. Focus your attention on setting up good games and contests, and use them to help all of us avoid the contest called war.

Southwest has created many neat games. It's a contest to make sure the plane leaves the gate on time, even with an exceptionally tight schedule. Employees take great pride in their performance, and are all dedicated to maintaining their record for keeping flights on time.

Here's How It Works

Creating goodwill contests and events can take any form you want and are limited only by your imagination. John Sortino, the guy who founded the Vermont Teddy Bear Company, used to celebrate the first day of spring with an employee softball game in the company's parking lot. He'd hold bocce tournaments every summer and give the winning teams a couple of days off. Employee skits at the holiday party were judged, with days off awarded as prizes. Sortino had great morale and happy employees.

Southwest isn't the only company that uses games to motivate its employees. Some others were mentioned in Chapter 3, Larry's supermarkets in Seattle, which have people competing with each other to collect the most tokens. Triad, that has people competing for hundreds of rewards with bragging rights, and Beverly, my wife, who has her kids competing to be Superstars.

A client oil company insisted on eliminating industrial accidents, a virtual impossibility, given some of the inherent dangers in the oil business. Management insisted, however, that it could be done.

The company was very serious and, to prove a point, promised to buy every employee a VCR and home video camera if they could reduce accidents to zero and hold the accident level at zero there for a full year. This incentive involved a fair piece of change for the company, seeing how there were more than 2,000 employees.

The executive position, however, was that it intended to prove a point with its challenge to the employees. There was much controversy regarding the definition of an accident, which was exactly the awareness that management was trying to create. Eventually, an accident was defined as an injury that required medical care. This satisfied employees, as it allowed some space for minor bumps or bruises. The campaign took five years, but it eventually worked. Management proved its point, and employees got their video cameras and VCRs.

Management at a Southern utility company gives away puffy stars for exceptional performance. They are made of yellow silk, are about two inches across, and are filled with stuffing to make them puffy, hence their name.

Rally the Troops

Rewards don't have to be trips to Hawaii or flashy new cars. Employees who get into the spirit of games and contests aren't all that interested in what the reward will be. Puffy stars, or other simple prizes that recognize performance, do just fine.

Employees compete for them, and keep their collections of past winnings displayed on the walls of their cubicles. The stars can be pinned to the walls.

Each star comes with a card that specifically describes what the recipient did to win the star. When I visited, I noticed that some employees had as many as ten stars displayed in their cubicles. I received a puffy star for the training seminar I facilitated. It's still pinned to my office wall.

Good games have clearly defined "us" and "them." Southwest, for example, defines "them" as the other airlines that can't achieve its rapid turnaround rate. "Them" can be a group outside your organization, or another group within. Keep the "them" simply defined.

You also can develop a game that allows your organization to define and compete against a common enemy.

A.C. wanted his organization to ship everything on its promised ship day. This sounds simple, but it took them more than a year to figure out how to do it. The starting point was with sales and the customers. Customers were poor planners, who often called the sales department and demanded rush orders. Individual salespeople, in turn, used their influence to move their customers ahead of other customers. This meant that some shipments would run late. Those customers, in turn, placed pressure on the sales department and the cycle continued.

The starting point was to inspire the team and convince it that it could operate differently. In this case, the "them" was the way the organization functioned. A.C. convinced the employees that they didn't need to operate the way that they had been. He convinced them that they could work ahead on requirements with customers, and that they didn't need to constantly jerk around the schedule.

It was a slow slog. A.C. gave the team a lot of encouragement. He wrote about its progress in the company newsletter. He gave constant encouragement and support to those who managed to work more closely with the customers and stopped changing around the schedule. Many within the organization didn't understand how disruptive and costly these constant changes to the schedule were. Everyone had to be trained to understand the implications of what was happening.

It took more than a year, but the troops finally rallied to the cause. It really worked, too. It's tough to get a good game going, but everyone loves to be a winner. A.C.'s small division started shipping on the promised date 99 percent of the time.

Once the shipping objective was achieved, the company launched a new advertising program, guaranteeing on-time shipments. Customers, who knew they could get their shipments on time, needed less inventory. That resulted in considerable savings.

A.C.'s business increased by 20 percent, and his reputation grew as well. Today, A.C. is a wealthy man and so are many of the people who followed his lead.

It Will Be Better Tomorrow

Promising a better tomorrow in order to make your operation more attractive to employees and potential employees might be a good idea, but you've got to be very careful about how you do it. You can promise, but don't over-promise.

The best way to avoid promising too much is to look only at the short term, say one month down the road or so. Don't guarantee the long term, as everyone knows you can neither predict nor control the future.

When Lee Iacocca, a man known for his superior verbal skills, took over the Chrysler Corporation in 1978, the company was a mess. At the time, Chrysler was one of the world's largest organizations. The company was spending $10 million a day, and had only $1 million in cash on hand.

Banks saw that the company was financially out of control, and refused to extend credit which would produce the cash needed to keep the company afloat. That's called, in simple language, bankruptcy.

Backfire

I knew a guy who had the nasty habit of promising his employees the moon, but never delivering. In fact, he'd often do the opposite. He'd hire somebody, then cut his salary or add extra hours to his schedule a couple of months later. Needless to say, this guy had a turnover rate like you wouldn't believe, and a group of very dissatisfied employees. Don't promise more than you can deliver. If you do, you'll ruin your credibility—and your workers' motivation.

So Iacocca went to the federal government, which agreed to bail out the financially desperate company. Of course, there would be many conditions placed on the auto company, including getting rid of thousands of employees. Morale throughout the organization was completely wiped out.

To try to motivate the survivors, Iacocca dealt only with the very short-term future of the company. He went to his unions and gave them a choice. Take $12.50 an hour and you'll have a job tomorrow. Insist on $17.50 and hour and there will be no jobs tomorrow.

Iacocca couldn't even guarantee that wage for the long term. The government support was to last only for a short period, in order to give management a chance to pull the company together. There were no guarantees that the company could be saved. Still, Iacocca managed to motivate workers by being hopeful for a better tomorrow and, as you know, the company pulled through and has prospered.

It is sometimes hard to tell the truth, but people really can deal with it. If they keep their confidence in you as a leader, they'll be motivated by hard truths. Never over-promise. It no doubt took some time for the company to get into bad shape, and it will take some time for it to pull out.

Building Positive Confrontation

Within any organization, there is an endless clash of ideas. The trick, for you, is to capture the best of those ideas without turning off the employees whose ideas are not pursued.

How do you do this? You've got to build positive confrontation.

Yes, There Is Such a Thing

A positive confrontation is confrontation in which both parties come out with solutions or ideas that can solve a problem or prevent it from happening again. Positive confrontations should be a goal of your organization. They don't involve name-calling or pointing fingers. They don't involve blame or "should-haves." They are forward-looking and, as the name implies, positive.

Defining Moments

Positive confrontations are those that address the impact of some action on the goals of your operation without being critical of the person or persons who caused the action.

You should focus on the idea of positive confrontations and teach your team the fine art of conducting them. Knowing how to confront one another positively will result in team members working together more effectively.

Consider a situation in which sales and production have agreed on a certain schedule and promised a delivery date to a customer. Problems begin to occur in production, and production staff knows that the promised ship date could be in jeopardy. Being conscientious, however, production attempts to make up for the lateness, and they don't alert the sales department to the impending problem. The date can't be met, however, and the shipment is missed.

Now everybody's upset. Production is upset because they couldn't make up for the problem, sales is livid, and the customer is not too happy either. The people in sales are sorely tempted to point fingers and put the blame where it belongs for the missed shipment.

How to Encourage and Control Positive Confrontation

Employees, in this hypothetical situation and in real situations, should be encouraged to practice constructive confrontation. The sales staff should say something to those in production rather than fume about the problem on their own.

To make it a constructive confrontation, sales must focus on what they will do to appease the customer, not what production should or shouldn't have done to avoid the problem in the first place. Production already knows they screwed up. Rubbing their noses in it will accomplish nothing.

Sales should let production know what their plans are to deal with the customers and what will be necessary for damage control. It also would be appropriate for sales and production to develop a better system of communication. Production should have been comfortable bringing sales in on the situation from the beginning, but, obviously, they weren't. If sales had been involved from the start, sales and production could have worked together and decided when to inform the customer of what was going on.

The purpose of positive confrontation is to discuss what will occur from this moment forward, not to place blame for things that have occurred in the past.

The Least You Need to Know

➤ Humans have an inborn motivation to improve their environments.

➤ When faced with terrible working conditions, use those conditions as motivators and get workers to try to make the conditions better.

➤ You hate to lose good employees, but promoting them within the company results in good benefits for you.

➤ You should work to create camaraderie and a sense of family within your organization.

➤ Games and contests can be great motivators within your company.

➤ Positive confrontation is not only possible but can be extremely productive.

Chapter 5

Cultivating Inquisitiveness

In This Chapter

➤ The different meanings of inquisitiveness

➤ Encouraging inquisitiveness in the workplace

➤ Getting past the negatives

➤ Looking past the day-to-day drag

➤ Encouraging people to want to work

➤ Finding ways to make the job special

➤ Making an old job new

➤ Finding pieces to the puzzles

You may have glanced at the title of this chapter and wondered what inquisitiveness has to do with motivation. On the surface, they seem like very different things.

When you think about it, however, inquisitiveness is an ideal motivator. Think about the people you know. The most interesting ones are probably those who are inquisitive. They're probably the folks who get the most done, too, and who look for better ways to do things.

Children are extremely inquisitive, and that characteristic motivates them to do all sorts of things. They explore, they put things in their mouths, they crawl behind the furniture, or wander away from the yard—all in the name of inquisitiveness. If kids weren't inquisitive, their learning process would slow down to a crawl.

Defining Moments

Inquisitiveness is the quality that drives a person to learn more about a particular topic, or about everything. It is what motivates someone to try to figure out a better way to complete a task. Inquisitiveness is a highly desirable quality that should be cultivated and encouraged.

And the same goes for adults, including the employees that you manage. So let's spend a few minutes investigating the concept of inquisitiveness and find out how it impacts on motivation.

What Is Inquisitiveness, and Who Cares About It?

When, just for fun, I clicked on my computer's thesaurus to look at some synonyms for "inquisitiveness," the word that came up first was "nosiness." Now, I don't know about you, but to me, inquisitiveness and nosiness are two distinctly different qualities.

Nosiness means that somebody is, well, nosy. A busybody. Interested in other people's business. When somebody is inquisitive, they're interested in what's going on, not because they're nosy but because they have a genuine desire to learn more for a good reason.

According to Webster's, a person who's inquisitive can be one of two things. The first definition says an inquisitive person is someone who is prying and unnecessarily curious. In other words, nosy.

Or, Webster says, an inquisitive person is one who is inclined to seek knowledge by discussion, investigation, observation, questioning, and so on. Or one who is eager to learn and given to research.

For our purposes, an inquisitive person is not nosy but one who is inclined to seek knowledge and is eager to learn.

Everyone should care about inquisitiveness because having inquisitive employees makes a huge difference in the workplace.

Cultivating an environment of inquisitiveness is very important to your success as a leader.

An environment that encourages and cultivates inquisitiveness is one that brings out the curious and creative elements in your team. It encourages your people to continuously learn and creatively develop new, innovative approaches.

Inquisitiveness is at the heart of competitive business, all of which is built upon continuous improvement.

Successful leaders understand this and never try to maintain stability or focus on the status quo. They're not focused on efficiency, either. Successful leaders are always changing things—always doing something differently.

They're focused on productivity, which is efficiency plus effectiveness. To be effective is to have the ability and desire to do something better. Inquisitive people are always seeking to do things better.

Competitive businesses are always looking for more money from consumers. It's how they stay competitive, right?

Consumers, however, will only put their money into things or ideas that they think will improve their lives. As a result, businesses are driven to find a better way and to continuously improve their products and services in order to convince customers to buy them.

Rally the Troops

Doing a job efficiently is desirable but shouldn't be a top priority. The top priority in your workplace should be for workers who are productive, which combines the qualities of efficiency and effectiveness.

Inquisitiveness and creative innovation lie at the very heart of the continuously improving standard of living that the human race, as a whole, has enjoyed over thousands and thousands of years.

PE Biosystems, a company in Foster City, California, has built a culture focused on inquisitiveness in its new product development area.

The company has no overall product development strategy. Rather, it has a large number of projects in progress at any given time. None of these many projects requires any initial approval from top management before they're launched. Anybody who has a creative or innovative idea can launch a project.

This implies considerable risk to the company. People tend to run in many different directions, and the company's resources go to fund many ideas that won't ever pay off. PE Biosystems, however, feels that this policy will be beneficial in the long run.

The thought process goes something like this…if you have lots of people and groups, all chasing good ideas with potentially great results, then at least one individual or group will hit on something big.

When that happens, the other groups will drop what they're working on and amass around the featured project, helping to push it forward. In this case, pushing it forward means pushing it into a marketable product.

PE Biosystems has created what essentially amounts to a survival-of-the-fittest strategy. Imagine a bunch of technicians, scientists, and engineers all working and competing to get a

Rally the Troops

PE Biosystem's idea policy is interesting. It creates a competitiveness among employees, each of whom is anxious to see his or her idea float to the top and grab the attention of the company. Competitiveness can be a great motivator.

following for their best thoughts. The ones that come up with the best results or solutions get the benefit of having everybody else jump on board to help with their projects.

This works out quite well for PE Biosystems because it creates a very fluid system that reinforces inquisitiveness and innovation.

The company has had annual sales the past few years of about $1 billion, and has experienced a 20 percent average annual growth rate throughout its 16-year history. Even more exceptional, however, is at the close of each fiscal year, it becomes evident that somewhere between 50 and 65 percent of sales are a result of products and services that didn't exist 12 months earlier.

Looking Beyond Discipline

To cultivate inquisitiveness in the workplace, you've got to change the way you think about leadership.

Many managers tend to spend a lot of time on humdrum issues such as basic discipline, process, and scheduling. Essentially, that's a waste of your time. You should be spending very little, or no time at all, on these issues.

Incorporate all the scheduling into daily activity and delegate it to your teams. You should be focusing on your company's goals, not the processes. Let your team concentrate on the day-to-day things. We'll discuss that idea in more detail later in the book. For now, just understand that in order to foster an inquisitive culture, you must first get your thinking processes way out in front of all the basic daily activity.

Defining Moments

Discipline, which is defined as "correction, chastisement, or punishment inflicted by way of correction and training," does have a more positive side. It's also defined as training that develops self-control, character, or orderliness and efficiency. Unfortunately, as used in business, the first meaning is normally the more relevant of the two.

Why Focusing on Discipline Doesn't Work

Discipline is negative. It's backward-looking, not forward. And discipline is always a reaction to something that shouldn't have occurred in the first place.

An inquisitive culture is positive and forward-looking. It looks outside itself into something new and different. An inquisitive culture stretches out into the future.

Unfortunately, you can't ignore discipline. It is a sometimes necessary evil. You can, however, diminish its impact. Your goal should be to build a culture that spends about 98 percent of its time focused on forward-looking, continuous-improvement issues. To do that, you'll need to spend about 98 percent of your time talking about, and acting upon, forward-looking business.

My consulting and training work doesn't always put me in touch with highly moti-vated, forward-looking teams. Many of the groups I work with are negatively focused on what is wrong within their company. They love to play what I like to call the "why-don't-they-do-something-about-this?" game. It's the most destructive game I see in business, and it's an activity that consumes incredible amounts of time.

It's a pleasure when I do encounter highly motivated, forward-looking teams. This occurs when I work with groups that have been built by great leaders.

If Not Discipline, Then What?

If you're not going to spend any—or much, at least—time focusing on discipline and other day-to-day routine matters, how will you spend your time? That's easy. You're going to rise above the daily grind and focus on the future.

When you do this, your team will follow. If you set the tone for your organization, your team will follow your example. It will rise above the negative, day-to-day stuff and focus on future issues also.

Negative events, thoughts, and ideas tend to be attention grabbers. What you need to do is to ignore the negative stuff as much as possible and start focusing on the positive.

Backfire

One of the dangers of sitting around waiting for somebody else to do something to improve the sit-uation is that, eventually, somebody will. And when that happens, where do you think it leaves you? Sitting on the outside looking in—that's where!

Don't wait for the magic "they" to come along. It's a tendency to wait for somebody else to come along to make things better, even when you have the power to do so yourself. Ignore those who constantly say things like, "They should do something about this," or "I wish they'd get moving on this." Understand that you and your team are "they" and start discussing new ways for your group to perform its responsi-bilities more productively.

Like most companies, the Unocal Corporation has always valued innovation. But at this El Segundo, California, oil and gas exploration company, executive leadership didn't feel that opportunities for greater innovation were happening fast enough.

The organization was becoming sluggish. People were focusing on the day-to-day rou-tine and not communicating enough. The goal had become to do the work for the day and get the heck out of there. Leadership, to its credit, saw the problems that were occurring, and was justifiably and wisely concerned.

The problem facing Unocal was basically an awareness—or lack of awareness—problem. People weren't aware of how their work was impacting other groups within the company. They were fragmented and not working as a whole.

The fundamental leadership question faced here was: "How do you rally people around a common purpose, making sharing what they know in their best personal interest?" The answer to that question lies in creating a new communications system.

Communication always occurs, sometimes even when you don't want it to. It isn't, however, always properly exposed to others.

What Unocal did to improve communications within the company was to develop new systems that made all the informal networks functioning within the organization more visible.

New training was developed and new reinforcement systems were put into place. Soon, employees within all the company's worldwide offices had developed more awareness of how their efforts related to the efforts of others. They had learned to consider who their communications might impact and how they could make the communications as effective as possible.

Here's How It Works

An important part of Unocal's training was to get employees to consider all the effects of their communications. Employees were taught to think about others who should be included before beginning any discussion, meeting, or even a conversation with a co-worker. This resulted in far better and more effective communication.

Unocal employees also were trained to ask larger questions. A normal question might be, "Who do we need in this meeting in order to resolve the issue before us?" To build a culture focused on inquisitiveness, however, you've got to look beyond the initial resolution. You've got to look at the impact that the initial resolution might have on other groups and how that result can be used to everyone's benefit.

At Unocal, additional forums and systems were built to take employees beyond the normal question. But the ability to communicate doesn't ensure that communication will occur. People must first realize that communication is vitally important and figure out with whom they can most effectively communicate.

That's what's happening at Unocal. Employees are asking, "Who else might care?" and are communicating with whomever the answer to that question happens to be.

As effective communication increases, workers become more confident. They're more aware of what other informal groups are doing. This awareness builds greater understanding of how important individual contributions are to the whole.

This overall understanding is building greater confidence in individuals, which translates into organizational confidence.

Effective leadership always pushes this concept. Informal groups exist in all organizations. To motivate, give the informal groups lots of exposure. Push people to ask the larger questions and encourage them to leap across the organizational barriers and into other groups. Encourage these actions and sell the idea that no one needs approval to leap forward and push ideas into other areas.

Kill Routines and Change the Job

Routine is an inquisitiveness buster, to be sure. Think about the times that you've had to do extremely routine jobs. You probably didn't go out of your way to be inquisitive—you just did the job to get it over with.

What you need to let your employees know, however, is that no job has to be a routine job. There are innovations possible with any task, no matter how routine it might seem on the surface. It's up to you, as a manager and a motivator, to get workers to start thinking creatively about their jobs. You have to empower them to do their jobs differently.

Backfire

The worst thing to do is to write off a job as routine or boring and let your workers know that that's how you feel about it. Remember that you set the tone. If workers know that you think a job is boring, they're sure to follow suit. Watch out that your attitudes don't rub off on your workers, even if it means changing those attitudes.

This Is Boring!

In almost every training program that I do, the problem of the routine job is raised. The general feeling is that there's no way to change these kinds of jobs. After all, they're routine by their very nature and there's nothing we can do about it. Wrong!

The job, whatever one we're talking about, was designed by some person to be repetitive and boring. That doesn't mean that there's not another way to do it, or that the method of doing it can't be changed. I've never seen it etched in stone anywhere that certain jobs must be universally done in the same boring, routine matter. I think, with a little creativity, every task can be improved upon and made more interesting.

If you can't think of any way to do that, then you'll have to deal with the results—poor morale, high employee turnover, and poor quality.

Decades ago, the automotive industry was highly regimented—read my lips: b-o-r-i-n-g. Employees were little more than robots. They were expected to do their job the way somebody told them to do it, and little more. They certainly weren't involved in any job improvement projects.

65

Other people were responsible for those kinds of things. Autoworkers simply did the same repetitive, assembly line job over and over.

That system produced a lot of cars. It also produced a lot of poor-quality cars and poor-quality working conditions that resulted in an adversarial management-labor system. Strikes were rampant.

Today, there still are plenty of assembly lines, and not just in auto plants. I see the lines in all kinds of industries. Progressive manufacturers, however, unlike the post-World War II-era auto industry, have altered their assembly line production methods.

The assembly worker now has the power to stop the line when something goes wrong. Also, the worker may well be involved in the industry as more than an assembly line worker. Doing the routine job still requires a major investment of his time. Many industries, however, include assembly line workers on things such as problem-solving teams, continuous improvement teams, or model changeover teams. They get employees involved and invested. They motivate and encourage inquisitiveness.

Here's How It Works

The human mind isn't designed for constant boredom and repetition. Watch a child sometime who's been assigned a repetitive task. She'll do the chore in a constant manner for a short time, then start looking for ways to make it more interesting. It's a natural tendency to try to avoid boredom and repetition, and one that all employers should use to their advantage.

Making People Want to Work

You hear a lot these days about people who don't want to work. To listen to some people, you'd think there's not one person left in the world who's remotely interested in doing a day's work. That, however, just isn't true. People want to work; they just want jobs that are interesting and challenging.

Good managers understand that and they make it happen. Special project teams include people from all parts of the company. Assembly workers are given time to meet with team members, engineers, and others. They discuss what's going right, and where the problems are. Then they come up with cost-effective solutions to the problems, which ensures that they won't happen again in the future.

In short, assembly workers, historically ignored as uninvolved in the job, do exactly what any responsible adult should do: They help to manage and operate the company.

In times past, their work had to be checked because their performances were unreliable.

Today, assembly workers are motivated and they help the organization produce quality goods. These same motivated teams might also be involved in model changeover projects, maintenance projects, new equipment installation, or startup projects.

The important point to understand here is that the assembly line job has been changed. Strong leaders had the vision and energy to go ahead and change the job that previously couldn't be changed.

Rally the Troops

Don't assume that people will resist getting more involved with the company. Some will, of course. Most, however, will rise to the challenge.

The result is that the same union people who couldn't be trusted are now helping companies to run better and more productively.

Assembly lines are still highly efficient ways to build cars, along with thousands of other worthwhile products. Progressive organizations still use them extensively, but they don't limit workers to being merely part of a line.

Progressive companies have expanded the duties of assembly line workers in order to make them more than just a body on the line. These companies have made the jobs different and more stimulating to the people performing them. They've made the jobs something that employees want to do.

Problem-solving responsibility is no longer the domain of offline engineering groups that are isolated from the workers. Instead, engineers and line workers operate hand in hand. They're teams that create better solutions.

Inspired leadership focuses its attention on the majority of workers, those who are willing and eager to rise to the challenge. This is how you foster inquisitiveness. Those who aren't willing to get involved should be downplayed and eventually purged from the system.

The Thomson Corporation, a publishing firm in Stamford, Connecticut, is very upfront about its expectations of each member of the company. All employees are kept up-to-date on changes within the company—even when the changes are only anticipated, not actual. This ensures that all employees will be prepared for any changes that occur.

The company teaches employees to expect change because change occurs when a company is very innovative. Instead of apologizing for change, Thomson provides employees with information about dealing with change and personal resilience. Training by design does not focus on a specific change initiative. Rather, training at the publishing firm focuses on the broader issue of how to increase the corporate capacity for any type of change. It teaches everyone in the corporation to cope with and benefit from change.

This kind of training teaches employees the characteristics they'll need to become more resilient and to survive during times of change.

Those characteristics include:

➤ Being focused

➤ Being organized

➤ Having a positive sense of their ability to deal with change

➤ Being positive about themselves and their environments

The survival of Thompson's employees, as well as the company itself, depends upon the ability of everyone there to continuously find better ways to do what they do. Thomson believes that being honest and upfront with its expectations draws people into the culture and makes them want to work. Sales numbers and margin improvement numbers suggest they are making it pay off.

Making the Job Really Special

In order to foster inquisitiveness, you've got to make a job really special. But how do you do that? Largely by doing what we've discussed so far in this chapter.

You get workers involved in the company. That makes their jobs special. Getting somebody involved is a universal way of getting people interested and invested in something, whether it's a job, a neighborhood, a nation, or whatever.

We know that keeping people involved in a society and its goals is the one sure way to assure that they'll contribute to that society and support its goals and purposes.

Here's How It Works

I once watched with wonder the rejuvenation of a run-down neighborhood in a mid-sized East Coast city. The rejuvenation occurred as neighbors got involved, and it all started when one family planted flowers in front of its home. Soon, three or four other families had planted flowers. All of a sudden, people were cleaning up junk piles and picking up trash from the streets. A neighborhood association was formed to ensure that the positive changes would continue. It was a joy to see, and a great example of the power of getting people involved.

You can also find other ways to make the job special. Think about some of these ideas:

➤ Add special activities to the job.

➤ Make time for special one-of-a-kind projects.

➤ Perform lots of cross-training.

➤ Team up with sister managers, where work similar to your work is being done. Do cross-training, then trade employees back and forth. This not only incites the team to action, it adds more security for you, the company, and your sister manager. The two of you gain power as you can share resources in an emergency.

Other things that progressive companies have done in order to make jobs special and attract and keep motivated, flexible employees are to break down internal hierarchies and get rid of job descriptions.

The hierarchy is a chain of command that slows things down. Job descriptions are limiting tools, not expanding tools. Progressive organizations are looking for employees who can work quickly and respond immediately to problems and situations. If hierarchies and job descriptions are preventing employees from being able to do those things, then it's best to put them aside.

Barclays Home Finance, based in the United Kingdom, flattened its hierarchy, created larger and more diverse groups of employees, and spent enormous energy on cross-training and developing work teams.

This company wants flexible, motivated people. It gets them by making things really special. The company has developed groups of people who can be moved from one part of the business to another with only very short notice necessary.

This gives Barclays a distinct competitive advantage. It has become one of the most profitable and productive organizations for its parent company and a leader in the highly competitive home mortgage market.

It hasn't cut prices, but it's become the market leader through quicker responsiveness and value-added services. Quicker responsiveness is a result of those flexible employees with flexible job descriptions. Value-added, unique services come from employees who are allowed to communicate freely. This freedom cultivates maximum creativity.

Employees at Barclays even helped to design their new office building, in which there are no private offices. Within this building, communications are rapid. People constantly hear conversations around them. Knowledge and

Rally the Troops

Workers should always be allowed to communicate their ideas freely, to each other and to management. This "brainstorming" process is an effective method of coming up with new ideas, while encouraging everyone to get involved.

intelligence travel quickly throughout the organization, producing the confidence needed to create quick and flexible, value-added, unique services.

Inquisitiveness definitely is encouraged and cultivated.

Everyone's Hunting for Something New

As you ponder your own responsibilities and environment, keep in mind that we're all hunting for something new. New things are exciting. They're great motivators. Don't try to encourage the status quo just because it's there.

In our society, the status quo is much less meaningful than the change that we embrace. Take a look at the jobs that you offer to others. What is the opportunity for discovery within those jobs? Behavioral scientists for the past century have argued that we cannot maintain motivated and inspired teams if their only responsibility is to do something repetitive. Satisfying jobs have to include room for growth and change.

Here's How It Works

Hamsters can maintain high levels of satisfaction by running in those little wheels in their cages for long periods of time. Dogs can maintain high levels of satisfaction by sitting on a chair next to the window, watching for the letter carrier to come up the walk. People, however, generally aren't satisfied with those types of tasks. We can't maintain high levels of satisfaction doing routine tasks, even if we're paid well to do them.

Too many managers I've worked with are focused on maintaining stability through building procedures and predictable processes. They spend lots of energy describing how the job is supposed to work, and teaching employees the rules. When employees start asking the inevitable "what-if-something-goes-wrong" questions, the typical answer from these kinds of managers is something like this: "Call us (read responsible management) and we'll have a look at the policy."

The implication to this kind of answer is clear. What these managers are saying is, "You do the work, but we really don't trust your judgment or your ability to make decisions."

There's no quicker way to stamp out inquisitiveness.

You can't build stability or ensure involved, motivated employees by spending a lot of time describing predictable processes. You build stability by training people to be alert to, to hunt for, and to deal with whatever is new, different, and unpredictable.

You build stability by training people to do the routine job and to exercise judgment while they do it. You also build involvement by helping people to deal with the unexpected.

An example of the "prepare for the unexpected" concept is with the takeoff and landing of passenger aircraft. Everybody wants these processes to be perfect and absolutely fail-safe all of the time.

No one believes, however, that they will be. Stuff happens, regardless. No matter how well pilots and controllers are trained, there's always a chance that something will go wrong and an accident will occur.

Backfire

Telling an employee to defer to management on anything of any importance is akin to a parent telling a kid to do something, and when the kid questions the command, saying, "Because I said so, that's why." There's no better way to alienate the employee—or the kid.

To build stability and predictability, you don't dwell on the possibility that something might go wrong. Instead, you train people to use sound judgment when the exception occurs.

Many times, these kinds of situations cause people to excel. All airline pilots, controllers, and everyone involved are given the best training available on how the system is supposed to work. This training is good enough for 99.9 percent of the job. Fortunately, most of the time, everything happens exactly they way it's supposed to.

Learning how to get the plane off the ground and back down again is basic training for everyone involved. After this training, though, comes the real training.

Training to deal with the "what-ifs" makes a big difference and builds a motivated team. Continuing reinforcement and continuing review of daily events focuses on new information.

All the new information is rolled into the real ongoing pilot training, and all of it's designed to help the pilot deal with the what-ifs. What if the plane does this, then what? What if the plane does that, then what? What has gone wrong in the past and what did we learn from that? What new things must we simulate in future training? The more what-ifs the pilot and everyone else involved can prepare to handle, the better off we all are.

Keeping people highly motivated and focused on the job is an ongoing process, not an event. Remembering that everyone is looking for something new and different will help you to keep things in perspective. Don't get too bogged down with the routine job stuff, but look to the what-ifs. Encourage workers to be creative and inquisitive.

Here's How It Works

If the airline industry crash rate for 1999 was exactly the same as the crash rate for 1960, then, considering the increase in air traffic over the past 40 years, we'd have an average of one airline crash every day. Fortunately, airline personnel have been dealing rather nicely with the "what–ifs," and finding solutions to problems that could result in crashes.

What's New for Me?

What's new for you depends on your work, your experiences, and other circumstances, but one thing is for sure: There always will be something new.

Bob Dylan told us back in the 1960s that the times they were a-changing. Guess what? They haven't stopped. And as the times and circumstances change, so will the way you'll need to respond to the problems and challenges that face you, your workers, and your business.

One of my clients distributes about a billion dollars' worth of consumer products annually to thousands of stores throughout several western states.

This company has about a hundred drivers, all of whom are members of the rough-and-tough Teamsters union. Most of their deliveries—about 60 percent—go to tiny mom-and-mop deli-type stores. My client and its Teamsters clearly need the mom-and-pop market.

The problem is it's getting harder and harder for small establishments to compete against the giant supermarkets, complete with deli counters, ready-to-eat packaged foods, salad bars, and so forth. Mom and Pop are keeping the stores open 18 hours a day, trying to keep up. They're losing the battle against the giants because they're working too many hours for too little pay.

All of a sudden, these drivers and management are faced with something new. They didn't set out to make something new happen, but circumstances dictate that they react to the situation.

It becomes in the best interest of my client, and of the Teamsters union, to make sure these little operations don't go out of business. They represent a lot of stops, you know, and the math is easy to do.

Fewer stops = fewer drivers

Here's How It Works

Nearly everybody faces new situations that they must respond to. Doctors have to treat previously unheard of diseases. Professional athletes come up against new competitors. Teachers get kids in their classes who have special needs or problems and they have to figure out how to make them fit in with the rest of the class. These are the challenges that ensure new things will always be occurring.

All of a sudden, there's a big shift in thinking. Teamsters have never cared about sales, only deliveries. Now they're trying to come up with ways to help keep the small stores in business because it's in their interests to do so.

Fortunately, Teamsters are in the ideal position to help the little guys stay in business. They know and understand how these small businesses work because they're constantly around them. They know how the stores are structured, how the products are handled and displayed, and so forth.

The routine part of the Teamster's job, making deliveries, has become secondary to the task of trying to keep the small guys in business. And union members have responded to the challenge. They've become involved in the effort, and are an inspired, motivated workforce.

Pilots and air traffic controllers need to know what to do if something goes wrong. Constant training and evaluation of the "what-if" scenarios keeps them inspired, motivated, and involved with the job, not just with routine flying.

Teamsters need to understand how to help the little guy compete against the big guys. There is always something new going on. You just have to be aware of what it is, focus on it, and keep your employees focused on the real issues that drive the business.

Is There a Puzzle to Be Solved Here?

All jobs, and many other aspects of life, are constant puzzles. At any point in time, we just don't know where all the pieces are.

This isn't necessarily a bad thing, however. Prepare for it by keeping your people aware of the unknown and always cultivate the inquisitive side of the team. Train for the known aspects of a job, but remember that all training should include discussions about the unknown.

Inquisitiveness is endless. It will only stop when human creativity ends, and that's a concept I don't even want to consider.

As a manager, you should encourage and welcome inquisitiveness. Don't try to turn it off, but do just the opposite. Make sure the jobs that you offer include as much puzzle-solving as you can possibly cram in.

The Least You Need to Know

➤ Inquisitiveness has both positive and negative definitions, but for our purposes, it's positive.

➤ Discipline doesn't foster an inquisitive environment and shouldn't be a dominant activity.

➤ Changing routines and making jobs more interesting goes a long way toward encouraging inquisitiveness.

➤ If work is challenging and exciting, with room for input and suggestions, your team will be motivated and eager to do their jobs.

➤ Every job can be made special by encouraging workers to look past the boundaries and think "outside of the box."

➤ We all want new experiences, and you can create these for your workers by letting them react to their environments.

➤ Encourage your team to try to solve puzzles and problems, and to be creative and inquisitive.

Part 2

Where, Why, What, Who, and When: The Biggest Motivators

When it comes to motivating your team, there are five words to keep in mind: Where, why, what, who, and when.

If you can get your workers to understand where you're heading, why you're trying to get there, what's the advantage for them to make sure they do get there, who wants them to get there, and when they need to be there, you'll be an effective motivator.

Part 2 explains why these ideas are so important and how you can get your workers excited about them. Buying into the "where, why, what, who, and when" concepts invests your team in the operation, and gets them involved in the greater goals of the team, the department, and the company.

It's extremely important, as a leader, to understand how important the five Ws are to your team, and to use them to move your team forward.

Chapter 6

Where Are We Heading?

In This Chapter

➤ Relating goals to where we are

➤ Making employees part of the "in crowd"

➤ Defining a good goal

➤ Making sure that your goals are worthwhile

➤ Setting goals that you can reach

➤ Staying on course by monitoring your goals

Considering the long-term trend of our existence, we can assume that we're always heading toward something better than what we have now, even though circumstances can be deteriorating in the short term.

As a society, we muddle through such events and periods as slavery and world wars. Still, I think we all agree that, for most of us living today, things are better than they were when man lived in caves and hunted animals for his food. To be comfortable, satisfied, and able to motivate ourselves, we need to understand much more than what's expected from us at any given point in time.

As individuals and members of groups, we need to understand where our organizations are heading. We need to be a part of planning for their futures, and we must feel comfortable supporting that future direction. We need to know how our smaller team fits into the larger direction, and we need to appreciate how our individual performances support the overall efforts of the organization.

In this chapter, we'll take a look at how we can achieve those needs and keep ourselves satisfied and motivated.

Linking the Goal to Where We Are Today

The direction in which we're all heading is a top-down process. While we all push and constantly try to modify that direction, we look to leadership to pull together our activities. It does no good to work against each other, so we look to someone with authority to keep things united, and describe some goal that makes sense to our group. This is true of all groups and organizations. Businesses, social groups, churches, and synagogues—you name it, and it looks for leadership. To give "where" real-world meaning, it must be related to current circumstances and make sense within the context of real-world circumstances.

Assume your goal is to motivate the filthy and starved ten-year-old urchin wandering the streets of some Third World city not to sell her stick-like, 60-pound body into the drug and sex trade that prospers around her.

To meet this goal, your top-down sales pitch should neither start with the Ten Commandments nor a justification of the consumer-driven markets that enable the existence of the sex and drug trades.

Backfire

Avoid confusing your team members with too much talk about "linking goals" or "real-world circumstances." These kinds of terms serve a purpose, but most employees relate better to straightforward talk about what will happen within the company, and how it will affect them and their jobs.

Start by offering food and a blanket, but only if the urchin agrees to stay at your safe shelter. This option is far more relevant to the world she knows than the Ten Commandments would be and you'll have a much greater chance of helping her.

"Where" Needs Constant Reinforcement

When you're talking about where you're heading to your team at work (something you should do frequently), explain the direction in terms that relate to the employees. Use team-oriented language such as, "We must increase quality because the expected quality level has increased, " or "We'll all be better off if we raise our quality levels above those of our competitors."

Avoid egocentric language such as, "I need for you to improve profitability." Also avoid words that are condescending such as, "The company wants us to improve our quality levels." Everybody knows you're blowing smoke when you say that sort of thing. The company doesn't want anything. It's people within the company who are clamoring to have something done.

While the long-term, overall direction is easy to explain, it's constantly confused and compromised by short-term realities. Frequent discussions are necessary to keep your people focused on the real cause, not the short-term diversions.

A common complaint I hear in my workshops is that bosses don't communicate the general direction of the company often enough to their employees.

Communicate often.

I've asked many bosses why they don't share their visions with employees and let everyone know where the company is headed. The answers I get vary. Some examples of what I've heard include:

Rally the Troops

Discussing with employees what is happening at the moment and how it's helping or hurting the cause will set you apart as a boss. That's not because talking to your employees about where you're heading is extremely difficult or tricky, it will set you apart simply because so few leaders do it.

➤ "They won't do their jobs correctly if they know they're going to be eliminated."

➤ "They may abandon us."

➤ "They don't care."

➤ "They only want a paycheck."

➤ "They really can't understand."

➤ "They'll tip our strategy to the competition."

➤ "It's not their company."

Bosses talk like this all time, even though history suggests that the exact opposite is a much better route to take.

People throughout millennia have proven they're willing to keep secrets, tolerate hardships, work hard, and fight for any number of causes if they believe that those causes are worthwhile. That's the crucial point. Your followers must personally identify with your cause before they can be motivated to support it.

Napoleon observed that, "People will die for a ribbon if they believe in the cause."

One of my clients owns a construction company that needed more involvement from its staff of project managers, engineers, and planners. Everyone worked, but not very hard. They were only superficially involved in business objectives, and the situation was producing disastrous results. Devoid of energy, the business's margins were very weak and it was losing ground against competition.

Company stock was privately held and the stockholders were under no obligation to disclose their financial conditions or future plans to employees. Yet, years of simply berating the team and demanding better performance or else had produced no results. Everyone could see that something had to change.

Backfire

Beware of disclosing unreliable information that turns out to be false. If you do that very often, your team will tune out most of what you say, thinking your information is unreliable.

What finally resulted in involved, motivated employees was a transformation in management's thinking. Leaders started openly sharing the financial health of the organization, the risks it faced because of obsolete and aged equipment, the future capital requirements that were necessary, and its future sales opportunities. In a forthright manner, management discussed with employees where the company was going and shared its strengths and weaknesses.

The response to the new approach was obvious within months. Everyone could see, and feel, the new energy in daily business discussions. Open communications even created additional interest and involvement from employees who were members of the construction union. This historically had been an adversarial, and rather cynical, group. The more open communications started in the late 1980s, and the company's confidential financial status has never leaked to the public. Profit margins have strengthened by about 20 percent, and the business is far more healthy than it was a decade ago.

Now, I'm not advocating that you disclose confidential or illegal corporate insider information on upcoming mergers or acquisitions and the like. But, short of violating laws, there no doubt is plenty of room for more effective communications with staff.

Needing to Be Part of the "In Crowd"

To make your employees feel that they're really part of the "in crowd," you must make sure that the job molds to fit them, while they mold to fit the job. Huh? Let's take a look at an example.

C.E. was a college junior when she first came to my company as a co-op employee. At our small company, keeping involved is easy. Company products include my worldwide seminars and whatever consulting projects our clients desire.

My staff is constantly doing research, reworking materials, dealing with schedules, reviewing correspondence, or writing up results from consulting projects. It's pretty easy to know where we're heading. Everyone looks at my calendar anytime they want to, and we communicate constantly. It's my job to keep them informed and involved.

C.E. slipped right into our operation and was just fine from the start. With a simple, brief overview of objectives and necessary changes, she could take over an entire manual and plow right through the thing.

Here's How It Works

People have a need to feel like they belong in all situations, not just those related to work. It's that need that causes most people to hang out with people who are like them in many ways. It's rare to find somebody who spends all of his time with people who are very unlike himself. Most of us like to be around folks who share our interests, values, and experiences.

College provided her with basic skills such as how to run the software we use. She was comfortable using her new skills, unafraid to make decisions, and willing to challenge things that made no sense to her. She knew immediately how her contribution fit into the total organization, and she was highly motivated to do whatever was necessary to ensure quality within our tight deadline requirements.

One night, I came in late while C.E. was still working. She was very upset. Her roommate had received a message from C.E.'s mother earlier in the day, saying that C.E.'s father, traveling home from a business trip, had driven into a freak ice storm, hundreds of miles from home. He had crashed his car and was in a small town's hospital emergency room.

C.E. and I had established effective communications long ago. I just sat there and listened while she related her sad story.

Like most college students, C.E. didn't have buckets of money for long-distance phone calls, or for anything else, for that matter.

I asked for the name of the town where her father was hospitalized. A few phone calls had me talking to the hospital's emergency room staff and, eventually, her dad. Another phone call got me hooked up with C.E.'s mom. Then I pushed a few buttons, dialed a code or two, and handed C.E. the phone. The family was linked in a conference call, and I simply left the room.

It was a simple task for me to do this from my well-equipped office. Sure, it cost a few dollars, but to do what I had done would have been impossible for C.E. to pull off from her dorm room.

Rally the Troops

A good way to make employees part of the "in crowd" is to allow flexible scheduling to accommodate family concerns. It isn't always possible, but employees say it's something that they really appreciate, and it breeds loyalty and motivation.

The point of that story is that sometimes you have to stretch things around a little bit. If you mold to fit your employees and their circumstances, they'll mold to fit you.

C.E. didn't stay on the phone for very long. Yet, molding her family concerns into the job for a few minutes probably helped her greatly. She wouldn't have been able to concentrate on her work while worrying about her father, so a modest investment was more than worthwhile.

C.E. stayed with us until her education was complete. She always made sure I was aware of the positive things her friends and family said about me, my company, and what we did. Of course, I knew that it was really C.E. out there creating all those impressions.

People will always work for money. They have to. Creating the "in crowd" is a different thing altogether. This gives you the power to inspire them. People will make their work an important part of their lives if there is space at work for their lives.

Just What Is a Good Goal, and Where Will We Find It?

First and foremost, a good goal is a realistic goal. There are many thoughts that are interesting and fun to talk about—maybe even worthwhile. But fun things are not necessarily realistic.

Rally the Troops

Good coaches know how to motivate their teams by setting high, but attainable, goals. A good coach might tell his team that its goal should be to win as many games as possible, but he won't make the team feel it's failed if it doesn't win every game it plays.

Here's an example. If I could only see what the world's stock markets were going to be 24 hours before anyone else could, I'd be able to earn zillions of dollars. I would then enjoy pumping those dollars into premium schools and educational programs for all. People would willingly accept this free education and go on to build fine homes for everyone; they'd negotiate all differences peaceably; stop polluting; eliminate hunger, corruption, tyranny, and crime; and then yada, yada, yada.

This might be fun to dream and talk about, but it incites little action and cannot be molded into an effective goal. It is too extravagant and unrealistic, and will remain so until someone figures out how to see the future.

Good Goals Must Be Attainable

Extravagance in itself does not mean bad goals. The real trick is to make the goal realistic enough so that it's reasonably attainable.

Seeing the future defies all known physical laws, so it goes beyond attainability and therefore cannot motivate. People can be motivated to follow extravagant goals, as long as those goals pass the attainability test.

Businessman Craig McCaw has launched five new companies since selling McCaw Communications to AT&T. He's founded Nextel, Nextlink, Internext, Nextband, and Teledesic. While these companies may have different customers, products, and objectives, McCaw sees them as integral parts of a larger purpose. He has some extravagant, but not absurd, thoughts.

McCaw feels the so-called Industrial Age is a low point of human evolution because it forced us to pile into cities, leaving relatives and friends behind. Industrialization, McCaw claims, has produced overcrowded urban areas.

He also believes the Industrial Age encouraged the breakdown of family structure, as people had to move to where the jobs were. The poorest countries lose their best talent and best potential leaders to the richest countries because the best and brightest people are those most able to move and seek their fortunes in prosperous countries.

Information moves far more freely than steel or timber, and that's where McCaw is going. He's planning to allow information to flow equally and freely to all people. Using the Internet and Teledesic's satellites, an African artisan, for example, can sell his sculptures directly and profitably to collectors in the United States and Europe. This allows him to cut out the middlemen and keep the profit for himself.

McCaw argues that the Internet will be able to slow, and perhaps reverse, the migration patterns that have been building over the past two centuries. If people can communicate more easily, they will be able to live where they like and be better able to create and work in useful jobs where they live.

Whether McCaw's vision is correct or not, it is at least understandable. It is also at least somewhat realistic. That is, the average informed person can perceive that his vision is possible. Investors and employees can understand the direction in which he's heading and determine for themselves if they want to be a part of that direction.

To motivate your team, make them part of the "in crowd." Give this a high priority. Don't use words like "make more profit," because people need more than that. Discuss larger impact. Find ways to describe where you're heading, using language that has a larger purpose that they can understand. Here are just a few examples:

Rally the Troops

Look for the visionaries on your team and appeal to their idealistic views. You can push these people a little further with your visions and goals than you'd be able to do with the more practical members.

➤ Your computer company is trying to change the world and give us all sorts of new ways to communicate and enjoy life.

➤ Your agriculture company is trying to give us the high-quality and safe food that we want year-round, at low prices.

➤ Your auto company is trying to give us highly reliable, safe cars that will run for at least 100,000 miles without need of repairs.

➤ Your airline company is trying to give us safe, reliable, and on-time travel.

All of these themes, and many others, are used constantly to motivate customers and employees. If you're running the customer service department, the job is more than simply handling customer complaints. The job is handling the complaints and then building systems to minimize future recurrence of the complaints.

The real job, then, is to handle complaints, determine why they occur, and help the company develop product improvements to make them disappear.

If your department assembles cars, then the job is to ensure the car is assembled without error or injury to your team. If you are commander of an armored personnel carrier attacking in Desert Storm, then the job is to make certain that you reach your objective and suffer no injuries in the process.

All activity must have some value. To motivate your team, incorporate discussions of the total value and broad purpose of your work; do not simply focus on the specific tasks that must be done.

Here's How It Works

Even children respond better when they know that a task they're performing is part of a bigger project. Consider the difference between asking a child to make a drawing of a dog, and asking her to make a drawing of a dog that's going to be displayed with a lot of other pictures of animals in a school art show. She'll be motivated to work a lot harder on the picture for the show than the one she's been instructed to draw for no apparent reason.

A Goal That's Understandable

Make the goal understandable within the context of your goal's larger mission. You may have an aggressive, risky, or even extravagant goal. It will still achieve a following if it has context.

Craig McCaw's goal for Teledesic to put 288 satellites in orbit by 2003 may be staggering in scope, considering the risky nature of satellite launches. This very aggressive goal requires a mind-boggling $9 billion in capital investment before Teledesic can sell any data transmission capability to any customer. This, of course, represents giant business risks.

Still, staggering in scope does not mean impossible. The motive for setting this aggressive, even extravagant, objective is perfectly understandable. If the satellites can be launched and the programming completed, then high-speed data connections will be available to any point of the globe.

Considering the scope and magnitude of the task Teledesic is contemplating, the dollar figure is reasonable. Furthermore, while no one knows if we really need all this additional Internet capability, one need only look at our historically insatiable desire to communicate with each other to understand why so many are being attracted to McCaw's goal.

Investors have been motivated to come up with more than 25 percent of the capital necessary for McCaw's project, as of this writing. McCaw seems on target to raise all the needed money, especially by recruiting giant partners such as Boeing Aircraft that have expertise in building and launching satellites.

Illogical goals, and those that can't be understood within the context of the total organization, are demotivators. They only create cynicism and distrust, and you should stay away from them. If you have inherited illogical goals, simply get rid of them. Kill them. If you can't kill them outright, ignore them until they die off slowly, over time.

Many businesses, for example, reward their customer service representatives for brevity with each customer contact. If it takes three minutes on average to resolve a problem, then, they figure, two minutes must be better. Brevity, however, has nothing to do with quality or customer satisfaction—critical anchors of any business.

At first glance, the goal of shorter customer service contacts seems to be a reasonable measure. However, it doesn't take the customer service representatives doing the job very long to figure out that the goal is a measure of efficiency, with nothing to do with effectiveness.

Dissatisfied customers who have been handled quickly or tersely simply call back and create even greater workloads. Furthermore, because brevity is rewarded, service representatives have little time to be proactive and take control of circumstances. They simply log those calls that they can't immediately resolve, and invite the customer to call back and check the status of their problem later. This creates even more dissatisfied customers—not to mention more calls.

Customer service representatives quickly become demoralized as they learn the drive for brevity is not understandable in the context of creating customer satisfaction, the heart of the mission statement.

This scenario has been with us before. In the 1950s, 1960s, and 1970s, millions of assembly line workers were rewarded for speed. As a result, we produced a lot of products that were of poor quality. We also produced a lot of demoralized workers. It took the quality revolution of the 1980s and 1990s to rebuild pride, morale, and motivation on the shop floor.

Here's How It Works

Can you imagine a great artist like Claude Monet being forced to produce paintings within a certain time frame in order to meet quotas? Or a composer like Ludwig van Beethoven being told he had to crank out four works in the next three months in order to meet his goals? Forced speed can be a real motivation buster.

A Goal That's Measurable

To give meaning to your goals, and to help them inspire people, create good, objective measurements that people can relate to their specific behavior. Measurement involves more than just determining if the goal is accomplished.

If your goal is to make reliable toasters and you only want to check toasters once after they're built, then everything is okay, as long as every toaster works reliably. However, because toasters are finished before they're checked, any failure involves high repair costs. To fix the new toaster, someone must take it apart and find the error. Even more importantly, the same error may be repeated with many more toasters before it's discovered. It would be far more effective to ensure toasters are being built reliably in the first place.

To build reliable toasters, measurements must be applied throughout the toaster-making process. They must be applied during design, parts manufacture, and assembly. Reliability for each component, and for the final assembly, must be defined.

Tests that measure all the stages of manufacturing must be developed. Measurements, commonly called milestones or checkpoints, must be created and applied along the way in order to evaluate progress.

This method would mean that toasters are built more slowly. It also insures focused employees and high morale because quality is being built into each unit along the way. Even though toasters are built more slowly, the total cost of building toasters would be lower because repair and rebuild costs are eliminated.

Making the Goal Worthwhile

Good measurement of a goal means creating a good scoreboard for that goal. Scoreboards are critical links that give meaning to the goal and the important milestone measurements.

Imagine any sporting event. There are many subgroups that make up the total show. There are fans, athletes, coaches, managers, owners, advertisers, officials, television broadcasting, leagues, and so on. All these groups are needed to make the event a success. What ties all groups together and gives the event spirit, while motivating the fans to put forth their hard-earned dollars, is the scoreboard. The scoreboard doesn't just announce the winner. It records and tracks how the game progresses.

Try to imagine a football game without a scoreboard. You'd have a bunch of big guys bashing into each other without direction. There would be no way to evaluate progress by checking elapsed time, scores, or penalties. It would be a mess.

Telling you who wins the game is the scoreboard's smallest contribution. Its more important contribution is the tracking of progress as the game is played.

It tracks team, as well as individual, contributions to the overall effort. The best scoreboards also help keep the game interesting by occasionally pulling up past individual player performances or the performances of other teams. They show replays and help the audience celebrate success for the home team.

Keep the scoreboard analogy in mind as you evaluate your work goals and think of ways to measure your team's performance. Develop measurements that can be posted for all to see, and keep the tracking system publicly posted in a central location.

Here's How It Works

Fund-raisers have long understood the power of tracking systems. Think about billboards you've seen that keep you informed of your local United Way's fund-raising efforts. This gets the community involved and makes everyone part of the effort. It's smart.

People get excited about tracking goals—I see it everywhere. Tracking goals is as important as noting when they're met.

Tracking should also note failures when they occur. Build in enough flexibility so that your scoreboard can also track failures. Just be sure that all your measures are relevant.

You can measure all sorts of things that have little or no meaning and do nothing to build and motivate a team. You can measure the number of bolts or nails used, phone calls answered, letters written, meetings attended, or pencils sharpened. None of these things makes sense because they're merely measurements of tools being used and not the work being done with those tools.

Measuring nails used by carpenters, while relevant, is not a measure of quality houses built. In the toaster example, working toasters are more important than toasters put together quickly. If your people are customer service specialists, resolving issues is the critical measurement. Importantly, taking corrective action to ensure the problem does not recur in the future is also a relevant measurement. If you are leading salespeople, measuring how effectively the salesperson cultivates the entire territory is more important than measuring success or failure with a particular sale.

Continuous Monitoring of Your Goals

Things are always shifting around. To maintain relevance, you must adjust your vision as reality shifts. This is also true for the goals you pursue in fulfillment of your vision.

Goals, as well as milestones or checkpoints, need to be constantly monitored and adjusted to ensure that they mesh with the ever-shifting reality.

Monitor the goal's validity while you pursue it. That's the only way to ensure its continued relevance. Build ways to monitor the goal with the same degree of energy that you invest in building the goal itself.

Let me explain the significance of this point further with an analogy.

Think about time passing and our need to measure the passage of time. A simple wristwatch usually is good enough. It can be adjusted and synchronized to some other instrument, say the television news announcer who serves as a master clock.

But where does the station get credibility? The station maintains its credibility by setting its time against one of the atomic clocks located in national laboratories around the world. In 1958, scientists throughout the world adopted the vibration rate of an atomic clock as the standard for defining time units.

This is as monitoring should be. Continuous micro-adjustment of the goal gives it long-term meaning. The overall system maintains high accuracy and relevance by constantly making micro-adjustments as necessary.

Backfire

A very common mistake among team leaders is to set goals and then refuse to adapt them as necessary. Goals sometimes seem reasonable and attainable at first, but it becomes clear later on that they're neither. If that's the case, don't be tempted to hang on to the bad goals out of pride or stubbornness. You'll damage your team's motivation and hurt your own credibility by doing so.

Build the same into your goals, and ensure they still support your overall vision. Here are some important questions to consider:

➤ Is the goal still on target and aligned with the vision?

➤ Can the goal be met?

➤ Are the measurements of progress still valid?

➤ Can additional measurements be created?

➤ Should additional measurements be created?

➤ What do people need to ensure they can achieve the goal?

If you answer these questions and keep the answers always in mind, you'll be sure that you're heading in the right direction.

The Least You Need to Know

➤ Your goals must relate to where you are now or they become irrelevant.

➤ Mold the job to fit your employees and they'll mold themselves to fit the job.

➤ Good goals are understandable, measurable, and attainable.

➤ Make sure that your goals are worthwhile and that they can be reached.

➤ Monitor your goals constantly to be sure you're staying on track.

Chapter 7

Why Are We Heading There?

In This Chapter

➤ Justifying the vision is the "why" of the "where"

➤ Looking at the big picture to explain goals and actions

➤ Getting others to support your purpose

➤ Making unpleasant tasks worthwhile as a way to assure the greater good

➤ Saying it well is as important as what you say

➤ Admitting and recovering from mistakes

We figured out in the last chapter where we're heading, or at least where we should be heading. In this chapter, we're going to look at *why* we're heading there. After all, it makes no sense to go someplace if you don't know why you're going.

When dealing with the "why are we heading there" question, we've got to address the things that cause us to do what we do. All our actions occur for reasons. Everything we do is prompted by some circumstance. It can be a thought, an event, or even a feeling. But there's always some reason that we do what we do.

When we decide where we're going, we're acting on a vision or a direction that we've chosen. When we ask why we're going there, we're justifying our vision or explaining why we've chosen the direction we have.

Here's How It Works

Judges consider all the time why people do the things they do. A judge will look at a case of killing in self-defense much differently than she'll look at a case of premeditated murder for financial gain.)

Why someone does something, or performs a particular action, doesn't have anything to do with the action itself. I know that it's a difficult thing to separate, but they really are two very different things.

Why somebody does something is all about motive. You have to look at what it was that made the person do what he did. Why someone does something is based on circumstances—the particular set of factors surrounding the action taken.

It's easy to motivate someone who can see an immediate, positive reward for his actions. If you say, "Sell ten of these machines and I'll give you a $5,000 bonus," you'll get people to sell the machines. The "why" for their action is readily apparent.

Leaders, though, keep others motivated to follow and perform when times are tough, as well as when times are good. The U.S. President always maintains popularity and public support when the economy is booming and peace prevails. Great presidents, however, maintain public support and popularity even if the nation is faced with adversity, such as war or economic recession. Abraham Lincoln, who led the U.S. through its darkest period in history, is still considered one of, if not the greatest president ever.

Looking at the Big Picture

To understand why you're heading in the direction you are, you've got to start with the big picture. Starting with the big picture, you can start to motivate people to follow you by explaining where you're going and why it's the best way. Tell your team how the action you're planning to take makes sense, both from your perspective and from their perspective. And explain those perceptions within the context of that larger picture.

Let's look at a real-life scenario that explains these concepts.

Milacron, the machine tool manufacturer we discussed earlier in the book, went through some really tough times in the early 1980s. Things were so bad, in fact, that all employees had to take a 10 percent pay cut in order to keep their jobs.

The across-the-board pay cut was painful for everybody, but given the business conditions of the times, it made sense. It was management's job to make sure everyone understood that the pay cut was in the best long-term interests of the company and of its employees. It had to clearly define the big picture and make sure employees bought into it.

Under such severe business conditions, it was not particularly difficult for management to get support for the pay cut, even though it was obviously an unpopular and radical course of action. Many employees had already lost their jobs through layoffs or early retirement buyouts. Employees understood the situation was very grim.

Leadership at Milacron was able to get employees to support the pay cut because it made sure that everyone understood the motives for the cut. During a recession, jobs are hard to come by. Making 10 percent less pay is better than having no job.

Milacron's management invested great energy in communications about business conditions. Employee meetings were set, and information on gross sales was shared with all. The overall objective was to survive for the short term and live to fight again another day. People will accept the need for a sacrifice if they support the greater cause.

Here's How It Works

The war effort during World War II is a great example of people who were motivated and willing to make sacrifices in support of a cause. There was widespread rationing of goods throughout the U.S.; factories converted to wartime production; women took over men's factory jobs, then bobbed their hair so they'd be safer at the machines. Everybody pitched in to do what was necessary for the cause.

People prefer good news over bad, there's no question about it. We can, however, tolerate frank discussion of bad news. Unwanted messages based upon the truth are better than wanted messages based upon misleading information. Using detailed slides and reports, Milacron's management described the deteriorating financial position openly with employees in public meetings. While employees didn't like what they were hearing, they understood why the pay cuts were necessary.

Milacron is publicly owned, so communication with its stockholders was equally important during this time. Management handled the communication by circulating press releases within the industry announcing an anticipated poor performance. This was done before the actual results were released.

When the final reports were released, and the company had registered a $10 million loss for the year, people were upset but not surprised. It is certainly undesirable for a business to lose money. It's more tolerable, however, if all interested parties understand the circumstances.

Good leaders don't make decisions in a vacuum and assume people will follow. Causing people to understand why things are happening maintains morale. Some important things to remember include:

➤ The circumstances surrounding your decisions are important.

➤ To have relevance, your decisions must consider, and be based upon, the surrounding circumstances.

➤ To maintain morale, surrounding circumstances must be explained to your followers.

➤ To create motivated followers, you must have back-and-forth communication so that you can be sure that they understand the reasons for your decisions.

➤ It's easier for people to accept the circumstances that led to your decision when they have a good understanding of the context in which those circumstances were created.

Dealing with "Why" Under Special Circumstances

Properly explaining the circumstances that surround and drive your decisions is particularly important, and potentially more difficult, when you're leading and motivating people outside your normal sphere of influence.

Defining Moments

A **matrix management system** is a dotted-line, informal reporting structure designed to give necessary attention to products or projects. The system pulls products or projects off to the side of the traditional business structure or standard line organization in order to give them special attention.

If you're charged with leading a group of people other than your regular team, you need to pay special attention to how you communicate. You'll need to address the "why" question often.

Say you're leading a special project that includes employees from all parts of the company. Typically, these projects are handled with a matrix management system, which puts "temporary" bosses in charge of groups of people in order to devote attention to that particular project or a particular product or service. Such a situation can be challenging. Employees might wonder why they should be loyal to you when they have a department and boss elsewhere. You're likely to get a lot of "why" questions.

Managers who work in project-based organizations need to establish authority and be able to motivate workers who don't normally report to them.

As part of my previous corporate life, I managed new product development for a $100 million product line for five or six years. Developing new, high-technology, precision metal-cutting machines is complex, requires advanced engineering, and involves significant costs.

Product design uses the disciplines of mechanics, metallurgy, electronics, hydraulics, and pneumatics. The machining systems are controlled with computers needing specialized software. Extensive prototype testing is normal, and while not a space shuttle project, new developments involve millions of dollars and the combined efforts of hundreds of people.

One of the major leadership hurdles with these developments is that the engineering talent is normally scattered throughout a number of different operational divisions.

While everyone answers to the same CEO, there are many layers and/or physical miles between the engineers and the project manager. This makes motivating difficult to accomplish.

Making the motivational challenge more complex, the necessary engineering talent may even be scattered throughout several different organizations and/or institutions and may not even answer to the same CEO.

Challenges such as these are typical of large projects that require effective matrix management. Many developments, including new skyscrapers, jet engines, automobiles, battleships, and computers, incur these complexities and difficulties. Each group of people necessary for such projects answers to diverse functional management.

Take a skyscraper project, which typically involves a number of different companies. Steel erection, electrical, security, HVAC, plumbing, drywall, painting, insulation, and other contractors all are involved in constructing the skyscraper.

Here's How It Works

If you've ever had a house built, you've probably gotten a taste of conflicting roles within a project. If the painters show up before the drywallers are finished, you've got problems. If the cement guys show up before the landscapers have graded the lot, you've got another problem. It's the same thing with a skyscraper, only a lot bigger.

The matrix manager, who's responsible for getting the skyscraper built on time and within budget, must organize and manage a transactional team. He must hold everything and everyone together.

A transactional team, like the one necessary to build a skyscraper, exists only long enough to finish the project. Its members are scattered throughout one or many organizations and answer directly to their own bosses, not the manager assigned to the skyscraper project.

Team members come together only for the duration of the project. What also is typical is that many team members have conflicting objectives and priorities, as they are working on several projects at the same time.

I've managed project teams consisting of some 350 members, all with conflicting priorities. Electrical guys only want to worry about the electrical stuff. Mechanical guys only care about the mechanical stuff, and so on. They sometimes lose sight of the fact that everything they do impacts on the work that others are doing.

When systems break down and issues aren't resolved as they should be, these projects become living hells. Everything runs late, there are major arguments about how and by whom things should be done, and cost runs out of control.

The people charged with putting the whole thing together usually suffer the most because they're supposed to be the glue that binds everything and assures that the job get done.

In my experience as a manager of new product development, there was always a short list. It was always "We just need to change these last seven things…"

The difficulty was that the last seven things never went away. As soon as one change was approved, another was added to the list. The product could never be declared complete, as improvements were constantly demanded and developed. It's like trying to reach a wall, knowing that the best step you can ever take covers only half of the remaining distance to the wall. Under those circumstances, you never reach the wall.

This short-list system was inherently flawed and demoralizing. New products can never be completed and introduced if sales and marketing insists on demanding more and more improvements and changes, while good employees are already busting their tails to do the best job they can.

The matrix management concept pools the best creative effort from individuals, but in the case of the project I managed, there was insufficient structure to channel the effort.

As manager, I could see that we were desperately in need of a model change system, which allows a certain period for project design and then freezes it at "good enough."

Once the design has been frozen (with the condition that it meets defined minimum standards), it's

Defining Moments

A **model change system** is one that halts project design at an assigned time, allowing the actual project to get completed. Any additional changes and enhancements are worked into a new model of the project at a future time.

tested, and any necessary changes must be scheduled to occur at a specific future time within the project. For instance, let's say you're designing a car that has a driver's side airbag. During testing, you realize the car would be more desirable if it also had an airbag on the passenger side. A passenger-side airbag is desirable but not mandatory. Because of that, using the model change concept, the car would be introduced to the market without the extra airbag, but adding it to next year's model would be a top priority.

Rally the Troops

It's surprising sometimes what you can accomplish if you remember to answer the "why" question first. Once you get people to understand and accept the circumstances around an issue, you can usually move in whatever direction you need to, provided that direction makes sense.

As product manager, I tried very hard to impose a model change system on my project team, and ultimately, the entire division of the company. Everyone on the team agreed the concept would provide welcome structure and would allow everyone to do their jobs more effectively. But neither individual team members nor their respective department heads had sufficient power to demand the system be imposed.

Even high-level executive management agreed the model change system would be helpful to the organization, but nobody was willing to put it into place. Being too far removed from the project, executive management was not willing to take a step that it felt could restrict innovation or otherwise cause the project to suffer. Everyone wanted the model change system, but nobody was either willing or able to put it into place.

It was very clear that someone had to take control of the matter and ask the "why" question. Somebody had to create the circumstances under which the organization could move onward. I decided to do it.

Because it was obvious that everyone needed to understand why a model change system would be beneficial, I created a monthly report that covered our progress. It was distributed widely to all team members and their managers. Executive management also was included in the distribution. Over time, the report gained credibility, as it provided valuable and necessary information about the project.

Once everyone was informed about the project and about the need for a model change system, I simply used one of the monthly reports to announce that the model change concept was being instituted. I said something like this:

"It has been decided that we will introduce a model change system. All engineering changes are frozen effective on April 15, 2000. After this date, all engineering changes will be part of model change 'A'. All changes for model change 'A' are due on or before August 15, 2000. All changes for model change 'B' are due on or before August 15, 2001."

Within 24 months or so, the team developed the disciplines necessary to properly evaluate priorities and merge market needs and engineering improvements into a more disciplined system. It is a classic example of how the "why" question, or the circumstance, drives the "where" question, which is the vision.

Backfire

Be sure that everyone on your team has a clear understanding of the "why" question, and that everyone has the same understanding of what's going on and why. If team members are confused, or have different ideas about what's happening, you risk your team splintering and falling apart.

Motivating with the "Why" Question

Circumstance, or effectively answering the "why" question, can and has motivated millions of people. It even has motivated entire nations.

The circumstance of slavery, for example, eventually drove the United States to rupture and caused a devastating civil war. Great leaders such as Martin Luther King Jr. or Mohandas Gandhi have motivated millions of people and produced grand movements and social change without ever holding formal office. They powerfully answered the "why" question as a means of creating a following for their vision of a better world.

To effectively motivate using the "why" question, keep in mind the following things:

➤ Focus communication on why the issue is relevant to the group.

➤ Describe how the total group will benefit if the circumstances change.

➤ Explain why and how the benefits will be greater when the circumstances change.

➤ Enlist subgroups or individuals to lobby others within the group and support the change you desire.

➤ Make it known that conditions will deteriorate if the current circumstances continue.

The "why" question is critical to all who must motivate, even government leaders with formal authority. Government leaders have power but not absolute power. Even dictators have limited power.

Government leaders must skillfully address the "why" question and follow the rules above to create support for their policies.

On October 19, 1987, the U.S. stock markets suffered their worst one-day percentage slide ever. The U.S. economy represents about 25 percent of the total world economy and an uncontrolled panic can paralyze financial markets in the U.S. and abroad. If this happens, we risk global economic disruption.

To avert such a situation in October 1987, the U.S. Federal Reserve quickly stepped in, offering to provide any funds needed "to support the economic and financial system." The Fed's statement (along with its assistance in obtaining loans for desperate brokers) averted a potentially serious crisis. The stock markets completely recovered within one year.

The Fed's pockets are deep. It can create money at will by adjusting the federal funds rate—the rate at which large commercial banks make loans to each other. Increasing the federal funds rate makes money scarce by making borrowing more expensive. Decreasing the rate has the opposite effect.

Yet, the Federal Reserve does not really control interest rates. It publishes the federal funds target rate and its member banks usually adhere to that target rate. The banks don't have to, but they do. Why? Because they support the Fed's motives.

The Fed always justifies its goals. As a result, the financial community trusts its judgment. That's the real source of the Federal Reserve's power and its ability to motivate the financial community.

It is a measure of the Fed's global prestige and its importance to the global economy that it normally isn't called upon to "put its money where its mouth is." Usually, as in October 1987, all the Fed has to do in order to produce results is remind us of what it is capable of doing.

Developing a Purpose

A purpose without support will not motivate. Because that statement is true and won't change, you need to develop your purpose and give it life by building a consensus around it. This is what the "why" question is all about.

Get your team lined up behind you and be ready to get them involved in whatever purpose you're trying to promote. Involvement from your followers will be critical to building support.

Consider the case at Alltel, a $3 billion information services and telecommunications company based in Arkansas.

In 1995, the company's 285-employee technology center was under considerable pressure because the company was growing incredibly fast. The rapid growth was causing declining productivity and poor morale.

Management addressed the problems that were occurring and agreed something had to be done

Backfire

Some managers think they can achieve their purpose on their own, without the backing of their teams. To do so, they try to force whatever the purpose may be on their workers. If you're ever tempted to do so, don't. All you'll do is cause resentment among your team, and your purpose will suffer badly.

to make things better. It knew that it had to get employees to buy into whatever plan it came up with, and to support the plan, whatever it would be. To do that, management implemented a program that involved all 285 employees.

It first created discussion and awareness among employees and management by breaking down the employees into groups of about 15 people each. Management laid out the challenges to each group and asked for ideas. It told employees that customer satisfaction wasn't as good as it should be and asked: What are we going to do about it? How can we improve the work environment? How can we help you develop professionally? And so on, and so forth.

Eventually, 170 specific action items emerged from these discussions. The items covered specific problems and concerns affecting employees' overall morale, performance, and working conditions. The groups also developed plans to address the specific issues.

Defining Moments

Participative management is, you guessed it, enlisting the participation of employees or other groups to help manage and solve problems. It takes more thought, planning, and time than does just ordering people around, but the results are always better.

The company then developed customized training sessions. These sessions challenged employees with real-life scenarios and encouraged them to brainstorm about how to address problems, build solutions, and handle issues in line with the company's mission. Employees learned more about how to work with each other to create the flexibility they needed.

The company's employees responded well to the training, and morale improved greatly due to employees' involvement. Results soon became obvious, as the renewed team drove its customer satisfaction scores to new heights.

Management achieved its mission of improving the situation by investing in participative management, which is more complex than traditional management. Participative management is more complex for several reasons:

➤ It takes more time.

➤ You really have to listen and mold all the input into some sort of cohesive idea.

➤ You can't ask for input and then shut people off; you have to deal with whatever you get.

➤ You'll need to listen to what you don't want to hear without criticizing the sender.

➤ People may come up with things you don't agree with, and you may have to accept some of these things.

➤ You may have to implement something that has a high probability of failure just to produce greater cohesiveness around something else.

Participative management is complex, but it produces higher morale and greater motivation than traditional management. It often leads to much better efficiency and effectiveness. In the long term, participative management will produce a more motivated, competitive, effective, and profitable organization. Getting people involved and making them part of your purpose will go a long way in assuring that your purpose will be realized.

Making What We Don't Want to Do Relevant to What We *Do* Want to Do

Rally the Troops

Parents, teachers, and others who deal with kids know well how important it is to make what kids don't want to do relevant to what they do want. For example, a teacher might tell her first-graders that they can't go outside for recess until they've cleaned up their art projects. That makes cleanup relevant to recess. A parent might make cutting the grass relevant to borrowing the car that night. You get the picture.

You can get people to accept very difficult missions if you can create circumstances that motivate them to support a larger mission that's more acceptable to the larger group. Let me explain.

For example, in 1979, militant Islamic students seized the American embassy in Teheran, Iran, and 52 Americans within the embassy were taken hostage and held for 444 days.

Although the incident was recognized internationally as an illegal act, the government of Iran claimed it could take no action against the students, for fear of risking harm to the embassy employees.

The militant students, according to the formal position of the Iranian government, allegedly acted on their own in protest against the United States for giving refuge to the ailing, deposed Shah of Iran.

This U.S. action, the Iranian opposition then feared, would lead to a CIA-backed coup like the one that put the Shah on the throne in 1953.

As the political crisis raged, the U.S. military planned and executed a rescue attempt that ultimately failed, resulting in the loss of a significant number of U.S. military personnel.

No soldier was forced to risk his life in that rescue mission. All who participated were volunteers.

The questions we want to look at are why the U.S. government might have decided to risk the lives of American soldiers in an effort to rescue other Americans, and why soldiers would volunteer to participate in the effort.

No one would argue that the life of an American embassy employee is worth more than the life of a U.S. soldier. There was no justification for trading one life for another in this rescue attempt. How do leaders, in instances such as the Iran crisis, get people to risk their lives?

Leaders achieve this very powerful position by carefully focusing on circumstances.

Take the embassy example. Americans are greatly invested in the idea of living in peace and freedom. We're willing to go to great lengths to maintain that goal—even to support risking American lives in military actions. We believe the risk is worthwhile because, while generally an undesirable thing, it supports a larger future purpose. It often appears to be the only remaining choice.

Here's How it Works

An extreme measure of linking an undesirable action to a desirable one is the case of a person who needs to have a limb amputated in order to save his life. While highly undesirable, amputating the limb will result in something highly desirable—life.

If you have to implement an undesirable action, link it to the greater desirable good. This will motivate others to follow and support the undesirable action.

In the business world, layoffs always create insecurity and poor morale. They are always disruptive and painful. While everyone hates layoffs, employees can and do accept them when they're put into the proper context. Furthermore, if the context is properly established, employees won't lose confidence in you.

Hopefully, you'll never need to ask people to do what they don't want to do. Reality, however, suggests otherwise. Being a leader doesn't mean that you only have to lead when everything's going as planned. There will be times when you're going to have to ask people to do something undesirable. When you do, be certain they understand that this is the last option available.

Remember the military analogy above. People will accept even war if they believe it's the last resort.

Here's How It Works

Franklin Roosevelt was forced to order many undesirable actions during his term as U.S. President. While he did what he needed to, he made it clear that he would rather not. He was often overheard to ask during wartime meetings, "Why did we have to be born in this generation?"

Here are a few rules to follow if you have to get your team to do something undesirable:

➤ Be sure that everyone understands that the undesirable task is the last viable option.

➤ Take responsibility for the final decision in these cases, but focus attention on the larger forces that are outside your control.

➤ Clarify that there are no other choices available, and explain what bad things will occur if the undesirable action is not taken.

➤ Be sure everyone understands that the action is the best alternative available.

➤ While you don't need to state it publicly, be certain that everyone knows how distasteful you consider the action to be.

Saying It the Best Way You Can

Picking the right words is a critical process. The right words are especially important when you need to explain why certain undesirable things must be tolerated in the short term.

When you must do that, think carefully before you start talking. Plan your presentations well, and don't overreach. No one likes bad news, and people tend to look for rainbows when skies get very dark. It's easy for your followers to interpret your hopeful wishes concerning the future as facts. If they do that, and your wishes don't come true, you end up losing credibility.

During the 1979 nuclear plant accident at Three Mile Island in Pennsylvania, officials tried to calm acute public concerns by being calm and reassuring. They wanted to convey that the nuclear reactor was "under control" and that radiation that had leaked was minimal and well within "safety ranges."

Backfire

Twenty years after the accident at the Three Mile Island nuclear plant, anti-nuke people, press people, utility officials, and public officials still debate the accident and how it was handled. Each side blames someone else for inept management of the situation. It clearly was a situation that could have, and should have, been handled with more thought.

While that was the public statement, officials inadvertently set off a panic when they suggested that pregnant women and small children consider leaving the area until the matter was resolved. Officials never told women and children to clear out, they merely suggested they consider it.

While trying to reassure and comfort, this warning produced the opposite effect. Concern escalated into panic. People misread the suggestion as an order and feared they'd be forced to evacuate the area. There was a lot of confusion, concern, and fear.

A subsequent visit by President Carter and his wife, Rosalyn, went a long way in calming the public's fears.

The President, who was formally trained in nuclear engineering, arrived at Three Mile Island for a first-hand briefing. He and his wife, with television crews in tow, walked through radioactive water while wearing protective boots, and went into the contaminated control room for all the world to see. The President's actions reassured a frightened public the reactor was brought back under control, and the crisis passed.

In preparing any presentation, especially one that asks people to tolerate something that's going to be objectionable, follow these rules:

➤ Say only what you know, and continue repeating only what you know.

➤ Deal only with circumstance; don't offer causal explanation unless you are certain of what you're saying.

➤ Don't offer false assurances, as this only makes people more insecure.

➤ Don't speculate or make predictions because people will immediately want to know the basis for those predictions.

➤ Have a high energy level and be confident when stating your strategy.

➤ Tell your team how it will be kept up-to-date with what's going on, and describe any review process or other action.

You can get a lot of mileage out of saying something well, even if it's something that nobody wants to hear. But don't think that a nice presentation will solve all your problems—it won't. People still will be upset—maybe angry. However, clearly explaining the "why" question in terms and language that employees understand will go a long way toward keeping your team motivated and your reputation intact.

Recovering from Mistakes

No matter how carefully you plan or how hard you try, you're going to make mistakes. You know why? Because you're human, just like the guy at the next desk, and the head of your company, and me.

When you make mistakes, the hardest thing usually is admitting them. Recovering from your mistakes normally is an easier process than telling everybody what you did in the first place. After all, once you start recovering from a mistake, everybody already knows you made it.

Rally the Troops

If you make a mistake, don't wait for it to be found out. Go ahead and admit it, because you'll be more respected for doing so than for waiting for someone to discover what you did.

Personally, I've had to admit and recover from more mistakes than I'd have liked—some of them pretty bad ones. Here's the story of a Ramundo mistake that's still painful to recall:

For more than a year, I'd been trying to build a department in the company I was working for. I'd already found a number of good guys, either by promoting from within or bringing them in from the outside.

J.A. was an inside guy. I got him promoted up to my department, and he'd been working out fine. J.A. was a little bit rigid, but he was a hard worker and he'd made an above-average contribution.

Because of a bad mistake I made, though, I was going to lose J.A.

It was all my own doing, and I still don't like to think about it. The worst mistakes we make are those that hurt others. My unprofessional mistake involving J.A. was caused by an observation I made at the wrong time and a poor choice of words.

I shared some opinions about his performance with J.A. in a manner that I thought he'd perceive positively. He didn't. He took my observations as being very negative, and he, understandably, reacted to them.

In hindsight, there really was no compelling reason for me to share my observations with J.A. at that point. I should have just kept my mouth shut. The whole incident amounted to a colossal screw-up, and it was all my fault.

Over and over, these types of mistakes teach the same, absolutely critical motivational lesson, which is:

Think before you speak.

As we all know, words once spoken must be dealt with. Losing J.A. was going to be a devastating loss to the department, and I couldn't prevent him from leaving.

If you do screw up, pull out all the stops and reverse things as quickly as possible.

Backfire

When you make a bad mistake—or any mistake, for that matter—resist the temptation to try to hide what you've done, or even worse, put the blame on somebody else. Doing those things will only put you in an even deeper hole and cost you whatever respect you still have.

Maybe I was going to lose J.A., but if I did, it wouldn't be for lack of trying. I counseled him, trying to get him to stay on the job. I called in favors and asked colleagues to take J.A. on in their departments (remember, that meant I had to admit my mistake—over and over). I thought that if he wouldn't work for me in my department, at least maybe we could keep him in the company.

My boss got involved and counseled him. I visited him at home, apologized to him with his wife present, and pleaded with him not to throw away his career with the company just because of the mistake I'd made.

J.A. turned everything down and submitted his resignation at the time when his workload, and that of everyone else, was at its peak. This caused an even greater problem, and it was pretty obvious that I was at the bottom of the whole mess.

When you completely mess up, don't be afraid to call in the reinforcements you've been cultivating. Even if it makes the embarrassment worse in the short term, your reinforcements allow you to make mistakes.

When J.A. resigned, I called three of my most trusted confidants into a secret meeting. I knew I needed their support to sustain the heavy overload that was going to fall on everyone, including them, when J.A. left.

I told them in a very forthright manner why J.A. was leaving. Although the crisis had been unfolding for six months or more, this was the first time I'd shared anything about it with anyone who answered directly to me.

Well, my confidants were extremely upset, not because their workloads would increase, but because they didn't want J.A. to leave. They also were angry at me for being the cause of J.A.'s resignation.

I didn't try to make any excuses or tell any lies, I just admitted that, yes, J.A. was leaving because I had screwed up.

I've thought about this encounter many times over the years. My trusted lieutenants knew all about the disagreement between J.A. and me long before I called that secret meeting.

The crisis, brewing for months, had gone on for far too long. Leaks were everywhere, and naturally, everyone in the department had heard about the confrontation. The rumor mill had been primed and was running well, yet no one in the department had shared anything with me. It makes perfect sense. If I had been in their shoes, I wouldn't have shared anything with the boss either. Importantly, though, my reputation was now trash in the department.

The three people in that meeting were my most loyal and trusted confidants. But I had hurt them, and the rest of the team as well. They needed reassurance. They needed reaffirmation that their confidence in me was not misplaced.

I knew I had been rendered ineffective, at least for a while. Because of that, I was forced to ask the three guys from the meeting to assume responsibility for the department. They were going to have to deal with the workload, the lousy morale, and everything else, because I couldn't.

To their everlasting credit, they rallied to the occasion. They took over the department for me, speaking privately with their colleagues, making phone calls, and cashing in favors. They adjusted our schedules, bought us time, and saved my butt.

When you make a mistake, deal with it quickly, in the best manner that you can. Don't lie, and don't make excuses. Just do what needs to be done and move on.

Here's How It Works

A famous example of taking the blame, even when it may not be due, is President John F. Kennedy and the Bay of Pigs incident. Kennedy accepted full responsibility for the incident, in which U.S.-backed Cuban exiles unsuccessfully attempted to overthrow Fidel Castro's regime. Historically speaking, some of the blame belonged elsewhere, but Kennedy was willing to shoulder the entire burden.

Some Words to Avoid—Always

As we learned in the previous section, there are some effective ways to handle a mistake. There also are things you can say that will only serve to make a bad situation worse.

These words or phrases, obviously, should be avoided—always:

➤ Any words that put blame on someone else should be avoided. Be sensitive to this, because even words such as, "But, he…," or "She said…" can be interpreted as blaming someone else. The phrase, "But it wasn't my fault," is a real killer. Just don't say it.

➤ Words that make excuses should be avoided. Phrases like, "I didn't think that…," or "Something must have happened that…" won't endear you to anyone. They just make it seem like you're trying to get out from under your mistake.

➤ Words that sugarcoat the situation won't be well received either. Saying something like, "I don't think this is as bad as you think," isn't a good idea.

If you screw up, you'll need to confess, be humble, and be willing to accept the reprimand that's bound to follow. If you can think of a constructive way to correct the mistake or fix the problem, it will go a long way in your recovering from the mistake.

The Least You Need to Know

➤ Knowing where you're headed isn't enough; you've got to be able to explain why you want to go there.

➤ Presenting the overall view of a situation often helps people understand actions that must be taken in order to achieve short-term goals.

➤ Your purpose won't take you far if you don't have others to support it.

➤ To get people to agree to do unpleasant things, you've got to convince them that it's for the greater good.

➤ Think carefully about what you'll say, before you say it.

➤ When you make a mistake—and you will—deal with it honestly, get it resolved, and move on.

Chapter 8

What's in It for Me?

In This Chapter

➤ Motivating workers to help you reach your goals

➤ Using benefits as a means of motivation

➤ Knowing what makes people want to work

➤ Good leaders and how they lead

➤ Letting employees know what you're doing for them

People generally are social creatures who care about others and the organizations with which they're affiliated. Society and culture, and what they stand for, are important to us and to how we motivate ourselves.

Leadership that's dedicated to high motivation recognizes the importance of society and culture and builds them into its development of constructive objectives.

Both C.W., a president with a client company, and I have young, adult children. We've talked several times about the possibility of having grandchildren before too long, and what it might be like. It's a pretty awe-inspiring thought.

C.W.'s former career was with one of the major American tobacco companies. While we've never discussed his past in any depth, I can tell he's a bit bothered about it. When the grandchild conversation comes up, C.W. mentions the need to internally "reconcile" his past employment history with his values and attitudes concerning family and society.

If our societal and personal goals and values don't jibe with our work values, it can cause a really difficult situation. Sure, we work for others to make money. And, yes, society is important to us.

We need to know and to understand how the goals we're asked to pursue at work help us achieve personal gain, as well as help to move society forward.

"What's in it for me?" is a personal question. While we all wonder about it, most of us don't go as far as putting the question bluntly to our employers. We trust that the employer realizes how important our personal self-interest is and will address it sufficiently.

As a leader who wants to keep her team interested, motivated, and involved, you've got to keep their vested interest at the forefront as you create goals and plan future direction and purpose. Don't wait for your workers to express personal concerns. Keep them involved and tell them exactly what they can expect to gain from their employment with your company.

Explain the personal benefits that they'll realize as the company meets its goals. Then, be sure they do benefit.

In this chapter, we'll learn about some famous business people who knew well how to motivate their employees by making their jobs profitable and worthwhile.

We'll also look at some of the things people work for—both tangible and intangible.

Workers who are satisfied with what they're getting from the job—whether it's the amount of their pay, the number of vacation days, or the personal fulfillment—will work harder and give more than those who aren't satisfied, and that's something that smart leaders never forget.

Henry Ford and the Saturn Car Division

If you're wondering what Henry Ford and the Saturn car division of General Motors have in common, you'll have to think past vehicles.

Both Henry Ford and Saturn realized the importance of looking out for the best interests of their employees and of keeping workers happy and satisfied.

In 1914, Henry Ford was criticized by many for his willingness to pay workers the absurd rate of $5 per eight-hour shift. The going rate in the auto industry at that time was $2.34 for a nine-hour shift, and Ford's breakthrough caused quite an outrage. *The Wall Street Journal* called the plan an "economic crime."

Ford, though, understood the importance money plays in motivating people; given a choice between working for Ford and working for the other auto manufacturers at the time, the best workers certainly would have chosen to work for Ford. Ford got the best employees, and they worked hard and built good cars.

He priced the cars low enough so that thousands of people who never thought they'd be able to afford a car could buy them. He sold so many cars that he was able, over time, to increase his workers' pay to $10 a shift. That made it possible for his workers to buy his cars.

He looked out for the interests of his employees, making the job well worth the time and effort his employees were giving him. When company backers insisted that the best way to maximize profits was to build cars for the rich, Ford refused to bend. Instead, he bought out the backers' interests in the company and forced them out.

Here's How It Works

When he was 16 in 1879, Henry Ford left his family's farm and walked eight miles to his first job in a Detroit machine shop. By 1912, he had 7,000 dealers selling his cars across the country. In 1914, the Ford Motor Company was producing a car every 93 minutes, and by the time production of the Model T stopped in 1927, more than 15 million of them—more than half of all the cars in the world—had been sold.

Ford's vision and willingness to look out for the best interests of his employees helped create a middle class in America. The country saw increased urbanization, higher wages, and free time in which to spend them. People flocked to Detroit for jobs, bought their own cars, and enjoyed them in their leisure time. Ford's pioneering efforts, which stressed looking out for his employees and making it worth their while to work for him, had a significant impact on our society.

A half a century later, in 1980, a new General Motors small car division called Saturn opened in Tennessee, stressing positive employee relations and the production of high-quality cars.

General Motors and United Auto Workers leadership worked hard to overcome years of built-up animosity and poor labor relations that were common in the auto industry. They've gone back to the basics as addressed by Henry Ford, once again focusing on the "what's-in-it-for-me?" question.

Saturn management and the local United Auto Workers have developed a mutual pride and sense of ownership in the company. Employee work teams made up of UAW members, engineers, and technicians meet frequently and are actively involved in finding ways to resolve issues and improve the Saturn product line.

The system obviously works. Saturn has developed a dedicated customer base and consistently gets high ratings from customers. Assembly line employees are showcased and frequently featured in brand advertising that touts the car's quality. Each summer, happy car owners join Saturn employees at the plant for a Saturn reunion.

Here's How It Works

An example of the cooperation between Saturn management and the union is seen in the makeup of the labor contract. Normally, these contracts are about the size of phone books, loaded with all kinds of picky stuff. The Saturn union contract is pamphlet size.

Saturn employees are involved in the total business, and the what's-in-it-for-me question has been answered. They're not just doing a job. They're invested in the company by a sense of pride and mutual effort.

Saturn understands that employees are not just cogs on some assembly line, performing repetitive tasks for pay. They're involved with the company's mission and purpose, and have achieved personal ownership in it through profit sharing and other gain-sharing methods.

The concepts of ownership and partnering are very important. When workers are inspired and motivated, they'll work hard to improve what they're a part of. Both Henry Ford and Saturn understood this and worked with employees for their mutual benefit.

Defining Moments

When workers have a **vested interest,** it means that they have an interest in, and enjoy benefits from, some economic or political privilege such as profit sharing, retirement plans, stock options, employee advisory boards, and so forth. It invests them in the company.

Vested Interest

Giving workers a vested interest in their company makes them a part of the total action and gives them ownership of the company's objectives. In short, it generally makes them better workers.

This is evident in our society in more areas than employment. People who own their own homes generally take better care of them than those who rent. Same with cars. Why? Because when something belongs to us, we're more inclined to care for it and work hard for it.

Henry Ford knew that when workers asked "what's in it for me?", they were asking about more than money. So, in addition to top wages, Ford gave his workers leisure time, the opportunity to own cars, and other benefits. He addressed all their wants and needs.

The what's-in-it-for-me question can and should be answered for workers in all jobs, from the most basic to the most sophisticated.

A client of mine manufactures high-tech blood diagnostic equipment. He needs to offer full 24-hour service coverage to his customers because small clinics that use his equipment normally can afford to buy only one machine. If it breaks down, they're out of luck until it's fixed. Shutting down the clinic could result in serious consequences for the people who are in need of blood tests.

When my client realized he had to go to round-the-clock service, he was faced with the problem of getting his workers to be willing to do it. He had to make it worth their while.

He decided that a permanent third-shift team wasn't a good idea. Technicians needed to keep in touch with one another to share innovations and changes that occurred rapidly within this business. A permanent third shift would always be isolated from daily mainstream activity and would quickly become irrelevant.

The only way to do it, my client thought, was to have a rotating third shift. Management announced that to better serve customers, everybody would be expected to pitch in and share the responsibility of keeping the all-night shift operating.

As you might imagine, this created a revolution. Communications quickly became strained as technicians protested the idea of a rotating shift. My client was worried because highly trained technicians such as these were in scarce supply. Losing a significant percentage of his workers would have been a disaster.

I was called in to help, and it was clear that the first thing we had to do was answer the what's-in-it-for-me question. The 24-hour service requirement wasn't an option; it had to be done. That meant we had to convince the employees and make it worth their while to work the rotating shift.

To do so, we explained why the change was necessary. Small communities didn't have backup equipment. If their machines broke down and nobody was around to fix them, things could be bad; it could perhaps even put lives at risk.

Then we personalized the message. Some of the workers lived in these small communities—many had family members there. Suddenly, 24-hour technical backup started to make more sense.

It made even more sense when we discussed the personal gains that the new system would bring. Because this 24-hour service was critically needed, customers are willing to pay a premium for it.

Rally the Troops

Consider carefully what will motivate your employees best before you announce a plan. If you offer something that doesn't satisfy the what's-in-it-for-me question, you may have to offer something in addition. And you'll find that it's difficult to take an offer off the table once you've made it, so you might end up having to give more than you had planned.

That meant that the company would make more money. In return, employees would realize higher wages or another form of profit sharing.

Now the team was really getting interested. All of a sudden, it was becoming clear that there were some advantages to the expanded hours.

We saved our best card for last. Most importantly, we told the workers, the new system put the company in a position to offer greater flexibility and more personal time off for the technical support team. Now we really had the attention of the workers.

The new schedule meant that each worker would get one week out of a six-week rotation in which she didn't have to come to work but would be on call. She'd earn her full salary for the week. On average, the person on call would only receive six calls per day. However, we couldn't predict when the calls would come in, and there was the possibility of more than six calls.

The technician could go anywhere she wanted to; to the beach, shopping, or wherever. She simply had to carry a beeper and a portable computer, stay within a 100-mile beeper range, and be able to get to a telephone within 15 minutes of the beeper sound (better technology has since made the last two requirements obsolete).

The technicians responded very positively to the incentives we offered, and the 24-hour service plan was soon in place and running smoothly. By giving the employees a vested interest, we gained their willingness to help advance the goals of the company. It turned out to be a winning situation for everybody.

Backfire

Bosses who refuse to interact with their employees on any level other than strictly work put themselves at a disadvantage. Generally, this kind of leader doesn't enjoy the loyalty and good will from employees that bosses who are not afraid to get to know their workers do. Employees like to be recognized as people, not just workers. Bosses who don't acknowledge that won't be as effective as they could be.

Making It More Than a Job

Ideally, the members of your team see their work as more than just a job. Hopefully, it's something in which they're really interested, that's fun to do, and is challenging and exciting. And, ideally, their work meshes with their personal lives and values.

I think it's a mistake to try to keep work and personal lives completely separate. I think that workers respond better to, and are more comfortable, when goals they encounter at work mesh with the values they live with in their personal lives. Most people have morals, are reasonably ethical, and are committed to something—whatever it might be. They want their work to reflect their personal commitments and morality.

They want their work to be more than simply a job.

Getting a Person Invested in the Company

Letting employees know exactly what's in it for them is the quickest and easiest way to get them invested in the company and its goals. You've got to let them know how they'll benefit from the company, and how they'll fit in.

Letting employees know how they fit into the overall scheme of the company accomplishes several things:

➤ It gives workers a stake in the organization.

➤ It gives workers a sense of the general purpose of the organization.

➤ It defines the authority and responsibility of the workers.

➤ It makes workers important links in the motivational chain.

Everyone wants to feel like they belong to something. We talked in Chapter 6 about making your team feel that it's part of the "in crowd." It's important to do that, because it invests team members in the company.

It's no fun to do a job without ever knowing how it relates to the general purpose of the organization. It would be like sewing seams on shirt sleeves all day long, but never knowing how the shirt turns out, or what it looks like. It would be like preparing a garnish that's the finishing touch on a beautiful dinner plate in a gourmet restaurant, but never getting to see how the garnish looks on the plate with the rest of the food.

Most people like the feeling of contributing to the greater good, whether it be in their jobs, for their families, or for their communities. When people can see that their particular job is important to the company's overall goals, they feel important and motivated to do their job well. After all, you won't have much of a shirt if the sleeves aren't sewn well.

Here's How It Works

The area in which I live was recently in a state of drought emergency. Nobody was allowed to water lawns, wash cars, or otherwise use water unnecessarily. It was interesting to see the whole neighborhood become invested in the water conservation project. It was a good example of the willingness of most people to contribute to the greater good, whether it be job-related, community-related, or whatever.

Letting workers know how they fit into the overall scheme of the company also helps to define their authority and responsibility.

The technicians on the diagnostic equipment in the example above had a responsibility to the patients who needed diagnostic work. We personalized goals in that example by explaining how the technicians' work benefited people in nearby, or even their own, communities. We explained how their authority (generated by their expertise) allowed them to fulfill their responsibility to the patients.

Knowing that the success of the company depends on the job they do makes workers important links in the company's motivational chain. It motivates them to perform well, because they don't want to be the link that makes the chain weak.

Making Sure Employees Understand Their Roles

We all talk to friends and family about just what it is we do at work—how we spend our time and fill our days. Be sure that your team can specifically explain how its role benefits not only each member and the team as a whole, but also how it benefits the entire operation.

Expect that your workers will accept their roles, and will react positively to your explanations of how they fit into the company. You'll be right most of the time.

If you encounter problems, consider that maybe you haven't explained the roles of workers well enough, or that for some reason, workers aren't understanding what you're saying. If people don't understand how they fit into the overall operation, chances are they won't fit in very well. Do the best you can to make it perfectly clear.

Reasons an Employee Will Want to Work

There are both basic and not-so-basic reasons why people work. Even people who we think of as not working, such as those on assistance, or those who are retired, do some form of work. All living creatures, people included, work to eat. We also work to protect and nourish future generations.

At one time, people were defined (by people, of course) as the only creatures capable of creating tools to help with the endless quest for food. Now, we've stopped being quite so egocentric, and we recognize that some animals also prepare and use tools with which to hunt for and gather food.

People, though, generally desire to do more than work for food. We want our work to satisfy inner curiosities, give us direction, challenge us, make us a part of something, and give us a feeling of satisfaction when it's done.

If we only wanted to work for food, we'd still be an agricultural society, where we, literally, worked for the food we produced. But, because we're able to understand and embrace the concepts of lifetime, investment, predictability, overcoming challenges, and accomplishing things, we prefer to work for more than just getting food. We work for the feelings mentioned above—we work for ideas.

Here's How It Works

Primatologist Jane Goodall was one of the first to observe, and create extraordinary video of, great apes using prepared stout twigs and reeds—their tools—to facilitate their hunts for termites in rotting logs.

Our challenge is to get our teams to work for the ideas that we think are important. We already know they're working for several things, including:

➤ A paycheck

➤ Benefits

➤ Perks

I mean, let's face it. If we took away those things, our work forces would shrink dramatically, wouldn't you agree? Our goal, however, is to get our teams to work for things other than those mentioned above. We want to invest them in what we think is important, and motivate them to help us meet our goals.

Let's take a look at how Estee Lauder, the queen of cosmetics, convinced her team to follow her ideas, and, as a result, created a beauty empire.

Lauder got her start by selling the skin products that her uncle, a chemist, made. She'd sell to beauty shops, resorts, and beach clubs. While the products were good, it's widely acknowledged that Lauder's selling techniques were the real force behind her success.

She understood that personalized selling would take her and her products where she wanted to be. Once she got her products into Saks Fifth Avenue in 1948, she put that personalized selling technique to the test, and it proved to be extremely effective.

When she hired salespeople to sell her product, she insisted that they use her personalized selling technique. Eventually, she mobilized legions of department store workers around her idea, setting Estee Lauder cosmetics apart from all the rest.

Rally the Troops

A leader who expects his employees to work only for a paycheck, benefits, and perks is likely to get workers who will do exactly that. A leader who expects more from his employees is likely to get more.

Lauder had to create a following of salespeople before she could create a following of customers. She needed to convince them that her sales methods were best, and that they should sell the same way. She was able to do that, and, as a result, she ultimately created an entire industry.

To push your idea forward and motivate others, you've got to be out in front of the idea and the followers. Your team needs to see what you're doing, and what you want them to do. Lauder made sure she did exactly that. She was famous for breezing into Saks on a Saturday to help the salespeople there improve their selling techniques.

Even after 40 years in the business, she still attended the openings of new Lauder shops. She was visible, she was available, and she was willing to work closely with her team to make sure they produced the kind of work she wanted.

Here's How It Works

Estee Lauder came up with the idea of giving customers a free gift at the sales counter, a technique that further motivated her salespeople. Now, they had something that would attract customers and make them happy once they had approached the counter. It gave salespeople confidence, and motivated them to get even more customers.

In short, Estee Lauder was a great motivator. She knew what she wanted, and she knew how to make others want to help her get it.

She achieved that primarily with her personal drive, energy, and charisma. Powerful leaders like Lauder consistently build involvement throughout the organization, and motivate the entire team by putting some real muscle behind the what's-in-it-for-me question. She showed her workers the power of her personalized selling technique, and got them to help her prove that it worked.

Ultimately, Lauder created a whole new methodology for selling high-end cosmetics. Like all great motivators, she was committed to the message—not the money that the message produced.

The money you make is a measuring stick of the message you're sending out. If people like your message, they'll buy the product and you'll see the money. If you're committed only to the money, not the message that you're sending through your product or service, the business won't work. The money has to follow the message—it can't lead it.

Put some real power behind your words to involve the total organization, and then let your workers know they've got your confidence. Once you've taught your team what you want them to do, and motivated them to do so, you've got to trust them with the ball. Hand it over to them, and let them run with it.

Let your team know that it's got your confidence, and that you believe it can make things happen for both itself and the organization.

Another Successful Leader, More Motivated Employees

Now, consider the Ritz-Carlton Group, the premium hotel company founded in 1983. The Ritz-Carlton has a great leader, president Horst Schulze, and it has motivated, dedicated employees.

Those two things—the president and the motivated employees—are closely and integrally related.

From the very beginning, Schulze insisted that his hotels provide the very best customer service possible. Like all hotels, the Ritz-Carlton was selling hospitality and guest services, working to get every employee to provide super-high customer satisfaction to every customer.

Schulze knew that this wouldn't happen on its own, or with a little help from somebody's magic wand. The only ways, he realized, that he could get employees to provide the kind of service he insisted upon were to:

➤ Provide excellent training

➤ Motivate employees to want to provide top-quality service

Schulze got down to work, and his work is paying off. The Ritz-Carlton shows consistently high customer satisfaction ratings—usually better than 90 percent.

How is Schulze able to attain such high and consistent ratings? Let's have a look. While you're reading, think about how you might adapt some of Schulze's ideas to your own company and your own team of workers.

For starters, Schulze understands that for his employees to want to provide superior service, they've got to be motivated. This is so central to the Ritz-Carlton that it's included in its mission statement. In the mission statement, management is challenged to make and keep

Backfire

Bosses sometimes expect their employees to understand the goals of the company without adequately explaining them, or they expect employees to be able to meet those goals without providing all the necessary training. Be sure you equip your workers to be able to reach goals—both personal and company. If you don't, you'll be demotivating them instead of making them want to achieve bigger and better things.

employees happy and motivated. It reads, in part, that all managers should "strive to meet individual (employee) needs, because our success depends on the satisfaction, effort and commitment of each employee."

The mission statement goes on to say that, "our leaders will constantly support and energize all employees to continuously improve productivity and customer satisfaction. This will be accomplished by creating an environment of genuine care, trust, respect, fairness and teamwork through training, education, empowerment, participation, recognition, rewards and career opportunities."

This is a great mission statement for several reasons. It acknowledges that the employees, not executive management, hold the key to the hotel chain's success. This empowers the employees, and invests them big-time into the organization.

It targets employees who want to share the chain's mission of providing top-notch customer service, and it states that it's the job of management to create a nurturing atmosphere that will encourage employees to work toward the goals of the organization.

I'd think that employees who read that mission statement would feel pretty good about their role within the corporation. I'd think they'd be feeling pretty motivated.

In keeping with its mission statement, the Ritz-Carlton chain puts its money where its mouth is, and spends significant resources (time and money) on training employees.

To begin, each new employee meets the chain's general manager. This is done to emphasize the importance of each employee, and of the contribution he or she is expected to make to the organization. The company estimates that it spends between $2700 and $3500 to train one employee. But, it justifies its high training costs with a staff turnover rate that's 40% lower than the industry average, and with the superior customer service its employees provide.

Rally the Troops

Take a look at the mission statement of your company. If it's not written in the spirit that you think it should be, it might be worth mentioning to an appropriate person.

I've run into a number of managers who just don't understand the importance of effective initial training for employees. Many, especially those in relatively low-paying industries like the hotel industry, believe that investing a lot of money in training isn't worthwhile. They think that, because their employees aren't highly paid, it's silly to spend a lot of money training them.

That's faulty logic, to put it kindly, and it's detrimental to the quality of the organization. It's not how much the employees are paid that matters. Doing what you need to do to build an inspired and motivated team is what matters.

The Ritz-Carlton has a system that serves to continuously push its mission. It's extremely important to the motivation of the employees, and serves as a constant reminder of the chain's goals.

All 10,000 Ritz-Carlton employees carry the hotel chain's "gold standards" on a "credo card." In less than 100 words, the message on the credo card challenges every staff member to put the guests' interests first, to pledge to provide the finest personal service and facilities, and to fulfill even the unexpressed wishes and needs of every guest.

The Ritz-Carlton also has 20 basic goals, which are constantly before the entire organization. All employees are expected to be familiar with the basics, and to consider them at all times.

Each day, one of the basics is selected as a topic of conversation in the quality meetings that every employee has daily with his or her boss. This keeps the basics in the faces of both employees and management, and forces everyone to consider how the basics apply to their jobs and to the overall operation.

Below is the Ritz-Carlton's list of 20 basic goals. It's a list of great goals that might serve as an inspiration for you to come up with something similar for your own organization. Such a list keeps your team focused on their responsibility to help create an answer to the what's-in-in-for-me question.

The Ritz-Carlton Basics

➤ The Credo will be known, owned, and energized by all employees.

➤ Our motto is: "We are ladies and gentlemen, serving ladies and gentlemen." Practice teamwork and "lateral service" to create a positive work environment.

➤ The three steps of service shall be practiced by all employees.

➤ All employees will successfully complete training certification to ensure they understand how to perform to The Ritz-Carlton standards that apply to their positions.

➤ Each employee will understand his or her work area and Hotel goals, as established in each strategic plan.

➤ All employees will know the needs of their internal and external customers (guests and employees), so that we may deliver the products and services they expect. Use guest preference pads to record specific needs.

➤ Each employee will continuously identify defects throughout the Hotel.

➤ Any employee who receives a customer complaint "owns" the complaint.

➤ Instant guest pacification will be ensured by all. React quickly to correct the problem immediately. Follow up with a telephone call within 20 minutes to verify that the problem has been resolved to the customer's satisfaction. Do everything you possibly can to never lose a guest.

Defining Moments

Keep in mind that the Ritz-Carlton is a huge operation. Your **mission statement** probably doesn't need to be this comprehensive and complex. A mission statement is simply a declaration of the goals and philosophies of a company. It doesn't need to be fancy.

➤ Guest incident action forms are used to record and communicate every incident of guest dissatisfaction. Every employee is empowered to resolve the problem and to prevent a repeat occurrence.

➤ Uncompromising levels of cleanliness are the responsibility of every employee.

➤ "Smile—we are on stage." Always maintain positive eye contact. Use the proper vocabulary with our guests. (Use phrases like "good morning," "certainly," "I'll be happy to," and "my pleasure.")

➤ Be an ambassador of your Hotel, in and outside of the work place. Always talk positively. No negative comments.

➤ Escort guests rather than pointing out directions to another area of the Hotel.

➤ Be knowledgeable of Hotel information (hours of operation, etc.) to answer guest inquiries. Always recommend the Hotel's retail and food and beverage outlets prior to outside facilities.

➤ Use proper telephone etiquette. Answer within three rings and with a "smile." When necessary, ask the caller, "May I place you on hold." Do not screen calls. Eliminate call transfers when possible.

➤ Uniforms are to be immaculate; wear proper and safe footwear (clean and polished), and your correct name tag. Take pride and care in your personal appearance (adhering to all grooming standards).

➤ Ensure that all employees know their roles during emergency situations and are aware of fire and life safety response processes.

➤ Notify your supervisor immediately of hazards, injuries, equipment or assistance that you need. Practice energy conservation and proper maintenance and repair of Hotel property and equipment.

➤ Protecting the assets of a Ritz-Carlton Hotel is the responsibility of every employee.

As you can see, the list of Ritz-Carlton basics provides employees with clear expectations. It also gives them empowerment by stating that employees can do anything necessary to resolve a problem with a guest. This shows employees that they're trusted. Again, the hotel chain puts its money where its mouth is, allowing employees to spend up to $2,000 without management approval to resolve guest problems. That's empowerment!

Empowered people are involved, and they contribute. The Ritz-Carlton encourages its staff to contribute ideas for improvement by posting white boards in the service corridors. Employees list their ideas on these boards, from which the ideas are transferred and delivered to management.

What Can This Job Do to Make Life Better?

Motivated employees will work effectively toward the goals of their companies. And, they are fully within their rights to expect that the job will benefit them.

It's a two-way street, after all. The Ritz-Carlton sees to it that its employees gain benefit from the goals that employees help to accomplish.

"Five Star Employee of the Quarter" awards give outstanding employees dinners in the hotel's restaurants, allowing them to enjoy the service that they helped to create. Annual awards give outstanding employees a week in a Ritz-Carlton hotel.

Rally the Troops

Make sure that you make the benefits of your employees' jobs very clear to them. Offer the best benefits that you can, and be sure that your team understands that they're good. It doesn't do any good to offer great benefits, if they're not perceived as being so.

The hotel chain also provides day-to-day benefits for its employees, such as a pension, dental and health benefits, and other things.

If you're not in a position to offer great salaries and benefits to your workers, don't be afraid to let them know that you'll improve their compensation as you're able to. This will help to motivate them to work toward your goals. If you can't offer the salaries and benefits that you'd like, consider perks.

Perks are little benefits that can be a lot of fun, and don't need to cost very much, if anything, to the company. How about a Friday casual day or theme day? Maybe the company can come up with some kind of shirt to give employees and encourage them to wear them once a week. Maybe it can throw a great summer picnic with all the trimmings.

Don't be afraid to be creative. Employees want to know what their job can do for them, and they generally appreciate any efforts you make.

As you've seen in this chapter, it's very important to make it worthwhile for employees to help you meet your goals. It's also very important to make them motivated to want to help you reach those goals. The two things, motivation and compensation, work hand in hand.

Employees who are satisfied with their compensation, whatever form it comes in, will generally be happier, more motivated workers.

The Least You Need to Know

➤ Workers who are motivated will want to help you reach your goals.

➤ Providing vested interests for employees is one of the most effective ways to get them behind your goals.

➤ It's very important to make your employees feel that they're a vital part of the overall organization.

➤ Understanding why people want to work helps you to know how to motivate.

➤ Know that your employees expect fair compensation, both monetarily and otherwise, for the jobs they're doing, and be sure that it's provided for them.

Chapter 9

Who Wants Us to Go There?

In This Chapter

➤ A powerful motivator: "Who"

➤ Dealing with really tough situations

➤ The motivating abilities of customers

➤ Resolving conflicts between customers, employees, and shareholders

➤ Working with your team when times get really tough

➤ Letting your team really own their decisions

➤ Thinking about relationships

"Who" can be a very powerful motivator. Think about it. "Who" has been motivating us all our lives. Remember when your mom would say, "Wait until your father gets home, young man," when you'd been giving her a hard time about one thing or another all day long? Your dad was the "who"—the motivation for you to settle down and quit giving Mom trouble.

What about the school principal? Or your teachers, girlfriends or boyfriends, husbands and wives, parents, bosses, and religious leaders. All these "whos" act as powerful motivators in our lives.

Basically, people tend to run with their immediate groups. Most people prefer to stay with the herd rather than to go off on their own. Sometimes, the consequences of this are dangerous. An effective leader often can convince people to do something as a group that they wouldn't do on their own.

Backfire

The people who followed Hitler are an example of people being convinced by a powerful leader to do what they might not have done on their own. Sometimes also, the herd takes on a life of its own: This is the case in riot situations, where people respond to the actions of the group and things spiral out of control.

Rally the Troops

To spark greater motivation in your followers, think about who benefits from the goals you set. The employees benefit, the stockholders benefit, and the customer benefits.

Effective leaders take advantage of the tendency of most people to run with the herd in order to get them to do what they want. If you can convince a significant percentage of the group to buy into an idea, the rest of the group will normally fall into place and follow.

When you're trying to motivate your team, you've got to think about the group. It's good to motivate one or two workers, but it's better to motivate everybody. To do that, you've got to give your team a "who." The "who" that will help you motivate your workers, usually, is your customer.

The ultimate goal of a business, after all, is to please its customers. If the business is a manufacturing outfit, it wants to make a good product in order to please the customer. If it's a service organization, it wants to provide a good service in order to do the same. A business that doesn't please its customers won't stay in business for very long.

Who Is the Customer?

Obviously, your customers are the people who buy the products or services your company supplies.

They're the people who buy dinner in your restaurant, or who buy and wear the tennis shoes you produce, or who pay you to treat their lawns. They're also, however, the people who help to shape your goals. They have a direct role in getting you to where you need to go. Customers are a big "who."

Let your customers guide and inspire your goals, and be certain that your workers know how important it is to satisfy customers. Make sure that your employees understand that they're invested in your customers' satisfaction.

Answering the who-wants-us-to-go-there question effectively justifies your goals, creates loyalty to those goals, and inspires greater exertion and energy in pursuit of the company's success.

It's an Imperfect Place

We all know that the workplace—like the world—is an imperfect place. No surprise there. There are all kinds of things that can happen to create less-than-ideal circumstances for you and your team.

Let's suppose, for example, that you have to rally your team toward some tough goal. Let's just say that you have to tell your workers they're going to have to work over-time. And let's say that this sure-to-be-hated announcement comes directly on the heels of a temporary but indefinite across-the-board pay cut. And, just for fun, let's say that both the overtime and pay cut announcements have hit just a month after a pretty significant layoff (excuse me, that's downsizing—or rightsizing, isn't it?) occurred.

Well, it doesn't take a rocket scientist to figure out that you're in a tough situation. Nope. Ain't nobody gonna be happy with you. The kicker is that none of these things are your fault. You're not responsible for the lay-offs, the pay cuts, or the overtime requirement. You're just the messenger, and you think you're about to be shot.

Yep, you've got a tough problem. Asking every-one to work harder, for less pay, just a few weeks after they watched you toss their friends and neighbors out the door is not going to be a walk in the park. In the total context of things, your announcement is likely to produce more cyni-cism than motivation.

I've worked with many managers who have had to lead through these kinds of unpleasant cir-cumstances. It's mighty tricky, but it can be done. Here's how.

The challenge is to put a positive spin on these deplorable events. Pretend for a minute that you're presidential press secretary Joe Lockhart trying to explain a tricky situation in which Bill Clinton has found himself to the Washington press corps. You'll need to be convincing and create a positive environ-ment for your remaining employees.

Backfire

Delivering bad news to your workers can be a tricky, difficult situation. You want your team to know that you're sympathetic, but you have to hold up your end for the company, too. Be careful not to lean too far in either direction, with the result of alienating one side or the other. It's your job to try to reconcile, not further divide.

In this instance, you're going to have to be the "who" that motivates. Your team is depending on you. Your leadership will have to do several things:

➤ Help your team to understand why the unpleasant and unpopular steps were necessary. If strong competition is the reason your company had to lay off work-ers and impose pay cuts, then tell your team. If you lost a major customer, say so. Helping workers to understand why the changes were necessary can reduce resentment and promote cooperation.

➤ Enable the injured team to heal. Your people have been hurt by the recent goings-on, as probably have you. It's hard to witness changes like those de-scribed above, regardless of your position. Effective, positive leadership can help to put negative events behind, and to focus on a brighter future.

Rally the Troops

Workers need for their leaders to be strong, especially in times of adversity. Be sure that you appear confident, in charge, and under control. Use strong, positive language, and be well prepared. Anticipate questions your team might ask, and know the answers.

➤ Move the team forward. It's probably difficult for your workers to have a positive outlook for the future at this time. Positive, hopeful leadership can help them to see that the future may not be as bleak as it first appeared.

Dealing with situations such as this one are tough leadership challenges, but they're not impossible. Good leaders can, and do, rise to such occasions.

Resolving the Inherent Conflict

All business organizations serve three groups: the customers, the stockholders, and the employees. All other organizations serve the same groups, except they might call them something different.

The essence of leadership is to keep these three constituencies in balance, which isn't easy. It's not easy because each group has different needs.

➤ Customers need the products, services, or other outputs of the company.

➤ Stockholders need company profits to support other interests.

➤ Employees need the jobs to support themselves and their families.

If you can understand, and get your employees to understand, that the pulling by these three groups, each in a different direction, forced the difficult situation discussed in the last section, you'll be taking a big step in maintaining or rebuilding motivation.

Backfire

Never try to create instant motivation and optimism by pretending that everything is okay when it isn't. You'll do far more harm than good, and there's no way it can work. It takes time to renew and rebuild damaged motivation and optimism.

You'll need to thoroughly address how and why the balance was disrupted, and what was done—or will be done—to improve the situation. Your workers won't like what you tell them, but they'll accept the truth. And they're entitled to a true and reasonable explanation.

People are fundamentally optimistic. They want to believe that things will improve, even when they're at their darkest. That's why terminally ill patients will seek second, third, and fourth opinions, or try unproven medical treatments.

As a leader, you need to facilitate your workers' optimism and assure them that things will improve. But don't sugarcoat the situation. Your team knows as well as anyone the seriousness of the situation. Follow these guidelines when dealing with a situation such as the one described above:

➤ Acknowledge that you're part of the team, and that the serious situation also affects you.

➤ Be sincerely empathetic. Don't fake anything, least of all empathy. You should understand what your team is going through. If you don't, you can't be a very effective leader.

➤ Choose your words carefully. If you're perceived as being flippant or uncaring, you'll alienate yourself from your team. Use phrases such as "This is a disaster for all of us," "This is no fun for anyone," "This is not why I wanted to be a manager," or "Some parts of my job are terrible, and this is one of them." Choose words with which you're generally comfortable and that fit your overall style.

➤ Share everything you can with your team. Give your workers the real story, with as much detail as you're able.

Your workers might not be overly sympathetic to your explanation of the situation, as described in terms of the customer-stockholder-employee conflict, but done properly, it will give them a better understanding of why the problems have occurred. And, hopefully, it will give them some motivation to help you solve those problems.

Why Is the Customer Willing to Pay for This?

Customers are customers because they're willing to pay a mutually agreed-upon price for the products or services your company offers.

For the company to make money, the price has to be high enough to cover all the associated costs with some money left over for profit. If the company doesn't make any money, it will eventually go out of business, and leave its customer in the lurch.

This is something employees can understand, but that doesn't mean they're going to like or support the steps that are sometimes necessary to achieve those goals. Serving the customer with a smaller workforce means more work for the remaining employees. Getting paid less to do more isn't going to be popular, either.

Again, it will up to you to reconcile the workers with the customers. You'll need to explain why it's so important to provide the best service possible to your customers, and reinforce the value of the customers.

You can use phrases like the ones below:

➤ "No doubt about it, our customers are being very tough on us, but they're no tougher than we are on our own suppliers. We expect the best from our suppliers, and our customers expect nothing less from us."

129

➤ "No question about it, our customers are seeking higher quality at lower prices. It's our job to make sure they get the best quality at the most competitive price we can offer."

➤ "It's true, we're taking a beating right now. But customers are not necessarily punishing us. They're rewarding our competition, which right now is a lot tougher than we are."

➤ "We're going to prove to our customers that going to the competition was, and is, a mistake. We're going to win back their business."

Your task is to cause your workers to understand that they must serve their customers with competitive quality and prices. If they don't, then the company will cease to exist.

Rally the Troops

Customers will always go for the highest value they can get. If that means enriching your competition, so be it.

All this needs to be explained. If your customer is leaving you for higher value (for example, a better price for the same product), he is not out to hurt your organization or to take anyone's job. He's merely enriching himself by working with others who are creatively offering more.

You'll have to explain all this to your team, and explain that you're doing what you can to get the customer back, as well as to hang onto as many jobs as possible.

To rally the troops, you have got to stake out a position and go for it.

Aluminum is a tough industry because it's very price sensitive. It's globally competitive, and it's very tough to break out of head-in-the-sand "commodity" thinking. After Paul O'Neill, CEO of Alcoa, had been on the job for a couple of days, he was asked what he was going to stress. He came up with a somewhat surprising answer: "Safety."

O'Neill reasoned that if the plants were safe, then such things as manufacturing processes, cleanliness, and quality were all under control. Controlled systems would eventually produce lower costs and allow the company to be more competitive. This would all eventually drop to the bottom line.

In meetings, and at every other opportunity, O'Neill would ask about safety and quality, not revenues for the week. He understood consistency and focus, and had chosen safety as the position he would take. It takes guts and self-confidence to stay the course, and O'Neill did an admirable job of it.

Stockholders as Motivators

Everyone agrees customers and employees are stakeholders in an organization. Most people understand the value that both of these parties contribute and expect that both will be rewarded by the organization.

Stockholders have a vested interest in the organization, too, and they can be very valuable motivators.

Outside investors get a lot of bad press, being blamed for layoffs and other employee woes. It's a common cry that companies these days are run only with the intention of pleasing the stockholders. Many perceive stockholders as hungry, get-rich-quick investors, who only seek to bleed cash from the company. To effectively motivate workers, you'll need to understand and explain the positive side of the company's financial structure.

Here's How It Works

Individuals and groups who invest in companies also are important "whos" when it comes to motivating those companies to reach and exceed goals. Investors typically are demanding greater and much faster returns on their investments. Those demands serve as powerful motivators.

Both "for-profit" and "not-for-profit" entities have some sort of ownership structure. Understand your structure and be able to explain it to your team. Not-for-profit associations, for example, are either owned by their members or responsible to benefactors. "For-profit" organizations might have private or institutional ownership. All the ownership groups are customers too, and all have needs.

Consider the "for-profit" organizations. In the United States, 85 percent of all the nation's "for-profit" assets are traded publicly and owned by the general population either through insurance institutions, mutual funds, retirement funds, or private direct investments.

All of these constituencies have invested their private money into these assets for a reason, and all have need for a return. Insurance companies must pay claims, retirement funds must support retirees, and mutual funds must enrich their investors, who themselves are investing mostly for retirement or other future needs.

Management has a responsibility to its shareholders to provide returns, and employees must be made to understand that stockholders need to be considered and addressed.

Be open and upfront about your responsibility to your stockholders when addressing your team.

Your team might not like it, but it can accept reality. Consider using explanations such as the ones below:

➤ "I understand that it's especially tough to watch our friends lose their jobs when we're still paying dividends to stockholders. However, our majority stockholders are institutions. Specifically, the Teacher's Retirement Fund of Minnesota (or whatever) is our largest shareholder. It must have a dividend to meet its ongoing obligations to the retirees, many of whom trained us and our children. They invested their members' money in us, and we have to address our responsibility to them."

Rally the Troops

Personalizing a situation is a great way to get people invested in your goals. If you can give the situation personal meaning to your team, members will be much more sympathetic to it and far more willing to work with you on your goals.

➤ "This company is 100 years old. One of our largest stockholder groups is our own employee retirement fund. We're all employees, too. Some of our friends who lost their jobs because of these tough economic times are already vested in the retirement fund. Yes, we're still paying dividends to the fund because it's our responsibility to do so. Certainly, if any of us were retired after a long career, we would expect the fund to continue to meet its obligations to us, even if times are tough."

You shouldn't expect your team to start loving the shareholders, but, hopefully, you'll be able to help them understand the company's position and obligations.

Only Improvement Drives Us Forward

Under the best circumstances, you're running your operations so that the kinds of conversations we've been talking about throughout this chapter never have to occur.

The best way to avoid all this unpleasantness is to keep your team focused on the prize. For business, the prize must be continuous improvement and continuous growth. There can be no status quo, and the task of leadership is to continuously push the team toward the idea of creating more and more opportunities for growth.

Leadership also needs to get the team to not just recognize the necessity for growth, but to accept responsibility for the decision to grow.

I was once consulting with a company, evaluating a takeover target. The chief executive officer was in favor of the takeover, but he hadn't shared that information with his executive team.

After considerable debate and discussion concerning the proposed takeover, the vote of the executive team was split evenly, four to four. The CEO could have cast his vote and made it five to four—resolving the matter. Instead, he abstained from voting. Rather than end the debate, he chose to prolong it.

This forced the executive group to re-evaluate. It had to plow through all the facts and figures again, and go through the entire thinking process again, analyzing all the pluses and minuses. Again.

The CEO knew his executive team had to live with its decision once it was made, and that it would have to create a following among the employees. The members of his executive team were his customers. He needed members of the team to buy into the decision, not just accept the decision. He let the team take its time and even played devil's advocate by arguing against his own beliefs concerning the matter.

Rally the Troops

Often, the most difficult decisions to make are those that end up being the most meaningful. If employees have to devote a lot of time and energy to a decision, you can bet that they'll own whatever their decision is. On the other hand, if you make a decision for them, it's your decision, not theirs, and they'll have no ownership or investment in it.

When the executive team finally voted again, the vote was five to three. The CEO added his own vote, making the final tally six to three. Now he had a significant majority in favor of the takeover, and he hadn't been forced to cast the tiebreaker vote. He had a following among his customers.

The CEO knew that his team needed to move forward, but he let its members do it on their own. He didn't push or impose his views, but let the process occur naturally. He showed excellent leadership in allowing the improvement (the takeover) to occur, but by not forcing it.

Killer Words: "The Boss Said..."

The worst possible way to try to motivate a team is to use phrases like, "The boss says we have to do this," or, "That's just the way the job is."

These are killer words. They kill your leadership role because you are, in effect, admitting you're not in control.

I recall some years back when I assumed control of a group of workers after the previous boss, John, was fired for poor performance. One good guy was immediately noticeable on the team. He was producing a lot, but he was burning out.

After a few weeks of getting acclimated to the job, I looked at the good guy's schedule and noticed that he was completely overloaded with customer face time, which is the time that an employee spends actually being with customers.

Backfire

Don't ever try to pass off a decision or an announcement as belonging to somebody else. Even if you know that what you have to say will be terribly impossible, go ahead and take responsibility for it. If you don't, your team will quickly see when you're trying to weasel out of a situation, and you'll risk losing large quantities of respect.

He had no time for anything else. He had no time to check, correct, improve upon, or follow up on anything that happened with the customers. Every week he had a new group of customers to work with and no time to rework his materials. I could clearly see why the good guy was burning out, and I knew that if nothing was done, he wouldn't stick around much longer.

So the good guy and I sat down for a chat and talked about what was going on and how the circumstances had come to be. Our conversation went something like this:

"This is the way John scheduled things," the good guy said.

"But what about program improvement, follow-up, or redesign? How do you do any of that?" I asked, with great concern.

"I don't," the good guy replied.

"What do you mean you don't?" I asked in amazement. "*Someone* has to ensure that we're maintaining quality standards."

"I agree," said the good guy. "I discussed all this with John and told him I was burning out and falling way, way behind on many support things that needed to be done."

"Well, how did John respond to all that?" I asked.

"He just told me that my job was to work with the customers, and the way things are done is the way they have to be done," the good guy replied

It was very obvious that my good guy wasn't going to be a good guy for very long. He was fried—big-time.

The immediate priority was getting him some relief. I borrowed some resources, fixed his schedule, and got him away from all the customer face time. I scheduled him for about a 50-50 development/customer face-time load—a far more reasonable work schedule than he'd had.

I also gained a lot more insight into why John had been removed from his duties, and I had to agree that it had been for legitimate reasons.

John had done nothing to build up the group or to take control of circumstances. He wasn't running the operation. He was letting the job, customer demand, and circumstances run the operation.

Essentially, he was sending a message to his people that we do what we do because "the boss said…"

He was removed from the position because he had failed to lead.

Here's How It Works

Being an effective and motivating leader isn't about being able to do everything or having all the answers. It's about knowing what you can do and what you can't, and about knowing where to get good help to do the things that you can't.

Linking "Who" to "Us"

If workers are being motivating by a "who," then they need to know just who the "who" is, and be able to link "who" back to them. Huh? Let me explain, using an example.

"We'll build anything for anybody, no matter what the location, type, or size," was Stephen Bechtel's motto. He repeated it endlessly throughout his career.

To me, Bechtel's motto is a perfect definition of who-wants-us-to-go-there, and how it links the customer back to "us," inside the organization. Throughout his 70-year career with his family's world-known construction company, Bechtel's imagination was fired by grandiose projects, the more seemingly impossible, the better.

Bechtel, who served for many years as chairman of the company, was able to inspire and motivate his whole organization with his progressive thinking. By 1997, his construction company was taking in annual revenues of about $11 billion.

Now a mature organization, its projects range from building a transit system in Athens to a semiconductor plant in China. But it was not always this way.

When Stephen took over the company after his father's death in 1933, its revenues were $20 million annually. Stephen, however, was determined to see the company grow. Not constricted by his thinking, he was dealing with global economics before most people even knew what it was.

In the early days of World War II, German U-boats were sending Allied merchant ships to the bottom of the ocean faster than the shipyards could build them. The U.S. Maritime Commission was desperately looking for companies to build 60 cargo ships for its allies. Someone recommended the Bechtel Construction Company, and the Maritime Commission invited it to submit a bid for half the job.

The company had no experience with shipbuilding, but Stephen Bechtel wasn't daunted. In fact, he insisted on submitting a bid for all 60 ships instead of 30.

Stephen Bechtel was a construction genius (he'd been the primary manager in the building of Hoover Dam), but more importantly, he knew how to organize and motivate people.

Bechtel Construction organized wartime shipyards, and oversaw the construction of 560 vessels in just four years—an astounding achievement.

It has built pipelines and power plants in the forbidding reaches of the Canadian Rockies, across the Arabian desert, and through South American jungles, as well as in more impossible places, like downtown Boston. The Central Artery project through the heart of Boston is under construction at the time of this writing. Overall, the Bechtel organization has built in 140 countries and on six continents. It even built a city, Jubail, Saudi Arabia.

People can be more than motivated when you keep their customers linked to them. Innovation and creativity are inspired, and can prevail throughout the organization. Stephen Bechtel's motto served to inspire and to link the "who" to the "us."

Here's How It Works

Stephen Bechtel's motto, "we build anything for anybody," permeates his company's culture and makes things happen within it. It links the customers to the company and its employees.

Who Is Traveling with Us?

Our relationships vary greatly, depending on whom they're with, and the situations that occur within them.

Ideally, our relationships with customers—with everyone, for that matter—are based upon trust, loyalty, and mutual respect. These aren't things that happen quickly. It sometimes can take years to build up a good relationship with a customer, or an employee, or a stockholder, or a supplier, or whomever.

Once you cultivate good relationships, make sure that you hang onto them and keep those people traveling with you.

Let's take a look at how the qualities mentioned above—trust, loyalty, and mutual respect—affect our relationships and keep us motivated.

> ➤ **Trust.** No relationship works well without trust. Trust takes a long time to establish but hardly any time at all to break down and destroy. If you have a trusting relationship with a customer, or an employee, or anyone, make sure you do all you can to preserve it. Don't cut corners, or tell a little lie, or cheat just a little bit in order to make things easier or get out of a scrape. Remember that little things can very quickly turn into serious trust-busters.

➤ **Loyalty.** It also takes a long time to build a degree of loyalty among customers, employees, stockholders, or whomever. And, many people don't fully under-stand or appreciate the value of loyalty. A loyal friend, customer, or employee is worth doing whatever you need to in order to hang onto him. You can always find another customer or employee, but loyalty must be earned over time.

➤ **Mutual respect.** As with trust and loyalty, respect is something that develops over time. Respect, like trust, can easily be lost, and is difficult to get back once it's gone.

Be picky about who travels with you, choosing people whom you can motivate and who will motivate you.

Be continually aware of who motivates you and your employees, and the manners in which they do it. Pay attention to who travels with you and the effects that they have on you and your team.

The Least You Need to Know

➤ "Who," whoever it may be, can be a very powerful motivator.

➤ Terrible situations are tough to deal with, but effective leaders find acceptable ways to do so.

➤ Customers tend to be big motivators.

➤ Nearly every company sees some tension in the dynamics between customers, employees, and stockholders.

➤ When times get really bad, let your team know you're on their side.

➤ Let your team make their own important decisions, so that they will be really invested in them.

➤ Don't take good relationships, namely those based on trust, loyalty, and mu-tual respect, for granted.

Chapter 10

When Do We Need to Be There?

In This Chapter

➤ Using "when" to motivate

➤ Forcing your team to look past the present and set goals for "when"

➤ Making sure your timing is right in a "when" situation

➤ Making sure you get the resources you need

➤ Avoiding resource overkill

➤ Knowing what you'll need, and how much

➤ Getting your team to buy into your work project

"When" is one of the more serious issues in motivation.

Think about all the "when" questions that motivate us, either willingly or unwillingly.

➤ *When* will you have it done?

➤ *When* do you need it?

➤ I'll show you *when* we get there.

➤ *When* are you going?

➤ And, of course, you want it *when*?!

Nearly everyone is pushed by "when." We use it to motivate kids all the time. Think about all the times you've said something like, "*When* you've finished cleaning your room, then you can go outside to play." Or, "We'll just see about that *when* your father/mother gets home." You see how "when" can be a pretty powerful motivator.

"When" certainly motivates us at work. Without it, we'd lose much of our motivation to finish projects on time, to come back from lunch, or to even show up at 8 or 9 a.m.

"When" is a word that causes us to reassess our priorities and deal with urgency faster than nearly anything else. It's a time issue, to be sure.

➤ When I was your age…

➤ When you finish that report…

➤ When are you leaving?

"When" always deals with time. Remember in Chapter 1, "Who Needs This Motivation Stuff, Anyway?" when we discussed how people, unlike any other creatures, are always motivated to pursue something? Whether it's sleep, recreation, work, or whatever, we're always moving on to do something else. That was the difference between my little neighbor, two-year-old Vivs, and Gimli, the furry thing that my wife calls a dog.

Gimli's motivations are limited to food, sleep, and comfort. Vivs, on the other hand, has seemingly unlimited motivations. She explores, searches, and learns constantly because she's motivated by curiosity to find out all she can about her big, new world.

Getting your team to pursue your goals is a matter of convincing them to move away from what it's doing to do what you want it to do. You've got to get team members to buy into the belief that the pursuit of your goals is more important than whatever it is they're doing at the time.

Using "when" is a great way to do that.

Anchoring "When" in Real Time—Like Today!

The ongoing leadership challenge surrounding the question of "when" is to create interest and willingness among your team members to work to change something.

Because change always runs against the current trend, whatever it is, you need to take some steps to get your team moving toward something new.

➤ Identify the current trend.

➤ Make sure that everyone on your team understands the trend, and what drives the trend.

➤ Justify the need for your team to move in a new direction.

➤ Motivate your team to constructively rise above the current trend and toward the new direction.

➤ Commit the necessary resources and allow your team to do its job.

What you have to do is move "when," which implies the future, into the present. You've got to get your team members to accept the change as something that's real to them. This moves the "when" into the present and allows you and your team to pursue it in real time.

Let's consider the steps listed above by looking at how Gillette—you know, the razor people—motivated its workers to design, introduce, and market a brand-new razor design. Then, we'll look at some other examples of how other leaders accomplished their goals by convincing their followers to target a future "when" as a viable alternative to whatever was happening presently.

The Gillette Story

It was a bold move for Gillette, coming up with the Mach3. The Mach3, just in case you haven't heard, is the world's very first triple-blade razor, introduced to the public in 1998.

Now, to you who are female, bearded, or wedded to electric shavers, this might not seem like a big deal. Believe me when I tell you, however, the Mach3 is a significant breakthrough in the world of whiskers.

Analysts were quick to say that Gillette was treading on thin ice when it spent big bucks to design, develop, and market the Mach3 at the time that it did. They pointed out that 1998 was a time of significant deflationary pressure and predicted that general price hikes were only going to average 1.4 percent or so for all of 1999.

That meant that there would be little or no room to increase prices on either existing or new products.

Gillette went ahead with its plans, despite the warnings, and put the Mach3 cartridges on the shelves for around $1.60 each. That represented a 50 percent premium over what was then Gillette's priciest blade, the SensorExcel double-blade razor cartridge.

Skeptics predicted that the personal care giant would be forced to cut the price shortly after introduction. Wrong again! The price held, and Mach3 became the leading blade and razor.

Gillette's market share by December of 1998 had climbed to almost 71 percent, the highest share it had achieved since 1962.

Remember that this all occurred within a deflationary market that experts had predicted would result in stagnant sales.

Backfire

While we all know that analysts aren't always right, it's important to remember that they're not always wrong, either. Don't ignore what could be good and important advice because it's not what you want to hear. You don't want to be held back from accomplishing your goals, but you don't want to do something that's downright stupid, either.

Gillette was running mightily and enviably against the tide, celebrating market share increases along with extraordinary price increases.

How did this happen? Motivation. Gillette management, which knew that the secret to creating this highly successful new product with the 50 percent higher price tag was to get its employees excited about the product, motivated its employee force to get behind Mach3 and go great guns with it. It got them to believe in the product and showed them how to look past the present to "when."

Here's How It Works

R.G. Bannister did what was thought to be impossible and ran a sub-four-minute mile in 1954. Once he accomplished what previously was considered to be beyond the reach of man, other runners were motivated by his performance, and new records were set. All these runners, and everyone who breaks records and does what was thought to be impossible, look past the present to "when."

Gillette accomplished each of the five steps that we mentioned earlier in this chapter. Let's take a look at each step and how Gillette did exactly what it needed to do to get its employees behind its new product.

➤ *Identify the current trend.* Being one of the major players, Gillette obviously understood what was going on in the personal care industry. Management knew the trends inside out.

➤ *Make sure that everyone on your team understands the trend and what drives the trend.* Gillette's management had to make sure that its employees understood what was happening within the industry and why.

➤ *Justify the need for your team to move in a new direction.* The only way to do this was for Gillette to have a darned good feeling of what its customers wanted, and that they'd be willing to pay in order to get it. You have to have a convincing vision to justify moving in a different direction than the current trend.

➤ *Motivate your team to constructively rise above the current trend and toward the new direction.* To do this, Gillette had to give its workers convincing reasons to change direction. It had to take them out of the present and motivate them to try something new.

➤ *Commit the necessary resources, and allow your team to do its job.* Once Gillette convinced its workers to get behind the Mach3, it had to be sure that it clearly demonstrated its support of the new product. This is very important. The employees need to see that management has confidence in the new direction. Gillette's management expressed its support of the new product by putting nearly $1 billion into the development and initial marketing of Mach3.

Alfred M. Zeien, CEO of Gillette, says it isn't always easy, but a company can buck the trend if it supplies, "new products that provide benefits people think are worth paying for."

Getting your team behind you to share that attitude is a central part of management's job, and what Gillette accomplished is an excellent example of how to do it.

What Gillette did was impressive, but it wasn't magic. It wasn't even all that unique. All the smartest leaders know that their job is positive leadership, and motivating their workers to anchor "when" in today.

Here's How It Works

Alfred M. Zeien, CEO of Gillette, says the best priority when setting new goals is to focus on creating additional value that people will be willing to pay for. That priority, Zeien says, has been used successfully ever since business began.

Other Successful "When" Stories

The Colgate-Palmolive Company was looking at the same deflationary market that Gillette had successfully outmaneuvered and was equally undaunted.

Employing the same tactic of introducing a product with the perception of added consumer value, Colgate priced its new toothpaste, Colgate Total, 25 percent above mainstream brands.

Colgate was banking on the assumption that its new brand would sell, based on the fact that it's the first toothpaste approved by the U.S. Food and Drug Administration as being effective in preventing the much-dreaded gum disease, gingivitis.

Total brand toothpaste moved into the number-one spot in the toothpaste world, grabbing almost 10 percent market share within a year of its introduction. As with

Rally the Troops

Take advantage of what's hot at the moment to create market value in an item or service. High-tech is exciting, sexy, and new, opening the doors to all sorts of creativity. As a result, manufacturers are coming up with all sorts of high-tech additions to ordinary products.

Gillette, the trick here was creating value, and creating it now. It is not about following the current trend; it's about setting the trend.

This is what effectively dealing with the "when" question is all about.

Effective leaders at Dr. Scholl's, a division of Schering-Plough Corporation, dealt with the "when" question by taking the lowly shoe-insert pad and using biomechanics to transform it into a remedy for leg and back pain. The new product, Dynastep, with its enhanced value to customers, is priced at about $14 per insert, twice as much as older inserts on the market. Within a year of its introduction, Dynastep had become the best-selling shoe insert and had a 29 percent market share.

The Maytag Corporation's environmentally friendly Neptune washer is a hit, even though at $1,100, it costs about twice as much as conventional washers.

Customers love the Neptune brand washer, and for good reason. It's supposed to, over the course of a year, save the consumer about $100 in electric costs and use 7,000 gallons of water less than a conventional washer. That, by the way, is as much water as the average person drinks in a lifetime.

Utility companies that think in the short term might not be so crazy about Neptune, but it's great news for consumers, for Maytag, and for our water supply.

Rally the Troops

If you find yourself faced with the need to create a sense of urgency in order to motivate, remember that timing is of the essence. Timing is so important in creating a sense of urgency, in fact, that, if you don't think your timing is good, you might have to figure out how to work it around to your advantage.

Companies and individuals are writing these kinds of success stories every day. They're all examples of lofty and optimistic goals set by people who are looking to "when" instead of "now."

And it's clear that customers and employees are responding to these goals because they see the value of a positive response, and because they've responded to the sense of urgency that the leaders behind these products have established. Leaders have convinced employees of the urgency to develop, produce, and market these types of products, and customers of the urgency to buy and possess them.

The need to create a sense of urgency extends past business situations. The issue of when, or creating that sense of urgency and priority, is critical in all kinds of situations in which leaders must motivate others to follow. The following story about the Gulf

War in the early part of the 1990s is a classic example of motivating by creating a sense of urgency.

In the early morning hours of August 2, 1990, hundreds of tanks and other Iraqi forces swept across the Kuwaiti border.

Within 24 hours, Iraq had complete control of Kuwait and had declared it to be an Iraqi province. Thousands of Iraqi troops then moved to Kuwait's border with Saudi Arabia, setting off the notion that Iraq intended to invade Saudi Arabia and take control of the region's oil supplies.

Less than a week later, 230,000 American troops were in Saudi Arabia as part of Operation Desert Shield. This situation, with all its political nuances and considerations, was a challenge for the leaders on both sides.

The United Nations, as well as the United States and many other countries, condemned the Iraqi invasion of Kuwait. Instead of backing down, however, Iraqi President Saddam Hussein accused the United States and other nations of following a double standard in their reactions to the invasion of Kuwait.

According to Hussein, if these nations condemned the Iraqi invasion, they should also condemn Israel's continued occupation of lands it had won from Arab nations in the Arab-Israeli wars.

By now, there were strong and opposing opinions on the invasion of Kuwait, the role the U.S. would play in the crisis, and, as always, the Arab-Israeli situation.

Opinions were clearly solidified, which meant that leaders on both sides now had the responsibility to create a sense of urgency in order to get their teams behind them to support their goals. Leaders needed to rally support for war and destruction, not for creating high value new products, as we've been dealing with previously in this chapter.

Here's How It Works

It's interesting that war and business situations appear to be completely different, and yet the leadership skills necessary in both of them are pretty much the same.

In November, after months of applying pressure on Iraq, and Iraq refusing to budge, the United Nations Security Council issued an ultimatum. If Iraq wasn't out of Kuwait by January 15, the UN authorized the use of "all necessary means" to get it out. World leaders, of course, interpreted this as an approval of war.

The challenge that U.S. President George Bush faced, along with leaders of countries such as Britain, France, and Italy—those that that would ultimately bear most of the burden of fighting Iraq—was to garner the necessary support from their governments and populations. Removing the Iraqi army from Kuwait would require a massive movement of troops to the area. It was a pretty safe assumption that lives would be lost in the process.

All through the massive buildup of military might in the Gulf region, public opinion, especially in the United States, was only marginally supportive of an invasion.

Given a chance to voice their opinions, the masses of people nearly always prefer negotiation to confrontation. President Bush, who was well aware of the importance of public opinion, challenged Hussein to a private meeting "anywhere in the world and at any time" to try to resolve the differences that were threatening to result in an all-out war.

Bush's leadership goal was to prove to the world that he had done everything possible to prevent war and to motivate people to support him if war became necessary. Bush was creating a sense of urgency among the American people and other people around the world.

Saddam Hussein outfoxed Bush by announcing that he would meet with the U.S. President near the end of December, just a couple of weeks before the UN ultimatum date for Iraq to be out of Kuwait. That was a smart move on Hussein's part, and a good use of timing.

Bush's security people couldn't allow the President to attend a meeting outside the United States just prior to launching a war. Furthermore, if Bush had agreed to the meeting, then launching a war on January 15 would be next to impossible.

The world would need some time to digest whatever would be discussed at the meeting, and it certainly would seem that the U.S. was rushing things if it kept on track with the UN ultimatum. Surely Hussein and his followers had anticipated that the United States would have to reject the offer for a meeting.

Backfire

If you don't consider timing when making important decisions or setting goals, you're asking to have whatever it is you're trying to do blow up in your face. Timing is crucial in all situations, especially "when" situations.

When the meeting was refused, the public relations pendulum swung toward Hussein, and away from Bush and the invasion. People claimed the entire situation was motivated by politics and oil, and that the U.S. had no business risking the lives of our military people over it.

Hussein had achieved a victory. He now could proclaim to the world that President Bush was a warmonger who was not willing to debate the issues, even though he had promised to do exactly that. Public support for the war effort declined.

This situation is an example of something that is absolutely critical to all leaders. President Bush was in a tough spot at this stage of the Gulf War situation, just as you may have been, or one day will be, with a business situation. He was in danger of losing the support of his people, which would have had serious consequences, both relating to the war and Bush's political career.

When this happens, you, as a leader, have the responsibility to create a sense of urgency, to establish the evidence, and to prove your point to your followers.

Proving your point, not merely stating it, is central to motivating your team to take immediate action. If you want something done now, and your followers see something else as more important, then you must create additional circumstances that demonstrate the urgency of your goals.

Here's How It Works

Sometimes you have to create circumstances to demonstrate the urgency of your goals, and sometimes somebody else will do it for you. The Japanese created the circumstances that proved urgency beyond a doubt by bombing Pearl Harbor in 1941 and forcing the U.S. into World War II.

Bush needed some way to regain momentum and to convince people that his goals of fighting and defeating Iraq were urgent and necessary.

To do so, Bush announced that U.S. Secretary of State Jim Baker would fly to Geneva, Switzerland. If Hussein wanted to send the Secretary of Iraq, then Baker would meet with him and negotiations could occur. Hussein was forced to agree because Bush had flipped the cards.

Now, world interest was focused on the Geneva meeting. Baker met with the Secretary of Iraq for six hours, fueling hopes that an all-out war could be avoided. Hopes were dashed, however, when Baker emerged from the talks and gave the following statement during a press conference.

"I have been in negotiations with the Secretary from Iraq for more than six hours. Never once did he even use the word Kuwait."

Iraq was clearly unrepentant and uncooperative, and plans to attack the country continued. Bush had successfully shown that Saddam Hussein had no intention of meeting the United Nations ultimatum, and he got the public support he needed to win Congressional approval for his position. The U.S. launched a devastating air attack against military targets in Iraq and Kuwait on January 16.

Defining Resource Requirements

Whether building new products or planning wars, one thing you can be sure about, is that all resources are usually committed elsewhere. Getting your share of them can be difficult, and when you have a project that needs to done by *when*ever (remember that "when" is always a time thing, and time is a powerful motivator), having what you need to accomplish your goals is of the utmost importance.

Defining Moments

Defining resource requirements *is* just jargon for figuring out what you need in order to accomplish your goals.

Be careful when you define your resource requirements. If you ask for too few resources, you may not be able to meet your objectives.

Overshooting, or demanding more resources than you need to accomplish your goals, is a waste of resources and can pull down the overall operation, while causing bad feelings against you and your team.

Consider the case of my friend Kate, a newspaper editor on a mid-sized paper in Pennsylvania. Kate, who's the features editor, decided to do a big series on teenage pregnancies. She knew that in order to do the series the way she thought it should be done, she'd need additional reporters, money with which to pay overtime, and other resources, such as use of the newspaper's conference room, company vehicles, photographers to accompany reporters to interviews and events, and so forth.

Other editors objected to losing some of their reporters to Kate, but she was extremely insistent, and she managed to convince the paper's decision makers to support her goals.

Kate got more resources—reporters, overtime pay, and newspaper facilities—than she really needed. The series was okay—I think one of the reporters even got a statewide award for one of the articles that appeared as part of it. But while Kate and her team of reporters were working on the series, other areas of the newspaper suffered. Reporters who normally covered important beats like the city school board, county and city government, and police were forced to give some of their time to the series. As a result, they missed some significant stories on their own beats.

By the time the series had run, there were a lot of people—editors and reporters—who were very unhappy with Kate and what they saw as her misuse of company resources. They claimed, and probably rightly so, that she could have done the same series with only her own reporters if she had managed the project more effectively.

People are still upset with Kate, even though this all occurred more than a year ago.

Measuring Requirements

So, how do you know what you'll need in way of resources? How could Kate have effectively figured out what she would need to have in order to successfully complete her series?

Start by breaking down your work project into small pieces. If somebody asks you to guess the length of two pieces of rope, one measuring one foot long and the other 25 feet long, you'll be far more likely to correctly guess the length of the shorter piece.

Kate could have done this by looking at one story within the series and figuring out what she needed in order to get it done. Then she could have determined exactly what the series would entail, and used her one-story resource requirements as a guide to what she would need for the entire project.

Backfire

If you're one of those people who find it very difficult to ask for help, and you insist on doing everything yourself, you're really making things far more difficult than they need to be. Not asking for help when you need it is risking that you'll run into serious trouble. That could damage your professional standing and reputation.

Another way to determine what you need is to ask people who understand the work project, or who have done similar projects, to help you create the time and resource estimates. People who have been there, done that have already gone through what you're attempting to do. They know what's going on. Remember, there's no use in reinventing the wheel.

If Kate had talked to another editor who had already done a series of similar length and scope, she could have avoided tying up more than her share of resources and creating bad feelings among her peers.

How to Create Buy In

Once you've defined a work project to your team, how do you get them to buy into the project and its goals? We've already discussed the importance of creating a sense of urgency for an important project and getting your team to look beyond the present, but how do you get team members to really buy into your goals?

Here are a couple of good ways you can do this.

➤ *Never ask people to perform goals—it's impossible.*

Defining Moments

Goals are the culmination of tasks performed successfully. Tasks are necessary steps toward reaching goals. You can't assign or perform goals, but you can assign and perform tasks in order to reach goals.

A lot of people confuse goals and tasks. A task is something that's done in order to reach a goal. You can assign tasks, but you can't assign goals. Think about a football coach who wants to win his league's championship—oh, let's go all the way and say that he wants to win the Super Bowl. Winning the Super Bowl is the goal.

A coach can't assign his team the job of winning the Super Bowl, but he can assign them tasks like improving a running play or a passing pattern. That will put his team on track to win the games necessary to reach the playoffs and, eventually, the Super Bowl.

➤ *Let members of your team evaluate the process, and tell you what they need to do to reach a goal.*

This is a sure-fire way to assure buy-in. If you invest your team in your goal by letting members tell you what needs to be done in order to reach it, you'll have a lot more willingness, interest, and help.

Once you've created buy-in for your project, it's easy to motivate your team to stay the course and do what needs to be done. You will have effectively used "when" to direct your goals.

The Least You Need to Know

➤ When can be a very powerful motivator, not only in work situations, but also in all areas of our lives.

➤ Looking ahead to "when" can inspire your team to think past whatever is happening presently.

➤ Timing is so important in a "when" situation that you may be forced to work around it in order to accomplish your goals.

➤ Be assertive enough to get the resources you need in order to complete a project, but avoid being greedy and taking more than you need.

➤ Break down a project into small parts, and rely on the experience of others when determining what, and how many resources you'll require.

➤ Give your team ample opportunity to get involved with a project in order to encourage buy-in.

Part 3
The Other Motivators

Where, why, what, who, and when are very important motivators, but they're not the only ones.

You'll also be able to motivate your team by understanding how to handle personal problems, being a good listener, building a sense of security, and handling discipline matters effectively.

In this section, you'll learn about the importance of being sincere (workers can spot a phony from clear across the shop floor), and how to be sincere—for real. You'll learn the right way—and the wrong way—to discipline employees, and why a clear discipline policy is necessary.

The members of your team are more than employees. They're real people with lives and problems of their own. Letting them know that you understand that goes a long way in getting, and keeping, them motivated.

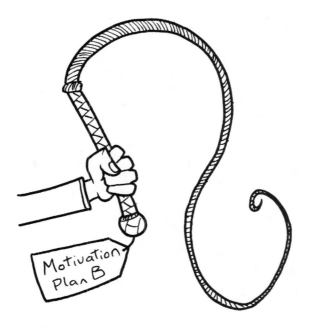

Chapter 11

Can't You See I'm Hurting?

In This Chapter

➤ Addressing personal problems among your workers

➤ Learning when and how to listen effectively

➤ Avoiding potentially dangerous situations

➤ Sincerity and insincerity

➤ Where to go for help when you need it

The duties of a supervisor are varied and sometimes entail much more than we think they should. These duties extend far beyond work into the scary realm of the personal and private.

When you have an employee with problems that aren't job oriented but are affecting the job she is performing, the matter needs to be addressed.

As you might imagine, these can be sensitive grounds, where you'll need to tread lightly.

In this chapter, we'll have a look at how you should deal with personal problems. We'll learn how important it is to listen, and discuss some cautions, as well.

So, pull up a chair and let's get personal.

Personal Problems Are a Part of the Package

There was a time when people were advised to leave work at work and home at home.

Frankly, I doubt that it ever occurred that way, but that's what we were told to do. Work was work and home was home, and ne'er were the twain to meet.

Fortunately or unfortunately, I'm not sure which, it's next to impossible to do that. The different components of our lives, by their very natures, overlap and mesh together. You don't necessarily have to take home a briefcase full of work every night, but it's hard to leave your work-related thoughts in the office.

Enlightened management is aware that people can't, and don't, completely separate home from work. And enlightened management is aware that they sometimes have to jump in and get involved with their employees' personal lives and problems.

Sometimes it's obvious that there's no choice. You're forced to jump in and get your hands dirty, as I was one morning when an employee called me, just before the start of business.

"Hi Greg," I said. "How are you?"

"I'm not that fine," Greg replied. "I'm going to commit suicide."

"Greg, where are you," I asked quickly."

"I'm at Perkins."

With that, he hung up the phone. I'm here to tell you that a call like this gets your attention in a big way. I immediately called my boss, who went right to the vice president of human resources for advice.

Unfortunately, the only advice we got there was to tell Greg that he was eligible for the company's medical assistance plan—hardly a comfort for someone who's considering ending his life. Not sure what to do, we shut down all the incoming phone lines, hoping Greg might call in again.

I also had staff people get the phone numbers of all the Perkins chain restaurants in the area and started calling them. We soon located Greg and had the police pick him up and take him to the hospital.

He spent three weeks in the psychiatric unit, which the company paid for. Ultimately, Greg was released from the company because he couldn't perform his job. We knew that it was important, though, to give him every opportunity to do his job. We felt, when we had to let Greg go, that we had done that. More importantly, we felt that we had done all we could

Rally the Troops

Some companies have policies in place for dealing with emergency situations like the one involving Greg. It's a good idea to find out whether your company has a policy, and, if so, what it entails.

to help him out, personally. It was obvious though that he had problems that extended way beyond our ability to help.

You need to be sensitive to and prepared to help out with personal problems when you encounter them. With most of your employees, however, personal problems won't be an issue. Not that they won't exist, but you'll never hear about them.

Most of your employees will never discuss their personal problems with you. Many of them, in fact, would rather have a root canal done than tell you about their personal problems. If they do, however, it goes without saying that you don't discuss their problems with anyone else, unless you feel it's necessary to do so to ensure the safety of the employee.

Backfire

Many people today have problems that are complex and potentially devastating. Don't try to handle problems that are bigger than you have the ability to deal with. Misguiding somebody can have disastrous consequences, so know when to punt.

It takes only one incident to lose the trust of your entire staff. I knew a woman named Barbara who was a supervisor at a large restaurant. She was a nice person, but she had a big mouth. An employee confided to Barbara that she was having marital problems and that she feared her husband was becoming abusive.

It was all that this employee, who was quiet and not very close to any of the other staff members, could do to bring herself to discuss these most personal of problems with anyone, much less Barbara, her work supervisor. So think how she felt a few days later when she overheard Barbara whispering to another employee about the information she had confided. She was devastated and quit her job almost immediately.

The employee didn't make a big issue of why she was leaving, probably because she was embarrassed about the whole situation. Word got around, however, and it became common knowledge that Barbara couldn't be trusted with confidential information.

How to Be a Good Listener

A great bit of wisdom advises that humans were given two ears and one mouth, and that they should be used proportionately.

Unfortunately, this gem is too seldom heeded. Most people love to hear themselves talk and have listening skills that could, to put it nicely, benefit from some improvement.

The thing about listening is that you have to make an effort to do it. It's not like hearing, which happens pretty much by default. Listening and hearing are two

Defining Moments

According to Kevin J. Murphy, author of "*Effective Listening*," **listening** is "the accurate perception of what is being communicated." Murphy says that unlike hearing, which is passive and something we always do, listening is active and something we choose to do.

different things. We can act like we're listening, look like we're listening, and maybe even believe that we're listening, when all we're really doing is hearing.

Fortunately, once you're aware of the differences between listening and hearing, it becomes easier to be aware of when you're performing each function. That's the first step to becoming a good listener.

Learning to be an effective listener takes some effort and some practice, but the results are well worth it. Listening may be an underused skill, but it's an important and valued one.

Knowing When to Listen

Sometimes it's easy to know when it's time to sit down and really listen to someone, because they'll tell you.

If somebody comes to you and says they need to talk, they're asking you for something. They're asking for some of your time, and for your attention. They're asking to be recognized. When this occurs, keep in mind that many people find it difficult to ask for help. When they do, you should treat the request seriously, and give them your complete attention.

In other circumstances, it might not be so easy to know when somebody wants your ear. Because many people do find it difficult to ask for help, they simply don't ask. As a leader, however, it's still your responsibility to recognize when someone has a problem. If you suspect that somebody wants to talk to you, but is reluctant or unwilling to ask, go ahead and offer.

Saying something like, "Hey Jerry, how's it going?" will open the door for conversation. If Jerry just mumbles that everything's okay, you can nudge the door a little bit further open by saying something like, "Geez, Jerry, are you sure? You seem a little preoccupied lately." With that, you're acknowledging Jerry, and telling him that you're concerned for him.

If he again doesn't respond, you can try one more time by saying something along the lines of, "well, if there's ever anything that you want to talk about, I'm around."

Now Jerry knows that you're willing to give him your time and attention, which makes it unnecessary for him to ask. You've put an offer on the table, and all Jerry has to do is take it.

Remember that you can't force somebody to talk to you. All you can do is offer, and follow through if he takes you up on your offer.

To be on the safe side, you should be listening all the time. As a leader, you need to know what's going on, and listening is probably the best way to do that.

Remember though, if you're going to be listening all the time, you need to be selective about what you listen to, and how you respond to what you hear. Guaranteed that, when you start honing in to what people are saying, you're going to hear some things you'd just as soon not hear.

Rally the Troops

Experienced leaders generally are pretty thick skinned and willing to ignore some of the abuse that comes with the territory. Be prepared to toughen up a little if you're planning to be effective.

You might hear a couple members of your team fighting, or maybe someone saying something nasty about their boss (you). You might hear some negative comments about the company, or its policies, or its managers (you again). If so, know when to walk away and ignore it. Not every comment that somebody makes is serious. People say things they don't mean all the time. They make mistakes, speak too quickly, and say things they regret.

Be willing to overlook—or "overhear"—a lot of what you pick up on your listening forays.

Developing Listening Skills

If somebody does take you up on your offer to listen, be sure you're there for him. You'll ruin your credibility by offering to sit and talk with someone, then not being available when he's ready to do so.

When you are in a situation of listening to someone talk about personal problems or issues, remember that your job is to *listen,* not to talk.

Most people are simply looking for someone to act as a sounding board. They need to know that you're really hearing what they're telling you, but they're not looking for a lot of advice.

If somebody really wants advice, he'll ask for it. Otherwise, your job is to be a good listener.

Listed below are some tips for good listening. Because listening is so important to managers, I'd recommend reading these twice.

> ➤ Listen all the time.
> ➤ Get out of your office. There's not enough going on in there to keep you in touch with the rest of the place.
> ➤ Start every day with your team. This makes you accessible, and keeps you up on what's going on.
> ➤ End every day with your team. For the same reasons as those listed above.
> ➤ Listen when you're in their work areas.
> ➤ Listen with your eyes, as well as your ears. Body language—gestures, facial expressions, and so forth—can tell you a lot.

How Close Is Too Close?

I think it's good to be close to your employees. Everyone knows, however, that it's not good to be *too* close. So, where do you draw the line? When is close too close? I've seen supervisors hug employees—same sex or different—with no bad results. On the other hand, I've seen gestures offered that were taken completely out of context, and resulted in huge problems for everyone.

In these most litigious of times, when even savvy fifth-graders can give you a definition of "sexual harassment," I think the best advice is "don't touch." I hope I don't even need to warn you of the dangers of becoming intimately involved with one of your employees.

I'm not saying that you should never give somebody a pat on the back, or shake hands, or that sort of thing. As you probably know, however, the workplace has become a minefield for sexual harassment lawsuits, and it's really in your best interests to watch out for them.

Sexual harassment is an unlawful employment practice under Tile VII of the Civil Rights Act of 1964. There are different kinds of sexual harassment, and the rulings are a little hazy, so, the best thing to do it to avoid any circumstances that might be misconstrued or misinterpreted as harassment.

Here's How It Works

Everybody from the President of the United States to elementary school-age kids are being accused of sexual harassment. We all know about Bill Clinton's problems, but think about this: A 13-year-old girl in Clay County, Missouri, sued her school district in federal court and was awarded $5,000. The reason: She claimed she had been sexually harassed for two years by elementary-age boys on her school bus.

We tend to think of sexual harassment as being a man thing, but it works both ways.

When I was about 35 or 40, I hired a secretary who was about 10 years younger than I was. I was married, had two young children, and damned serious about getting my career moving.

Imagine my surprise when, about a month after she was hired, she came into my office and sat down. I hadn't asked her to come in for anything, and I was a little surprised, but didn't think too much about it. After all, it was perfectly feasible that there was something she wanted to discuss with me.

There was something she wanted to discuss, but it didn't have anything to do with the phone call I'd asked her to make earlier in the day.

My secretary looked me in the eye and asked me point blank, "do you fool around on your wife?"

I stared at her, all flustered and puzzled, and came up with a very clever reply. "What?"

"You know, do you mess around with other women?" she asked again. "Anyway, if you do, I just wanted you to know that I'm available, if you're interested."

I mumbled something completely unintelligible, and went back to work. She left the office, and never mentioned sex again. She worked with us for two or three years, and did a fair job. I just chose to ignore the whole incident. It simply never was discussed again.

Lots of things happen in and around offices. You don't need to get involved with everything that's available.

Another manager was confronted with a similar situation, but chose a different course. He and his office secretary, both divorced from their spouses, started a private relationship. At least they thought the relationship was private.

One day, without warning, the manager was offered another position in another division of the company. He interviewed for the job, but the position was way below what he had currently. He turned it down.

One day not long after, Mr. Big-Shot Company President passed by the manager in the hallway. He looked at the manager and said, "I really want you to take that other job. We need you there."

The manager saw the writing on the wall and took the other job. Of course, what the president really wanted was for the manager and his lover/secretary to be separated. People were talking about it, and it was affecting the morale and productivity of the entire team. The manager eventually left the firm.

Some managers can pull off close relationships with their employees better than others. No one, however, can afford to take chances concerning sexual harassment or other negative behavior.

You Can't Fake Sincerity

If you really care about the members of your team, and you really want to be a good and effective leader, they'll know it. If you don't

Backfire

Don't ever, ever assume that your private life is private in an office situation. Somebody always finds out what's going on, and then somebody else, and soon everyone knows. If you don't want people to know you're doing something—don't do it.

Rally the Troops

If you ever do become involved in a relationship with one of your employees, it's better to confront the matter openly, even if it means that one of you has to find another assignment.

really care, and you've got many priorities that rank above being a good leader, they'll know that, too.

To be sincere is to be genuine, without false appearances or gestures for the sake of the gestures.

To be sincere is to be honest. If you don't like being around people, then don't assume that you can be an effective leader. You can't. Your employees are most likely more perceptive than you give them credit for, and will certainly see through your façade.

Trying to fake sincerity is like trying to fake love. You might get away with it for a little while, but pretty soon the people affected are sure to catch on.

Dangers of Pretending

Workers are pretty much aware of what's going on. If you try to pretend that your interests are with your people, when actually they're with getting yourself a promotion and the accompanying raise, they'll see that, and you'll soon be cut out of the loop.

If you lie to your team by pretending, your team will lie to you. They'll see you as a hypocrite, and they'll tell you what they think you want to hear not what you should hear.

To pretend that you're sincere in your interests concerning your team—or about anything else, for that matter—is to risk alienating yourself.

It's unhealthy, and it's unwise.

Learning to Be Sincere—for Real

Anybody can learn to look someone in the eye when they're talking, nod his or her head at all the appropriate times, and give a sympathetic squeeze of the hand.

Not everyone, however, is going to feel real compassion and sincerity for his or her employees. What makes the difference?

A lot of how you feel about your team depends upon your general attitudes toward life and people.

What do you believe about the world around you? Do you think that people are fundamentally good, and are trying to do things the way they should? Or, do you think that most people couldn't care less about anything other than themselves, and probably wouldn't cross the street to hand you a glass of water if you were dying of thirst.

My work has caused me to travel to many places, and I've seen many different perceptions about life and people. In Lahore, Pakistan, resources are terribly limited. Extreme poverty is everywhere and there is little infrastructure.

While visiting there on business, I witnessed an auto accident. The drivers were discussing what to do in the aftermath, and I asked my host whether they would call for a police officer.

My host replied very matter of factly, "well, if they do, they'll just need to bribe him and they'll still have to resolve the matter themselves." Because of those circumstances, he said, they were not likely to be calling for the police.

The lesson here, is that most folks in Lahore, like everywhere else, are simply trying to get through the day and make life a little better for themselves and their families. How we live each day has a profound effect on our outlooks, and how we see the world around us.

Here's How it Works

People's perceptions and attitudes are shaped by many factors, most of which you'll never know anything about. You shouldn't be judgmental of people and their attitudes, because you can't know what happened to create them.

Our personal attitudes are what they are. I think we can work to change them, and, as a result, we may be able to change our sincerity levels. I'm not exactly sure, however, just how much sincerity you can learn.

It seems to be a classic nature/nurture argument of whether the quality of sincerity is something with which you're born, or something you learn and acquire.

You'll need to decide that for yourself.

I do know, however, that people certainly will respond to both sincerity and insincerity. Being sincerely concerned and caring about your workers will cause them to be motivated. They'll want to do their best for you, and you'll get excellent results.

On the other hand, if you're insincere, they'll see through you, and be much less than effective, reliable workers. You can motivate your team by having confidence in their abilities and their work. Team members will respond to your help with their personal issues, and your team will be stronger for your efforts.

Locating Resources You Might Need

Trying to locate resources in a time of crisis is a bad idea. Become familiar with the resources available to your company before you need them, and you'll be a valuable source of help when need arises.

Rally the Troops

Check out the Federal Information Center, which provides information and referrals for federal programs, agencies, and services. It can be reached by calling 800–688–9889.

Start with your own personnel department. Does your company offer professional support for its workers? Maybe there are counseling services available, or access to mental health facilities.

If your company is small, or doesn't offer services for another reason, check out the human services agencies listed in your telephone book. You'll find all kinds of services listed there, dealing with issues as diverse as housing, emergency shelters, foster care, pregnancy, legal, crime prevention, and education.

Many churches, synagogues, and temples offer support groups and counseling services, and your area chamber of commerce will have names of such services. Knowing in advance what's available will help you to be a better leader in the event of a crisis, or in a situation in which someone needs help.

And, being able to offer assistance will portray you as caring, and someone who is willing to get involved in order to help.

The Least You Need to Know

➤ You're sure to encounter personal problems among your employees, so you'd better know how to deal with them.

➤ Listening is an underused, but extremely important skill; all leaders should work to develop their listening skills.

➤ Getting close to your employees is okay, but these days you must be very careful to avoid even the appearance of impropriety.

➤ Trying to appear sincere when you're not is insulting to your employees.

➤ There are many services and agencies available to help with personal problems; know what they are and how to reach them before they become necessary.

Chapter 12

Where's the Security Blanket?

In This Chapter

➤ Understanding the basic need for security

➤ Learning where security starts and how it can be cultivated

➤ Continual knowledge is a great way to increase security

➤ Creating a sense of security in an insecure situation

➤ Dealing with people who reject security

Everyone needs a sense of security and/or predictability. I'd argue that it's a basic human need, not that much unlike food and shelter.

Scientists have determined that security and predictability are important factors not only in the development of emotional well-being but of brain development in children as well.

Security, along with predictability, lessens stress levels among children. When children don't have security and predictability, their stress levels rise, increasing the level of a naturally occurring steroid within the body. This steroid can destroy brain cells and cause other brain-related problems if it occurs frequently and in high amounts.

Continually high levels of this steroid have been associated with some developmental delays and neurological impairments in kids.

Humans have this need for security because we don't operate purely from instinct. All of us, even small children, anticipate and reason. We like to know what's going to

Defining Moments

Security is the sense of being safe and cared for. It's being able to anticipate what will occur and what your responses will be. It's a feeling of being comfortable within your environment without excessive doubt, anxiety, or fear.

happen and what to expect so we don't need to be constantly prepared to react. Security doesn't necessarily cause motivation, but a lack of security sure can cause people to become demotivated. Security is an important contributing factor in creating motivation.

What Is Security, and Where Does It Come From?

Security is the sense that we're free from excessive risk or danger. It's a feeling of safety within the environment, and freedom from doubt, anxiety, or fear.

Think of the times that you feel most secure. They probably occur in familiar settings in which you know what to expect and are with people who know you. Security is being at home with your family, knowing that everyone is safe and accounted for. Or maybe it's being with a group of close friends with whom you don't have to pretend or put on airs.

Now, think about times and situations in which you feel insecure. Here's an example of one that's guaranteed to make you sweat. Consider this:

It's the first day of your new job as a manager with a large corporation. You walk into the building in which you'll be working, and head for your boss's office. You feel okay about that because you and he hit it off during the interview process and you're very comfortable with him. His plan was to stay with you this first morning, make sure you get introduced to everybody, and show you where everything is.

Rally the Troops

Something to remember is that when you're feeling insecure, you can still create the impression of being secure and confident. Remember that everyone experiences moments of insecurity. If you act confident, you'll feel more secure and be able to gain more control over the situation.

Wouldn't you know it, though—he's out sick. You don't know what to do now. Eventually, you get hooked up with your boss's boss, who you also met during the interviews, but with whom you had very limited contact. She's very busy and seems a bit reluctant to have to give you her time. She agrees, however, to introduce you to your team and make sure you know where you're going and where everything is.

You're feeling decidedly out of your element by now because things aren't going the way you'd anticipated. Then, it goes from bad to worse when you meet your team and find that most of the people you'll be managing are downright resentful of you because they really, really liked their last boss, who they feel lost his job unfairly due to office politics.

To top it all off, the outfit you carefully chose that morning is unlike anything anyone else in the building is wearing, and you've discovered a huge run in your panty hose.

All of a sudden, any sense of security or predictability you might have had is completely gone.

Security comes from a sense of confidence. We need confidence in our self, confidence in our environment, and confidence in our leadership in order to accomplish our goals and effectively lead others.

How to Build Security

Effective leaders serve as security blankets for their teams.

Your team must believe that, as their leader, you'll take care of them. People follow leaders into war because they believe, correctly or not, that the leader will protect them. If your team feels that they can't count on you as an advocate and protector, they will lack the security that they need.

So, how do you build security among your team? You have to make the members of your team confident in your ability and willingness to lead. They must trust you enough to let you know about problems or other sources of insecurity. You have to let your team know that you care, that you'll treat each member fairly, and that you won't do anything to hurt them.

Building Security for the Individual

Trust is an integral part of building security among your workers. They've got to be able to trust you enough to share a confidence. And they've got to know that you won't betray that confidence.

It's unusual and difficult for employees' work and personal lives not to overlap. It's very hard to leave your personal life completely at home and your work life completely in the office or shop.

As a supervisor, you're almost sure to, at some point, encounter a situation where an individual's work performance is being affected by a personal problem. It's unavoidable, and you need to be ready to deal with such things.

Best scenario is that the employee recognizes that the personal problem is affecting her work performance and makes an effort to talk to you about it. That means three things:

Rally the Troops

To build security among individual employees, never betray a confidence; let each employee know that she is important, both as an individual and to the team; and be available for your employees, as necessary.

➤ The employee trusts you enough to share confidential information.

➤ The employee recognizes that her work performance is being affected by the problem.

➤ The employee cares enough about the job to want to do something about her performance.

Often, however, employees won't willingly share issues. That doesn't necessarily mean that they don't trust you or they don't care about their job performances. It could just mean that they don't like to share personal information because they're embarrassed, or for some other reason.

In those instances, if job performance is being severely affected, it might be necessary for you to try to find out what's going on. Your focus, however, must remain on job performance, not the personal issues. You're a manager, not a psychologist. Leave it up to the employee to introduce personal issues.

If she obviously wants to talk about something, but seems hesitant to share personal information, you'll have to reassure her that you would never betray a confidence and that you're sincerely interested in helping, both for the sake of the employee and the sake of your team. Always stay focused on the job performance, and try to help the employee to get back on track with her work objectives.

This sort of personal attention can be beneficial because it lets an employee know that she is valued, both as a person and as a worker. It also shows that you're available and willing to get involved with your team on a deeper level than just day-to-day operations.

If one of your employees has a concern about what's going on at work, listen to what she has to say, and be willing to share your perceptions about whatever problem is causing the concern. If your employee is worried about getting laid off, for instance, tell her what's going on in the company that may, or may not, lead to lay-offs. If there's no reason to worry about being laid off, your employee will be deeply reassured. If there is reason to worry, you'll only make things worse if you try to cover it up or lie about it.

Most people can accept bad news, but nobody appreciates being misled or lied to.

I had a situation as a supervisor where a female employee, Caryn, confided in me concerning a problem she was having with a guy from a different department.

She was hesitant to discuss the problem, but I was grateful that she displayed the level of trust necessary to get the situation out in the open so that we could deal with it.

Caryn was concerned that one of the cleanup guys in our shop was getting a little too familiar. She had always been friendly to him in the course of doing her job, but apparently he had misinterpreted her gestures. He was becoming overly familiar, to the point that it was making Caryn very nervous.

Here's How It Works

Even children can appreciate and benefit from being told the truth and learning how to deal with it. Remember the air-raid drills public schools conducted during the Cold War? Kids were informed in basic terms about the risk of nuclear war and taught how to deal with the risk.

Caryn, no doubt, regretted being as friendly as she had, but there was no way to undo that. She was embarrassed and felt as though she had created this situation and now was stuck with it. She was definitely feeling insecure about the situation and felt that something needed to be done.

I was glad that Caryn was comfortable enough to discuss the problem with me. If she hadn't been willing to do so, I may not have found out about it until it worsened to the point that it became dangerous. Of course, I told Caryn I'd make sure something was done about it.

We could have made a big deal about the situation—gone to personnel, got the guy fired, whatever. I was concerned, though, that doing so would have put Caryn at risk even more than we already feared she was. We didn't want to antagonize the guy, just get him to leave Caryn and any other employees he was bothering alone.

Rally the Troops

Make sure you let your workers know that you're accessible to them. If you're willing, but they don't know that, you're not going to get many takers.

To accomplish that, I went four or five levels above the guy's head. I wanted to talk to a fairly sophisticated supervisor who could assess the problem properly and take appropriate action, not somebody who would insist on playing it strictly by the rules.

I was afraid that this situation might turn out to be a more serious problem than just misread intentions. I was concerned that it could get ugly for Caryn. I could take care of her in the shop area, but what about the parking lot or other areas where she might meet up with him?

After much consideration, we decided to go after the guy for being out of his work area. We didn't say a word about Caryn, or in any way let him know that she was involved. His supervisor was told to take care of the matter, and the guy was told that he couldn't wander around outside of his department, which would keep him away from Caryn.

It re-established Caryn's sense of security because she knew he would no longer be able to come into her space.

If your workers don't have a sense of personal security, they'll never be able to do their jobs as effectively as they should. It's really important that you, as a supervisor, are able to establish and maintain a sense of security for them.

Building Security for the Team

While individual security is important, a sense of security within your team also is vital to cooperation and to getting the job done.

One of the most important things you can do for your team is to let them know what's going on and what risks are before them.

You might think that would make team members insecure, but it doesn't. Just as with individuals, your team will appreciate knowing where it stands and what lies ahead.

Lying to your team is the worst thing you can do. It always will come back at you negatively. You can build great security for your employees by telling them, and proving to them, that you'll never lie to them. Knowing that makes you their ally and someone to be trusted. Too many managers feel that by holding back information (aka lying) they build team security. The exact opposite happens. Your people will know exactly what you're doing, and they'll become insecure wondering what's going on that can't be shared with them.

Here's How It Works

A family-owned newspaper merged its two staffs and laid off about 20 percent of its workers. All managers were forbidden to say anything about the action prior to when it occurred. The laid-off employees were given the news when they arrived at work, along with 30 minutes to clear out their desks and leave the building. This action caused great distrust and resentment toward management from the remaining employees. It took years for the staff to recover and be able to again work effectively. If you hold out on your employees, you can't expect that they'll trust you. If they can't trust you, you'd better be prepared for big problems.

Some managers withhold information—or lie—because they want to protect their teams, but that's wrong. Your employees aren't a bunch of children who can't handle facts. They're adults who deserve to know what's going on so that they can deal with it and prepare for it.

Knowing what's going on gives your workers the opportunity to come up with ideas and solutions. It makes them part of the effort to improve things and makes them feel like valuable members of the team.

All that creates a sense of security.

Building Security for the Corporation

Many people don't realize that corporations need security, just as the people who work in them do, but when you think about it, it makes perfect sense.

If the corporation itself is not secure, how can the people who work there—who actually make up the corporation—be secure?

Corporations become and remain secure by establishing their places within their markets, using sound business practices to keep themselves profitable and operational, and having solid bases within which their employees can operate and work.

What are some of the characteristics of secure corporations? Let's have a look.

➤ Secure corporations take modest risks that allow them to move forward. They don't, however, take outlandish risks that jeopardize the health and/or future of the company and its employees.

➤ Secure corporations create a unique presence in the marketplace. This gives them stability, a good customer base, and the opportunity for growth.

➤ Secure corporations don't compete on price, but they do compete on creativity and innovation, and they encourage all employees to contribute to, and be a part of, that creativity and innovation.

➤ Secure corporations don't grow just for the sake of growth; they grow for the sake of making themselves unique and valuable.

➤ Secure corporations eliminate all the reasons why customers would consider going elsewhere.

➤ Secure corporations make sure their customers understand exactly what the corporations are doing for them, and are of constant and excellent service to customers.

➤ Secure corporations don't wait for their customers to come to them for help; they go to their customers with suggestions for improvement.

If a corporation can do these things, it will be secure and able to keep its employees secure. We often underestimate the value of security and the role it plays in all areas

Rally the Troops

We often think of security as something that is more necessary for children than for adults, but that's a mistaken notion. Adults who aren't secure themselves will have an extremely difficult time providing security for children, or living and working effectively and productively. We all, regardless of age, require security and predictability.

of our lives. The need for security extends to everyone, and to all of our organizations. We all want to know that everything that's important to our lives is secure, because if they're not, we can't be secure.

We seek security for things such as

➤ Our children's schools

➤ Our workplaces

➤ Our places of worship

➤ Our banks

➤ The places where we shop

If all of these establishments are secure, then we feel that our lives as we know them will go on. We have predictability. If you are going to be a motivator of people, you will need to do your part to create security in some of these institutions.

Knowledge and More Knowledge

The best possible security for individuals, teams, and corporations is to have continuous learning. Knowledge paves the way for growth and success, which creates and maintains security.

The desire and quest for constant learning should be a part of every corporation's corporate character, and should be stressed among all employees.

Defining Moments

Corporate character is the makeup of a corporation, just as personal character is the makeup of an individual. Every company, no matter how big or small, has its own character. Some of these characteristics evolve naturally, while others are intentionally created.

A knowledge-seeking corporation will continue to look for and learn ways in which it can create greater bonds with its customers. That results in the corporation being a value-added organization, which is another means of building security.

Learning and knowing everything that it can about its customers, its markets, pertinent business climates, and so forth, gives a company security. It does so because it makes the company better able to anticipate and deal with what lies ahead. It helps it to prepare to stay strong.

Constant learning helps a company to look beyond its own strengths and weaknesses to those of its customers. This might sound strange, but in the long run, a company that helps its customers is helping itself.

Let's say that your corporation manufactures blue jeans that are sold in major department store chains across the country. Constant knowledge seeking pays off, and you learn that two of your biggest retail chain customers are in big trouble for different reasons. It's not looking good for either of them, and you know that losing them as customers is going to greatly and negatively impact your business.

Because you've bothered to learn, and you know what's going on, your corporation is in a good position to do something to prevent the loss of your major customers. Maybe you can offer some sort of assistance in helping your customers to stay profitable. It's clearly in your best interests to do so, but you'd have no chance of doing so if you weren't aware of the situation.

Several of the Chrysler Corporation's suppliers offered assistance to the ailing company during the early 1980s when it was in danger of going bankrupt. The suppliers shipped in much-needed machinery, even though they knew that they might never get paid for it. You know the ending: Chrysler was bailed out, and those loyal suppliers have been reaping the rewards of their service to the company ever since.

Knowledge is equally important to the individuals and teams within your organization. Knowledge empowers and encourages, which creates security and motivation. Smart managers always encourage their employees to increase their knowledge. Some ways you can do that might include:

➤ Reimburse expenses for additional training and/or education.

➤ Encourage ongoing in-house training in varied areas for employees.

➤ Provide and encourage participation in enrichment programs in which employees would learn about topics that aren't necessarily job-related but that would contribute to overall happiness and security.

➤ Allow time off from work for those who take training programs.

➤ Make attendance in training programs mandatory.

Rally the Troops

Remember that it takes strong links to make a strong chain. If one area of your overall business is weak—even if it's a customer—it will affect the entire organization. Keep an eye on all aspects of your business and try to keep all the links strong.

Some managers don't encourage their employees to continue learning because they feel that the acquired knowledge will threaten their positions. What these managers must understand, however, is that they must keep learning too.

Knowledge works for everybody—not just the guys at the top or the ones at the bottom. Everyone will benefit from acquired knowledge, and the overall organization will be stronger.

How to Give Security When You Don't Have Any to Give

If your organization isn't secure, it's going to be next to impossible to pass along security to your workers and your customers.

If the ship is going down, what you need to do is find the lifeboats.

If there's reason for employees and customers to feel insecure about their company, then it's up to company managers to improve the situation.

If you don't have any security to give, you'll have to create it.

Defining Moments

Value building is the process of continuously determining, defining, structuring, and creating additional profitability for the customer.

Form a think tank and create something new. Value-building organizations are always think tanks, continuously researching their customers and creating new knowledge. A value-added company will not be insecure because it will be constantly expanding its knowledge.

Making yours a value-added company will provide security to your employees, and your customers, as well.

Value-focused organizations are always aware of and seeking additional knowledge on the following issues.

➤ What specific problems do we solve, and what others should we solve?

➤ How are we currently helping our customers to increase their sales, and what more can we do to help?

➤ What return in profits do customers achieve with our solutions, and how can we increase those returns?

➤ What kind of immediate savings will the customer receive from our solutions, and how can we increase those savings?

➤ What costs, either direct and indirect, do we, can we, or should we eliminate?

➤ How can we enhance our customers' positions with their customers?

➤ How does our product make our customers' lives easier or better?

➤ How can we increase quality?

➤ How can we decrease waste?

➤ How can we add security and make the customer more durable, reliable, or stable?

Knowing the answers to these kinds of questions will make your customers feel secure about your organization. Once they are secure about your company's expertise, you can adhere to these eight steps for effective business analysis.

All organizations with reputations for being learning institutions use some version of these eight fundamental steps. The steps assure that the organization will continue to grow and change constructively.

Eight Steps for Effective Business Analysis

Map out business functions for your customers. Chart the flow of critical customer business processes. This means figure out why your customers do business with you. What is it they like about your company? People say they go to McDonald's, for instance, because they know they'll find a clean environment, entertainment for their kids, speed, consistency, and so forth.

Rally the Troops

When you get some time, check out *The 7 Universal Laws of Customer Values: How to Win Customers and Influence Markets*, by Stephen C. Broydrick. It's a good read with lots of valuable information.

Identify and quantify the customer's total acquisition and ownership costs. Assign appropriate costs to the customer's success factors. Examples include warehousing, delivery sequencing, handling, downtime, uptime, unavailability of product, invoice processing, skills deficiencies, bad parts, poor quality, errors, and so forth. For McDonald's, disposal of all the packaging the restaurant chain uses is as much of an issue as the quality of the food.

Measure how your contribution relates to all the customer's processes. Find the critical success factors.

Match your organizational expertise with the customer's weaknesses, and use the expertise to strengthen those weaknesses. McDonald's did this by forming the Ronald McDonald's houses for sick children and their families.

Drive cost out of the system. Build value-added services and concepts. Money earned in all of the McDonald's restaurants is used for the Ronald McDonald House charity project. Find ways to create savings for your customer while creating dependency between your company and the customer, as McDonald's does by allowing the parents of sick children to stay for free at the Ronald McDonald houses.

Evaluate, prioritize, and establish potential opportunities for joint improvements and savings. McDonald's is currently experimenting on how to further reduce its packaging. If things work out, the restaurants should soon be able to start using some environmentally friendly packaging made from potato starch.

Document These Total Values in Economic Terms

Create profit improvement plans that jointly benefit your customer and you. This provides greater security for employees, and continuous value to customers and stockholders.

Following these steps will create security among your customers. When your customers have a sense of security about your organization, you'll have a secure company. A secure company has secure employees and stockholders, and everyone can work effectively, realizing the most gains for the entire corporation.

Dealing with People Who Don't Want Security

Everyone needs a sense of security. Some people, however, aren't going to admit this. In fact, some people will deny it vehemently. And they sure won't acknowledge that they're looking to you to provide security for them.

The danger is that this type of person can threaten the security of your entire team. She can throw off the dynamics of teamwork by feeling like she has to prove something. It's in the best interests of everyone to have an overall feeling of security among the entire team.

So, what do you do when you encounter these people among your workers? You make them realize that it's natural and okay to want to security. And you unobtrusively show them that you're the person in the organization who helps them achieve security, and that the security they achieve will be of benefit to them and the entire organization.

Before you can help these people, however, you've got to be able to identify them.

Recognizing Who They Are

People who deny the need for security are likely to be those who operate with high risk. Some sales people, for example, insist on working 100 percent on commission. It's almost an affront to them to be offered a salary. They reject the chance to have the security of a predictable income, preferring instead to be solely responsible.

Here's How It Works

I'm sure that you've encountered people who claim to reject security. They're often belligerent, difficult to work with, or seem to have "a chip on their shoulder."

People who reject the security of working within a team will be loners and may have difficulty working with others in structured situations. They'll have a need to create the structure within which they work and insist that the work is done on their terms.

They'll want to be responsible for all the outcomes, and they'll seek total control. They may be people who "shoot from the hip," or loose cannons, who can't be trusted to work within the corporate frameworks.

It's very important to be able to recognize these security rejects because they often turn out to be problems within the organization.

Understanding Why They're Like That

I'm sure that psychologists have field days figuring out why some people seem to reject security and live lives that are filled with risk and unpredictability.

Well, I'm no psychologist, but based on what I've observed, I have some pretty clear ideas why this occurs.

People who reject or won't admit to needing or wanting security often are driven by some idea, concept, or theme. The driving force can be so powerful that it's an obsession.

If security gets in the way of this force, it's got to be sacrificed. For instance, let's say that John, who has a perfectly fine job as a mechanical engineer, decides he's going to be a rock star.

He becomes completely obsessed with being a rock star to the point where he gives up everything that's been giving him security up to this point. He leaves his family, quits his job, and blows off all his relationships and obligations.

It's not that John no longer wants security; it's just that his rock star obsession won't allow him to have it. He feels that he can't be a rock star if he's a mechanical engineer with a house, a family, the obligations that go with those things. So, he gives up the things that have provided him with a sense of security in order to purse his obsession. Usually, it doesn't work, and John will end up regretting his foolishness.

Another reason people might reject security is because they have an overwhelming need to create their own environments.

They might be preoccupied with the thought of somebody telling them what to do, and are completely unable to accept authority or directions. These kinds of people have control issues,

Defining Moments

A **driving force,** which depending on the degree, can be an obsession, sometimes serves as a positive thing. It's what causes some people to realize their dreams and accomplish goals they wouldn't be able to accomplish otherwise. But it also can be a dangerous, destructive force if allowed to become consuming.

175

and they affect their abilities to work within a team. Obviously, these kinds of people can negatively impact your team.

Some other possible causes that people might reject security include

➤ General suspicion of others, especially those in authority positions

➤ Major distrust of their environments

➤ Overwhelming need to be recognized and applauded for anything, even if it's inappropriate or detrimental to the team

➤ Difficulty in addressing issues of dominance and submission

➤ Difficulty in defining role models

People with these kinds of characteristics can be very dangerous to your team and to the overall organization. Once you've identified them and have a basic understanding of why their particular attitude exists, it's in your best interests to try to do something about it.

Backfire

It's crucially important to recognize the difference between a loose cannon, unmotivated, discontented-type of worker, as opposed to a person with serious emotional or mental problems. It's great to want to help your workers, but you can get yourself in serious trouble by thinking you can help people when you're simply not qualified to do so.

Helping Out When You Can

If you can make somebody understand that being secure within the organization will help her to be a better worker and will benefit the entire team, you'll be doing the employee, your organization, and yourself a big favor.

If you have somebody who's causing problems, try to talk with her about it. Try to make her realize that security isn't a bad thing, and that accepting it will make her a more effective employee with more future opportunities.

Personalize the issue by showing the employee how accepting security will benefit her job performance and her career in the long run. Recognize that, deep down, there probably is a desire for security, even if it's clouded by issues or past experiences.

The Least You Need to Know

➤ Security is a basic need, not unlike food and shelter.

➤ Security comes from trusting in ourselves, our environments, and those around us.

➤ Continual attainment of knowledge is one of the best ways to keep employees and corporations secure.

➤ Even if security is lacking, there are things you can do as a leader to create a sense of it.

➤ Some people won't admit to needing security, and may even go out of their way to avoid it.

➤ People who avoid or reject security often are detrimental to the stability of the organization, and their attitudes should be addressed.

Chapter 13

Fair Discipline— Or How to Spank Nicely

In This Chapter

➤ Knowing the difference between discipline and punishment

➤ The discipline/security connection

➤ Using discipline to keep your team inspired

➤ Making sure everyone understands the rules

➤ The dangers and benefits of hot stoves

➤ Dealing with hot shots

Discipline. The D word. While the word conjures up all kinds of images—none of them pleasant—it's really important to realize that the concept of discipline is not necessarily a negative one.

The word "discipline" is used interchangeably with "punishment," but they're really not the same thing at all.

Discipline is training intended to produce a specific character or pattern of behavior. It's a systematic method used to obtain obedience. In short, discipline is an insistence for consistency (try saying that a few times—really fast!).

That's all a mouthful, I know. But I think you get the idea. Discipline is what keeps everybody on the same page. It's the rules that we make and the incentives we use to get people to follow them. Discipline is society-wide, not restricted to schools or places of work.

Discipline is what makes us stop at stop signs and red lights, even when we're in a big hurry and would rather go right on through. The incentive we have to stop there (other than our personal safety) is the threat of being cited and ticketed if we don't. As a leader, it's up to you to establish and enforce discipline among your workers.

Discipline must be continuous. If your start time is 8 a.m., then it's 8 a.m. for everyone on your staff—every day.

If your workday is 8 a.m. to 5 p.m. for everyone on your staff, you should be at work by 7:45 every morning, and never leave before 5:15.

If you have a one-hour lunch, and you're a smart leader who's building a sense of urgency among your employees, you'll take 45 minutes—tops. Hey, nobody said being a good leader was easy!

As a leader, it's up to you to be the discipline poster boy. If you wander in and out of the building, paying no attention to posted schedules, you can't be too insistent that your team strictly follows the rules. And, as we'll see in the next section, a team without discipline won't be a motivated team working to its fullest potential.

Avoiding Discipline Can Destroy a Team's Motivation

As we've established earlier, motivated people want a leader they can trust. They're not looking for a friend or a confidant, although you may occasionally have to be those things. They're looking for someone on whom they can depend to guide them, to tell them what's going on, and to set an example of behavior.

John, a very insecure schoolteacher, is unable to be any of those things to his students. He tries hard—that's not an issue—but he just doesn't have what it takes to be a good teacher.

Backfire

Make sure that whatever rules you establish are uniform for everyone. If you force some people to comply with the rules but let others slide, you're asking for a lack of motivation at best, and maybe even an all-out uprising.

John teaches science, and he goes out of his way to create an effective environment for the kids. He's always got animals in the classroom, and all sorts of displays, and that sort of thing. The problem with John is that he doesn't understand the children.

He plays with them and teases them, and then he gets upset when they start to do the same to him. The kids don't respect him.

Furthermore, they don't even like him. They complain about him frequently, and John's been finding himself in a lot of trouble.

The kids in his classes haven't been performing on standard tests as well as they should be. Parents are complaining about John, and the school principal is after him. He's fighting back with his union representatives, but, ultimately, John is going to lose this war. His teaching career, I predict, will screech to a grinding halt, and he'll have to find another way to fill up his days.

The reason John has all this trouble is that he avoids discipline. He doesn't understand that discipline creates a healthy, motivated environment in which kids (or workers) are able to perform at their best.

When there is discipline, everyone knows what to expect and the rules are the same for everyone. That provides security and predictability. As we learned in Chapter 12, "Where's the Security Blanket?", security and predictability are two important components of motivation.

John thinks the kids in his classes won't like him if he insists on a disciplined environment. He doesn't realize, however, that he's weakening his classes, their academic performances, and his own career by trying to avoid discipline.

Study after study has shown that children who are raised in disciplined homes thrive on that discipline. That's because they know what to expect. There are no surprises. They know that bedtime will occur at the same time each night, that dinner will be at 6 p.m., and that they're not allowed to eat cookies in bed. They know that the rules that apply to them apply also to their brothers and sisters.

Defining Moments

The whole issue of **discipline** is closely interwoven with the issues of security and predictability. When everyone adheres to the same code of discipline, there is a sense of security, and everyone knows what to expect. Security is a feeling of being safe and having a good idea of what to expect. Discipline provides the framework for those feelings.

These kids are secure in the knowledge of what to expect. They can operate better because they're free to focus on what they're doing, rather than worry about what might occur, or wondering if there will be dinner at all that night—regardless of the time.

The same concepts apply to workers. If they know what to expect, they're able to focus on the job at hand and perform to their fullest potential. And that's a great source of motivation.

Necessary Rules for Creating and Maintaining Discipline

Creating a disciplined environment takes some thought. It's not the kind of thing you can make up as you go along. Every company, however, needs to have some rules to ensure a disciplined environment.

Rules establish guidelines for employees, and let them know what you expect from them. They set limits and convey what you, as a manager, feel is important.

If your company has an employee handbook that states all the rules and guidelines, make sure that everyone on your team has a copy of it. If you have your own rules that apply to your department, make sure they're listed someplace where everyone can see them.

Avoid the temptation to overgovern. Many leaders impose far too many rules. When your company rules take longer to read and digest than your financial statements, it's time to streamline. Get to the heart of things. Having too many rules dilutes the really important ones.

Some managers and bosses thrive on rules. They want to tell their employees how to dress, when they can eat, how much coffee they can drink, how many cigarettes they can smoke, and when they can go to the beach with their kids.

The risk these people run by making so darned many rules is that, in order to retain respect and credibility, they've got to enforce them. All of them. That can get to be a huge task. Do you really want to do clothing checks or keep tabs on cigarette breaks? Don't you have better things to do?

Here's How It Works

John Sortino, the founder of the Vermont Teddy Bear Company, kept rules for his employees to an absolute minimum because he didn't want to spend all his time enforcing them. There were only three rules for his employees, but they were strictly enforced. His rules were: no stealing, no lying, and all employees had to follow the laws in terms of discrimination, harassment, and so forth.

If you make 100 rules, you're ultimately responsible for enforcing 100 rules. You can pass off the job to somebody else, but it always comes back to you eventually. So, remember that when you're tempted to get out your pad and pencil and start jotting down things like "Bathroom breaks are limited to three per day," or, "Only vegetarian meals may be consumed in the lunchroom."

The rules you probably want to pay the most attention to are those that affect the daily work behavior of employees. They need to know what time to show up and when they can leave. They need to know about lunch breaks, smoke breaks, and coffee breaks. They need to know what's expected of them.

Sure, you'll think of other guidelines that you'll want your team to follow because they'll make your operation run more smoothly and efficiently. Just be sure of the following things when you set up and maintain a discipline program:

➤ Make sure you and your team are on the same track concerning discipline. Make sure everyone has the same understanding of the rules.

➤ Make sure that the rules you have apply to everyone and are enforced equally.

➤ Make sure that a policy is in place for dealing with those that violate the rules. You can't make it up as you go along.

➤ Make sure that you enforce all the rules that you make—all the time. To not do so is to risk losing respect among your team.

Discipline is important to an operation, and it doesn't have to be a negative thing. It's not something that you should wield like a whip, using it to keep your employees in line and getting them to do what you want them to.

If your employees are motivated, they'll want do their best, and discipline will be a minor issue. An important factor in getting and keeping them motivated is to have an environment with discipline. So, you see, it's really a win-win situation.

The discipline you create will help to motivate your employees, and motivated employees will be disciplined because they'll want to work effectively.

Rally the Troops

When setting up a discipline program for your team, be aware of any previous rules that you might not know about. You'll need to make sure that your rules don't conflict with any that had been in place previously.

➤ Avoid impatience, anger, or sarcasm.

➤ Be sure present orders do not conflict with previous ones and that they conform to the proper line of authority.

➤ Make it clear that you will not interfere unnecessarily but that you will retain control.

Being Sure Your Expectations Are Understood

You can have the most comprehensive set of rules and guidelines in the world, but, if your team doesn't understand them, they won't do anybody any good. You can't enforce a discipline policy if your team doesn't understand the policy. There's nothing worse than knowing that somebody wants you to do something or behave in a certain manner, but not knowing what it is.

Backfire

If you sense that someone is having trouble understanding your discipline policy, take him aside and discuss it in private. If you call attention to it in front of other employees, you'll appear insensitive. And if that happens, you'll be perceived as insensitive, regardless of whether you really are or not.

The point being, if you're going to have rules and regulations, make sure they're designed so that everyone can understand them. Furthermore, make sure everyone *does* understand them.

In order to communicate a discipline policy effectively, you've got to be sure that you understand it first.

Once you've got it down, consider how to communicate the policy to your team. The best way to do that depends on the caliber of employee to whom you're giving the information.

Tailor your communications to the intelligence, ability, and experience of your subordinates.

Make the policy precise and accurate, without overloading your workers with excessive and useless details. But provide enough detail to ensure they can assume ownership in the goal and the process.

Steps to Take Before Resorting to Discipline

We've pretty much been using the word "discipline" as a noun. We've talked about it as a means of training or a method intended to produce a certain type of behavior.

In this section, however, "discipline" becomes a verb. I could have substituted the word "punishment" in the header for this section, but I wanted to make a point about the two meanings of the "D" word.

Defining Moments

For most of our purposes, we think of **discipline** as training intended to produce a certain type of behavior. When the rules established for use in that training are ignored or broken, however, leaders must impose discipline on those that didn't adhere to them.

Used as a verb, discipline becomes the action taken when rules have not been followed. In a sense, it is the consequence of the violation of the discipline code. So, we could say that discipline becomes necessary when discipline is ignored, but that gets sort of confusing.

Let's just remember that "discipline" can be used as either a noun or a verb. And, while the verb form can mean punishment, "discipline," when used as a noun, is by no means a punishment.

If you have kids, you understand that if you disciplined, or punished, every time a rule was ignored or broken, you'd spend much of your day doing so. As it is, good parents spend an inordinate amount of time correcting their children's behavior.

Correcting and punishing, however, are very different actions.

And the same goes for employees. If we wanted to, we could spend an inordinate amount of time correcting and/or disciplining our employees. But that's hardly the ideal. What we want to do is to motivate them to work at a level that will require fewer corrections, and to assure that they'll correct themselves when necessary.

Occasionally, however, you'll be in a position where you need to deal with a discipline matter. Hopefully, it won't be anything too serious, but these things happen. Naturally, some infringements of the rules are more serious than others. Coming in late from a lunch break is a violation of the rules, but, obviously, it's a lot less serious a violation than someone falsifying an expense voucher.

Because there are varying degrees of violations, there need to be varying degrees of punishments. For the sake of simplicity, we'll talk about reprimand and punishment, with reprimand being a sort of preliminary step.

I've come up with two lists. The first is a checklist of steps to take before reprimanding an employee. The second is a checklist to use before punishing an employee.

A Checklist Before Reprimanding an Employee

Consider these questions before reprimanding an employee. The answers you come up with will serve as your guideline for whether the employee should be reprimanded, and to what degree.

➤ Have all the facts concerning the discipline matter been determined?

➤ Has the employee been disciplined previously for the same type of violation?

➤ Has the employee been informed of the rules or standards that he's accused of violating?

➤ Has the violated rule been consistently enforced with other employees?

➤ Will the planned disciplinary action benefit the company, production, and/or the employee?

➤ If a warning was given previously, was the employee made aware of what would happen if the case of future violations?

➤ Did the employee have sufficient opportunity to correct or modify his or her behavior?

➤ Were there other persons involved in the incident?

➤ Was the infraction a willing mistake?

➤ Was the infraction something beyond the employee's control?

➤ Were personal problems involved?

➤ Is the disciplinary action planned commensurate with the infraction?

➤ Do you have the authority to carry out the planned disciplinary action?

➤ Is the action you're contemplating based on an established, well-thought-out plan?

A Checklist Before Punishing an Employee

Punishment, of course, is more severe than a reprimand, so the matter should be given careful thought. Consider these questions carefully, and then draw your conclusions. The matter of discipline is quite subjective, so two people may have very different answers to these questions, even if they're being asked about the same situation. The most important thing is to be fair and consistent.

➤ Did the employee have an opportunity to tell his side of the story?

➤ Did you investigate all sources of information?

➤ Did you conduct all interviews privately in order to avoid embarrassing the employee?

➤ Did you exert every possible effort to verify the information?

➤ Have you shown any sort of discrimination toward an individual or a group?

➤ Have you let personalities affect your decision?

➤ What is the rule that was broken intended to accomplish?

➤ If the rule was observed as written, was the purpose of the rule realized?

➤ Is the rule realistic?

➤ Is the rule easy to understand?

➤ Is the rule outdated?

➤ Can the rule, as it's written, be complied with under the present circumstances?

➤ Are the penalties too light? Too severe?

➤ Do the people living under the rule consider the penalties as being just?

➤ Are the penalties being enforced?

➤ Do all people affected by the rule know the rule?

➤ Is the rule periodically brought to the attention of those expected to follow it?

➤ Do all people affected know the purpose of the rule?

➤ Is the rule affecting groups that don't need it?

➤ Should the rule be extended to cover groups not now affected by it?

➤ Are certain affected groups allowed to violate the rule without incurring the penalties?

There may be other things to consider as well, but your answers to these questions should give you a good sense of whether you're on the right track for whatever sort of punishment you're planning to impose.

Good leaders don't go out of their way to punish employees. They do, however, punish when necessary, and they do it as fairly and cleanly as possible.

Be sure that you have a clear procedure concerning punishment, and that you use it. And keep the following tips in mind.

Rally the Troops

There are some good books and manuals out there for dealing with employees. It's probably a good idea to have one handy in case you need it. Check out *101 Sample Write-Ups for Documenting Employee Performance Problems: A Guide to Progressive Discipline & Termination* by Paul Falcone.

➤ If you anticipate trouble with an employee down the road, document anything applicable about his behavior, attitude, or work. Keep records of all events, such as raises, promotions, disciplinary matters, and so forth.

➤ Don't be a lone wolf. If you're having trouble with an employee, be certain to keep your manager and other interested parties (such as personnel and legal) informed as necessary.

➤ Make sure the employee knows what the problems are, and make sure he's notified of them in writing. Be very specific about what's going on, and inform him of possible consequences. Get him to acknowledge in writing that he's been informed. Make it clear in advance that you intend to fire the employee. Write specifically, "If (whatever) happens again, you will be released from the payroll on that date." If the employee refuses to sign the document, make a note and have a witness.

➤ If you have to fire somebody, make sure there's a third person in the room when you do it. State the reasons for the termination clearly, and don't get into a nonproductive discussion or debate. Say what needs to be said, wish him luck, and close the discussion.

➤ Don't lose your cool. Nobody likes to fire someone. Unfortunately, it's sometimes part of the territory. Be as calm as you can, and don't let the employee bait you or get you upset. The whole process should take about a minute.

➤ If you think there's a potential for legal trouble with an employee, notify your lawyer well in advance.

Rally the Troops

Many parenting experts advise that stressed-out parents should remove themselves from potentially explosive situations with their kids by leaving the room for ten minutes or so. This gives the parent some time to cool down before reacting to the situation and allows him or her to get some perspective on what's happening. The same theory applies to supervisors and employees.

Ouch! Hot Stoves Burn!

We all have times when we lose our tempers and say or do things we later wish we hadn't. Usually, these slip-ups can be mended, or at least patched, with an explanation and an apology.

Sometimes, what we say is so hurtful that the damage it causes can never be repaired. These slip-ups then rise to the category of tragic mistakes and are sometimes incidents that we regret for the rest of our lives.

Hot stoves do burn, and sometimes cause more damage than we can fix. So, before you say something hurtful, or impose disciplinary measures on an employee, try to take a step back and look at what you're doing.

If it's clear that you're going to have to discipline an employee, then use what I call the hot-stove rule. If you consistently apply this rule to applicable situations, your ability to handle disciplinary situations will dramatically improve, and you may find the whole thing a little less difficult to deal with.

The hot-stove rule mandates that all discipline be four things:

➤ Predictable

➤ Immediate

➤ Consistent

➤ Impersonal

Let's have a look at each of those characteristics, and see how they can improve your discipline style.

Predictable

If workers know and understand the rules, then disciplinary action will be predictable. Everyone will understand what situations will warrant action and what the action will be. There will be no surprises. In addition, they'll be able to feel the heat of the stove starting to build long before the disciplinary measure is taken.

Immediate

The hot stove burns as soon as you touch it, and to be effective, discipline should be administered as soon as possible after the violation that prompts it. Immediate action makes it clear that the discipline is a result of the employee's behavior and removes the association away from you. This helps to keep resentment against you to a minimum.

Consistent

The hot stove burns everyone in the same way. Discipline must be applied equally, as well, regardless of who's involved. If the circumstances are the same, then the discipline must be the same. There are always extenuating circumstances that you must consider when imposing penalties; but, with comparable conditions, don't play favorites. Also, don't overlook poor behavior one time and reprimand for it the next. Consistent application of appropriate discipline will clearly establish the limits of acceptable behavior for your people.

Impersonal

Any disciplinary action should be impersonal. It must be perfectly clear that the action is because of something a person did, not because of who he is. Your criticisms should never be directed personally against an employee. Avoid saying things like, "You're always the one causing trouble," or, "I made a big mistake when I hired a troublemaker like you." Most people can understand punishment for something they did. Nobody, however, appreciates criticism that is personal and hurtful.

Bringing a Hot Shot Back Down to Earth

Every now and then you get an employee who thinks he's a real hot shot. He'll think that he's better than the other employees, and sometimes even better at the job and smarter than you. When you encounter a hot shot, you've got to know how to bring him back down to earth.

Jeff was one of my best hires. He was always perfectly dressed and well-spoken. Jeff was going places—and he knew it. He was a classic hot shot.

He didn't like getting his hands dirty, and he made it very clear that his job was training people how to run production machinery, not getting down and dirty to maintain equipment or do *those* types of jobs.

Well, the machinery was dirty, and he had to train shop types—operators, lower-level folks who didn't share his style and presence. He thought he was above all of them.

Rally the Troops

The danger with hot shots is that they often think they can get away with things that other employees can't. You've got to be watchful of that, and make it clear that nobody has special privileges.

Jeff had been on the team for about six months when he approached me and said, "My equipment isn't ready for training next week. Where are the porters to clean it up, and how do I get fresh coolant in the tanks?"

I just looked at him for a moment, and then said, "Let me show you how we get the porters to do it."

I got up, took off my jacket and tie, and put on my lab coat. Jeff followed me out to the shop floor, where the coolant tanks were filthy and stinking. I didn't let him help a bit as I vacuumed the tanks and filled them with clean fresh coolant. I spent about an hour with him, and never let him do a thing.

When we had finished, my shirt was ruined and my trousers were filthy from the shop grit. But Jeff's machine was clean and ready for him to use to train our customers. I said, "That's how we get this stuff done around here."

The hot shot got the message, loud and clear: Get off your throne or get out of here. He quit within two weeks.

There are other ways to bring hot shots back to earth, and you've got to find one that suits your personal style. Disciplinary action works sometimes, but you might think of something even more effective, like I did with Jeff.

The Least You Need to Know

➤ There's a big difference between discipline and punishment.

➤ Discipline breeds security, and security contributes greatly to a motivated team.

➤ Even the best set of rules won't work if your team can't understand them, so make sure everyone is on the same page regarding policies.

➤ Think before you speak or act because hot stoves can burn someone badly.

➤ Use the four components of the hot-stove rule to discipline effectively.

➤ Hot shots can bring down your team, so learn how to deal with them.

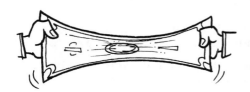

Chapter 14

We've Gotta Talk Money, but How Far Will Your Dollar Go?

> **In This Chapter**
>
> ➤ Using money to indicate status, power, and happiness
>
> ➤ Using money to motivate
>
> ➤ The shortcomings of incentives and commissions
>
> ➤ Looking at a variety of factors when gauging performance
>
> ➤ Motivating with points

Money, as I think we all know, can be a mighty powerful motivator.

People work for money, lie for money, cheat for money, engage in illegal business for money—even kill for money. Money is a pervasive force in our society that affects almost everything we do. It enables us to do things we want to, and it frustrates us when don't have enough to do what we'd like.

In just a few recent conversations with friends and colleagues, I recall discussions about the cost of cars, houses, gas, taxes, and many other things. All of those conversations centered on things we were motivated to get, and goals we wanted to achieve. All those goals required—you guessed it—money. We talk, and think, about money all the time. It's impossible not to because we deal with it on a daily basis.

Every time you buy a newspaper, a cup of coffee, or a sandwich, you're dealing with money. Every time you get a haircut, read the stock reports, go out to dinner, cash your paycheck, or hire somebody to mow your grass, you're dealing with money. In an open, market-driven economy, money is the largest and most widely accepted measuring system. It's unavoidable in our daily lives.

In our society, money and the things we buy with it also serve as measures of status. We tend to gauge (often inaccurately) intelligence, power, and worth by how much money somebody has. We also assume—not always correctly—that a person with a lot of money is a successful person. We think people who have money must be happy, although we know that's often not the case.

With all its good and bad points, it looks like money is here to stay. Our society pretty much runs on money, which is the reason it can be used so effectively as a motivator.

Money can make people do a lot of things they wouldn't do ordinarily, both bad and good. When used properly, however, it can be an effective support tool in getting your team to give their very best efforts.

The Role of Money in Motivating People

Money is a really funny thing. For many people, it's nearly an obsession. No matter how much they have, they always want more.

People who don't have much money often are sure that if they only did, their lives would be great. All their worries would go away and they'd live without care.

People who have gone from rags to riches, however, like many of the big lottery winners, for instance, find out that money doesn't solve all of life's problems. It can solve some, but often causes others.

Studies show—and don't you wonder why we need studies to tell us what's already so perfectly obvious—that people who are really impoverished are not generally happy people. They have all kinds of worries and fears that people with money don't. Some include:

➤ Not having enough food for themselves and their families

➤ Not being able to pay for medical treatment when they need it

➤ Losing the place where they live and becoming homeless

➤ Not having adequate clothing

If you give a person with these worries enough money to assure a decent standard of living, they'll be happier than they were without money. But studies also show that, once a person has everything that he or she needs, having a lot of money doesn't assure greater happiness. We reach a sort of zero level. Having enough money for the basic necessities of life keeps us from being miserable. Having a ton of money, on the other hand, doesn't create guaranteed euphoria.

Many wealthy people end up having money problems of different kinds. They lose their money because they never learn to manage it properly. Or they worry about what to do with it.

Here's How it Works

I remember watching Johnny Carson on *The Tonight Show* one time when he was going through one of his divorces. I often think about what he said, which was something like, "When you have money, people think you have no problems. All money means is that you don't have money problems. You still have all the others."

Still, even people who realize that money can't buy happiness seem to want it. Corporations recognize that want, and they use money, or other forms of gain sharing, to motivate their employees.

More than 2,000 major corporations in America are now offering significant gain-sharing systems—such as profit sharing or stock options—for all of their employees. And the number of companies going this route is growing. Why? Because employees respond to gain sharing. They want their piece of the pie.

These systems give employees a vested interest in the overall goal of creating higher profits, which creates corporate strength.

Employees work harder and smarter for a company in which they personally share the profits that the company earns. It makes perfect sense. We all work harder and smarter for that which we own.

The most enlightened companies are building gain-sharing systems. Unfortunately, not all companies, or the executives that lead them, are this enlightened. In fact, the gap between executive pay and worker pay has been steadily increasing over the past couple of decades. This has been well publicized, and it's risky. When the "haves" have too much, and the "have-nots" have too little, the middle class shrinks. A too-small middle class is a prescription for disruption in any society.

Top executives earned 209 times the earnings of factory workers in 1996, surveys show. Five years earlier, they earned 100 times more. The pay disparity more than doubled in just five years.

U.S. corporate executives typically earn about twice as much as their counterparts in countries such as Germany, Japan, Canada, and Britain.

According to *Forbes* magazine, the highest paid executive in the U.S. earned more than $225 million in 1997. Forbes' compensation figures include salary, bonus, non-cash stock gains, and other benefits such as country club memberships, car allowances, and life-insurance premiums. The 10 highest-paid U.S. executives in 1997 and their earnings follow.

193

➤ Sanford I. Weill, Travelers Group, $227.6 million

➤ Stephen C. Hilbert, Conseco, $124.6 million

➤ Richard M. Scrushy, HealthSouth, $106.8 million

➤ Ray R. Irani, Occidental Petroleum, $104.5 million

➤ Lawrence A. Bossidy, AlliedSignal, $57.5 million

➤ Andrew S. Grove, Intel, $52.6 million

➤ Charles W. McCall, HBO & Co., $52.1 million

➤ Robert B. Shapiro, Monsanto, $51.8 million

➤ Philip J. Purcell, Morgan Stanley, Dean Witter & Co., $47.7 million

➤ Henry R. Silverman, Cendant, $44.1 million

To make matters even worse, these escalating CEO salaries coincided with layoffs from many companies. In 1995, for example, AT&T top guy Robert Allen collected $10 million in options after announcing plans to cut 40,000 jobs. Is it any wonder that workers are unhappy?

Here's How It Works

While many executive salaries are spiraling out of control, some companies have capped executive pay in relation to workers' pay. Others, Ben & Jerry's Ice Cream, for instance, tried to cap executive pay but ended up paying a CEO more than they wanted to because they weren't satisfied with the candidates who responded to the position at the lower salary.

Some companies are at least sharing gains with employees. Not to the extent that their executives are raking it in, of course, but employees in some firms are seeing some benefits. It's smart for organizations to try to bring employee and executive pay closer together. If the gap between the highest and lowest salaries is glaringly vast, authenticity becomes impossible to build. Under these circumstances, workers become discouraged and demotivated because they feel their efforts are neither appreciated nor rewarded.

If companies choose to share gains with only a select top few within the organization, they should expect a good degree of cynicism among the lower levels of the organization.

On the other hand, if money or other gains are shared properly to motivate employees, it can create a sense of worth, ownership, and pride. It can be a good incentive to do the job better, work harder, and be recognized and rewarded for it.

Why Commissions and Incentives Fail

There are different ways to motivate people with money. You can offer salaries based on job performance. You can offer bonuses and incentives and raises for meeting certain goals. Another way money has been used to motivate people is by paying commissions or incentives. This method is, however, diminishing in popularity, and for good reason. There are many forms of commission or incentive pay.

To pay a commission or incentive is to give money for certain, specific things that are measured. The factory worker who is paid so much for every widget he produces is paid an incentive. The salesperson who's paid a percentage of the money taken in on the sale of each widget sold is earning a commission. The incentive or commission percentage is agreed upon in advance by the employee and the employer. If Bill receives a 10 percent commission, for example, he'll get $10,000 for every $100,000 dollars in sales he produces.

If he sells a machine for half a million dollars, Bill gets $50,000. Factory workers get paid piecework, a form of incentive pay, for producing shirts. They get paid incentives for producing any number of widgets. Realtors get commissions for selling homes. Car salespeople get commissions for selling cars. Marketing people get commissions for selling advertising.

Many, many people work "on commission," or "on incentive," or get a combination of salary and commissions or incentives.

All commission or incentive systems are classic, fixed-ratio systems. If you'll think back to Chapter 3, "Incentives—The Heart of Motivation," you'll remember (hopefully) that the fixed-ratio system is a method of reinforcement that rewards an individual for a certain behavior that's already been exhibited.

>
>
> **Defining Moments**
>
> A **commission** is a certain percentage of the amount of money taken in on sales, paid to the person who made the sales. An **incentive** is paying a person a certain amount of money for some specific thing that he does.

A real estate agent earns a commission after she sells the house. The commission is the reward for the work done, and reinforces the behavior exhibited. Some other examples of the fixed-ratio system include:

➤ Rewarding the shipping department with a catered lunch in recognition of 30 accident-free days.

➤ Giving everyone a gift certificate for a local restaurant after the company achieves 30 consecutive days of zero-defect work.

195

➤ Paying the sewing machine operator three cents for every shirt sewn.

➤ Paying the assembler $1 for every widget assembled.

➤ Paying the migrant worker 50 cents for every box of peaches that's picked and packed.

When using a fixed-ratio system, including a commission or incentive system, everyone has to be aware up front of the terms of the agreement.

You can't decide after the salesperson has sold the piece of machinery that he'll get 10 percent commission instead of 8 or 12 percent. You can't tell the workers, after they've achieved 30 consecutive days of zero-defect work, that the reward has been changed from a gift certificate to a free cup of coffee in the lunchroom. You can't tell a migrant worker that his incentive has been lowered from 50 to 25 cents after he's picked the peaches.

Backfire

If you promise a child an ice-cream cone when she finishes cleaning her room, you'll get her to clean her room. If you don't deliver when she's finished, however, you won't get her to clean her room the next time, and you'll make yourself less than trustworthy in her eyes. The same principle applies with employees and the fixed–ratio system.

The terms have to be set up ahead of time and honored as set. Otherwise, the system won't work. If you again think back to Chapter 3, you'll remember the lengthy discussion about how important authenticity is to motivation. A system that promises something but doesn't deliver has no authenticity, and will do nothing to motivate workers. In fact, it only will make them angry and resentful, and serve to demotivate.

Another example of a commission system is the piecework system. This system is based on the efficiency of the workers.

A factory worker gets $5 for every ten shirts produced, or the farmhand gets $1 for every bushel of vegetables delivered to the produce truck. Does it work? I guess so—to a point. It probably makes that farmhand work harder to pick more tomatoes or peppers. It probably at least keeps the factory worker attentive to her sewing machine and the shirts she's sewing.

The commission and incentive systems, however, do have downsides.

One of the biggest problems with these systems is that they focus workers on themselves, instead of on being part of a team. The "us" factor flies out the window and is replaced with "me, me, me." This is a perfectly natural, although undesirable, byproduct of these systems.

If not carefully controlled and monitored, commission and incentive systems—especially commissions—can cause fierce competition among workers and animosity between workers and management. Every time management rejects a piece of work due to quality, the worker loses out on incentive pay. This often creates hostility.

And while some competition can be healthy and productive, it can lead to big problems. Employees tend to protect their own interests, and sacrifice the interests of the company, and even those of their colleagues. I've heard stories of salespeople going to elaborate lengths to take away their colleagues' customers. Unless there's a strict code of conduct that's in place and enforced, watch out when workers have a lot to gain through the commission system.

Another downside of the commission system is that it assumes the playing field is level. As you know, it seldom is, even when it appears to be.

The 1973 oil embargo, for example, created a boom in the oil drilling industry, while causing a big bust in the automobile and aircraft manufacturing industries.

Many machinery manufacturers sell their machines to both the oil industry and the auto and aircraft industries. Between 1975 and 1980, salespeople with these manufacturers who were selling to the oil industry got rich. Salespeople who were selling to the auto and aircraft industries got poor.

The success or failure of these salespeople didn't have much to do with their sales ability. Their successes and failures were the results of social and political upheaval, well beyond the control of the salespeople or their companies.

> **Rally the Troops**
>
> An unlevel playing field is a dangerous thing within a company, or even an industry. Unfairness in the system breeds hard feelings and negative reinforcement, which serves to bring down the entire company or industry.

Those who got rich reaped the benefits of the oil embargo, something that many of them never fully understood. Those who went under were victims of the embargo, whether or not they knew what it was all about.

We see this kind of thing all the time.

When real estate agents are on the top of the world—selling more houses than they ever dreamed of—is it really a credit to their selling abilities? Sure. But, more likely than not, it's more a credit to a booming economy, a generation coming of age and into the housing market, or, just a great housing market.

The real estate market is a classic example of one that moves in cycles and fluctuates greatly. A real estate agent might sell 40 houses one year and only ten the next. Much of her success or failure depends on the economic climate of the area in which she's working, the availability of homes, the amount of construction occurring in the area, and many other factors.

While her selling abilities don't change throughout these cycles, other conditions, over which she has little or no control, do.

Organizations constantly modify their commission systems to adjust for social and political factors.

Here's How It Works

In a very slow real estate market, sales will drop off at all levels, and even the best real estate agents will sell fewer homes than they can when the market is hot.

This effort to level the playing field isn't new—it's been going on ever since the commission system came into use. The problem is, it's extremely difficult—next to impossible—to do because we can't see future social change.

Because it's so terribly difficult, we have to consider the possibility that a fair commission system may be beyond human reach.

As long as the organization is unable to control all the social variables, the playing fields will remain unlevel. The success of all organizations, to some degree, is always beyond the control of the people within that organization.

What Should You Be Measuring?

So, if not incentives and commissions, then what should you be measuring? How can you determine the best way to motivate and reward your team for the work they do? What kinds of things should you look for to determine whether you're on your way to reaching your goals?

The best advice I can offer is to measure many factors in addition to just sales or units produced. Think of your organization as a sports team, and your efforts to achieve customer satisfaction, or whatever goal you're working toward, as your season.

Let's use baseball as an example. A team can't know whether it will get to the World Series—the ultimate measure in baseball success—until it gets there.

But it can use certain things as measures to determine its chances of getting to the Series.

If the Chicago Cubs have a great batting average (yeah, right), for example, it doesn't guarantee that the Cubs will go to the World Series. The batting average, however, serves as an indicator to other teams that the Cubs are a team to watch. And it indicates to the Cubs that a trip to the Series could be within their reach.

Errors, strikeouts, base hits, home runs, games won, and so forth all serve as good indicators. They're all objectively measurable and related to the goal. None of these things guarantees a trip to the World Series. However, high numbers in the desirable areas, and low numbers in the undesirables, serve as indicators of a team's chances of reaching the Series.

In the same regard, you can't measure customer satisfaction until you get results. You can predict that customers are going to love the new machine your company has designed and is manufacturing. But you can't know for sure until it's been sold and customers have been using it for while.

While you're waiting to see how much your customers like the machines, however, you can measure lots of things that might contribute to overall customer satisfaction. Some of them include:

Rally the Troops

Remember that all aspects of a business affect its overall performance, and serve as indicators for how well the business will do. Don't overlook little indicators, because they all play a part in the total operation.

➤ Good quality of the equipment

➤ On-time delivery

➤ Excellent customer service

➤ Adequate training in use of the machine

➤ Reliability of the machines

➤ Follow-up support regarding the performance and operation of the machines

None of these things guarantee customer satisfaction. However, if these things are being done successfully, they'll indicate a high probability of customer satisfaction. Even if there are problems with the machines, you'll have a better chance of keeping customers satisfied—although maybe not happy—if you've done everything right up until the point the machines were delivered.

When trying to motivate the people on your team, you should make it a point to measure the things they do well.

You might look at the gross sales Jack has generated, for instance, or the number of complimentary letters that customers have sent in about Becky, or the number of times you've observed Jeff go out of his way to help another team member. Maybe you'll take a look at the number of special projects team members have completed, or how many times they've stayed late to finish something.

When you measure these things and apply them toward an overall standard, you give employees incentive and motivation to keep doing well and to improve. Be sure that everyone knows what kinds of things are being measured, and recognize those that achieve high levels of success.

None of these things can guarantee a successful workplace. All of them, however, are indicators that steps are being taken, and things are happening, to produce an effective workplace and motivated teams.

Fight for Points Instead of Money

While I don't like commission and incentive systems, I do like point systems. Points given for performance don't tend to result in the "me, me, me" situation that commissions do.

When somebody does something well, you can reward them with points. If Joe has higher sales than Becky, Joe gets more points. If Becky has invested more time in support service goals, however, she gets more points in that area than Joe.

Tasks completed will have different levels of importance, so they'll have more point value than others. Build a grid sheet on which to keep track of points, and let everyone see where they stand.

A point-based system allows you to measure and reward many things. It expands the basic incentive or commission idea, by allowing you to do far more than use just money as incentive. Points give you a bona fide system of gain sharing, because you're using money to reward total performance, not just a narrow part of the overall performance.

Rally the Troops

Points are more indicative of a baseball game than a competitive business situation. They tend to encourage a team spirit and are great to use in team situations.

When setting and measuring objectives on which your point system will be based, a good objective is:

➤ Measurable

➤ Reproducible by all with appropriate training

➤ Observable by all (everyone knows when the batter gets a home run or an out)

➤ Continuously monitored

➤ Modified and updated continuously

➤ Job-related

➤ Realistic

The Least You Need to Know

➤ Money is a powerful motivator, but it doesn't guarantee happiness.

➤ Gain sharing is good for employees and management, because it inspires workers to do their best for the company.

➤ Commissions and incentive systems are widely used, but they tend to create "me" conditions instead of team conditions.

➤ Many factors should be considered when judging how well a person is performing.

➤ A points system, which lets everyone see what's being measured and how, is a good way of keeping employees motivated.

Part 4

Your Role in Motivation

As a leader, you play a very important role in motivating your team. In fact, someone who can't motivate cannot be an effective leader because the ability to motivate is central to leadership.

In this section, we examine the role of a leader in motivating his or her team. You'll learn about the kinds of relationships you should have with team members, and the kinds you should never have. You'll also learn how to communicate well with your team, and how to inspire team members to do their best and reach their goals.

There are certain things you should know about your workers, and in this section, you'll learn what they are and how to find them. You'll also learn about some things that are guaranteed to turn off any employee.

The Leadership Role

In This Chapter

➤ Exploring the leadership/motivation connection

➤ Knowing what to tell your workers about yourself

➤ Gauging how much is okay to tell

➤ Watching out for secrets in the workplace

➤ Spreading the word with a carefully placed whisper

➤ Good listening is a skill we all should aspire to

➤ Being a confidant and mentor

There's an old saying that claims "behind every great man is a great woman," or something like that. I'd like to add my two cents and put on the record that behind every great company is a great leader.

Great leaders—the likes of General Motor's Alfred Sloan; General Electric's Jack Welch; the late Roberto Goizueta, former CEO of Coca-Cola; and others—evolve into more than leaders. They're legends.

These kinds of leaders ride into ailing, chaotic companies on white horses and save the day—and the companies. Sloan not only saved General Motors—his concept of decentralized management has influenced and left its mark on every large company.

Welch reorganized and remade General Electric, as well as set the tone for how American businesses should respond to, and deal with, the threat of foreign competitors.

Goizueta is remembered for his radical concepts concerning market share, his foresightedness in bringing people of all nationalities and cultures on board, and his ability to make Coca-Cola such an international success after the old Coke/new Coke fiasco.

Leaders such as these change the way businesses are run; affect all industries, not just their own; and establish themselves as business legends.

Of course, not everyone can, or will, be the kind of leader that Welch is, or Sloan and Goizueta were. Most of us will never have the opportunity to reorganize giant companies. We all, however, can lead to the best of our abilities and work to make a difference in our own corners of the world. We don't have to come up with revolutionary methods of doing things in order to be good, effective leaders. But there are some things we must do.

In order to lead effectively, we must first have four essential characteristics. First, we must be honest. People need to perceive that you know the rules and are willing to follow them—at least when the rules are reasonable.

Second, we must be competent. We've got to know what we're doing, and our followers need to know that we know what we're doing. This doesn't mean we must know how to do every job that our workers perform. But we must have the ability to understand those jobs.

Third, you must be forward-looking. Being a leader means moving people into the future. That means that we, as leaders, must have the ability to see and describe what the future should be.

Fourth, leaders must inspire. You've got to be someone who your workers admire and can look up to. Ideally, your people should be proud to tell their friends and families that they work with you. They must be proud of what they do and of the methods you use to lead them.

Leadership and Motivation

Leadership—both good and bad—can motivate. If you've ever worked for a really awful boss, as too many of us have, you know that it can be a pretty powerful motivator. The problem is, it motivates us to do the wrong things.

Bad leadership motivates workers to form tight bands of self-defense. It motivates them to huddle together at the watercooler, plotting strategy and figuring how to avoid the boss's next move, whatever it might be. They're motivated to defend themselves in a hostile environment.

Bosses from hell can be motivators, all right. But it's not the kind of motivation you want for your team. And it's certainly not the kind of motivation that produces high productivity or enhances your career.

Here's How It Works

Many workplaces have yet to become kinder, gentler places, due to plenty of bad bosses out there. If you've got one, take comfort in the fact that you're not alone. There's even a book about bad bosses. It's *Crazy Bosses: Spotting Them, Serving Them, Surviving Them.* The author is Stanley Bing.

Now, take a minute and remember some of the positive leaders with whom you've been acquainted. Maybe you're thinking of a parent, a teacher, a college professor, a mentor, or a special, talented boss.

If you've had the good fortune of knowing people like this, then you've probably experienced firsthand the motivation they can inspire.

Good bosses are good leaders, and their workers respond to their leadership by becoming motivated, inspired teams. Whether or not a boss is a good leader is of utmost importance to the success of the team.

What Should Your Workers Know About You?

You've got to get to know the members of your team, and they've got to get to know you.

This doesn't mean you all need to be—or should be—best buddies, exchanging intimate details of your lives and hanging out together on the weekends. Your workers don't necessarily want to be your friends. They do, however, want you to be friendly. A degree of familiarity among co-workers and their leaders is desirable.

If you've ever had a boss who was completely aloof and unattainable, you know what it can do to the morale of a working team. An unapproachable boss is not an effective boss because you can't lead if you're removed from those you're leading.

This has less to do with physical presence than it does with demeanor. An effective leader who has built relationships with his team can lead from China, if need be. But an aloof and removed leader who refuses to get involved and never gets to know his team will have trouble leading from the middle of the shop floor.

Your workers will be very curious to know who and what you are. When you first meet them, you'll need to give the "official" information. If you're just coming onto the job, give them some of the résumé stuff: Where you worked before you came on board with them, the number of years you've been in the industry, and that sort of thing.

Backfire

Don't ever use your influence as a boss to try to get your workers involved in your interests. It's okay to talk about the service organization that you chair, but it's not okay to prod workers to get involved with it. If you try to do so, you'll end up causing a lot of resentment among your team.

Tell them what they can expect from you. If you're a stickler for everybody being on time, make that perfectly clear. Discuss your management style and give them an idea of how you'll be running things. People like to know how life will be. It's part of the security thing, remember?

If your workers don't have the vaguest idea of what kind of person you are, or what kind of manager you'll be, it will be difficult for them to feel secure about you. How do they know you won't walk in some morning and change all the rules?

The information you give your workers should make it perfectly clear to them that you're a person who can be respected, both professionally and personally.

Don't brag, but let them know what you've accomplished and how you accomplished it. Include personal as well as professional achievements.

If you work every other weekend for Habitat for Humanity, or you've led the community's March of Dimes campaign for five years straight, there's nothing wrong with letting your team know about it. This kind of information gives them an idea of the kind of person you are and what's important to you.

Rally the Troops

The trouble with letting your employees know about odd habits or preferences you have is that the news quickly becomes the team's focus. Let's face it. Having a boss claim to have been abducted by aliens seven times in the past five years captures the imagination much more than talking with him about how to reduce waste in the company's production department.

You might relate such information in a way that encourages your team to get involved with your cause or merely tells them about the event. You can make the information less about you and more about the group with which you're involved, and still convey a sense of who you are.

Your team doesn't expect you to be a saint, and probably will be decidedly uncomfortable if you try to pass yourself off as one. If you spend every evening and weekend volunteering in nursing homes or delivering soup to homebound invalids, you can feel great about yourself.

However, don't constantly remind your team what a great guy you are, or expect that they'll mirror your behavior.

On the other hand, if you give your workers the impression that most of your free time is spent organizing Ku Klux Klan marches or torturing small animals, you're not likely to be chosen as boss of the year. You will, however, succeed at making your team extremely nervous and unsettled.

Position yourself near the center of the bell curve when you present yourself. Avoid extremes of any kind, and be encouraging, cordial, and levelheaded.

When to Tell

Unless it's your first day on the job and you want to give your team a little information about yourself, you obviously won't call a meeting to talk about yourself.

Your workers would think it was pretty bizarre if you gathered them together to go over your personal likes and dislikes, family history, and current marital situation.

However, you can reveal your personality casually, in appropriate settings. Talk about yourself during informal situations such as office lunches or breaks at the coffee machine or watercooler.

If the team goes out for a drink after work every Wednesday night and you're invited, feel free to stop by on your way home. Just make sure that these get-togethers are all-inclusive. If they're not, you could be accused of taking sides or playing favorites.

Once you've let people in on some of your personal information, the word will spread. Don't feel like you have to tell every employee the same things. Once you tell Mary that you have a son the same age as her daughter, she'll mention it to Jack, who will tell Tom during lunch, who will tell Jenny on the way to the parking lot. Employees are interested in their bosses, just as bosses should be interested in employees.

How Much to Tell

Deciding just how much to reveal to your employees about yourself and your personal life can be like walking on a tightrope.

Here's How It Works

Some people are much more skillful at meshing personal information with professional situations than others. Some people reveal personal information seamlessly while maintaining a professional demeanor. Others find it harder to separate the two things and have a much more difficult time talking about themselves.

You want to be friendly and sociable, but you don't under any circumstances want your employees to become your confidants. Basic information is fine, but extremely personal or otherwise confidential information is inappropriate to share with employees.

Let's have a look at some things that are okay to talk about, assuming the circumstances warrant personal discussion.

➤ **Family circumstance.** This is a big part of who a person is, and you certainly can tell your employees whether you're married or not, what part of town you live in, how many kids you have, and so forth.

➤ **Your age.** It's okay to tell your employees how old you are. The only thing to watch for is possible resentment if you're much younger than the members of your team. It might not be a factor, but it could cause some resentment.

➤ **Personal interests.** If you love to read, and team members see you heading out for your lunch break every day with a book under your arm, it's fine to talk about that interest. If you're committed to saving the Chesapeake Bay or the local wetlands, it's okay to talk about that, too. Personal interests make managers human, and you'll probably find out some of your team members share the same interests.

➤ **Hobbies.** Are you a tennis player? Golfer? Fisherman? Hiker? Drummer in a rock band? Everybody likes to talk about their hobbies, and finding that you have common hobbies can be a powerful bind with your team members. So, go ahead and let on that ornithology is your thing. You might get some good tips about the best bird-watching spots in the area. Just be sure your hobbies fall within the accepted norm. A drummer in a rock band is one thing, but an exotic dancer in a well-known strip joint would be quite another.

➤ **Religious affiliation.** This can be a little tricky, but I don't see anything wrong with letting your employees know how and where you worship. Just be sure not to put any pressure on them to join your flock—whatever that flock might be.

➤ **Children.** Chances are that at least some, and probably many, of your team members are parents. Nothing binds people more quickly than sharing information about their kids. You know as well as I do that having kids gives you a never-ending supply of stories, joys, and frustrations. Kids are a valuable common denominator among workers and bosses, especially if they go to the same schools, have the same teachers, play on the same teams, or share the same interests.

➤ **Your spouse's occupation.** People who know you tend to be curious about your spouse and family. It's okay to talk about what your spouse does for a living, but don't supply any more personal information than your husband or wife is comfortable with you giving. Some people don't mind sharing personal information, and they overlook the fact that their spouses are more private and prefer to keep their personal lives private.

Talking about these kinds of personal things makes it more likely that your people will share the same sort of information about themselves with you. If you're going to work together harmoniously, it helps to know something about each other.

If you're going to motivate your team through your leadership, it helps if your team knows what kind of person you are and what they can expect from you. Sharing personal information assures team members that you consider them to be valuable. Not sharing any personal information comes across as being snobbish, or implies that you don't feel your team is worthy of knowing about you.

You don't need to get carried away and tell all, but sharing some personal information with your workers is generally a good idea.

Backfire

Be sure that you don't share overly personal or intimate information with employees. There's a fine line between appropriate and inappropriate behavior you know. If you overstep that line, you'll likely find yourself in big trouble.

When and What Not to Tell

Don't talk about yourself or your personal life in formal gatherings or during any kind of business meeting, unless there are special circumstances that make personal information applicable.

A meeting with your company's shareholders, for instance, is neither the time nor the place for you to tell that funny story about how your dog got loose the other night and had the whole neighborhood in an uproar before you finally managed to capture him.

I said in the last section that it's okay to reveal your religious preference, and I'll stand by that, just don't ever try to sell your religion—or any religion, for that matter. Don't ever criticize any religion, either. If you've got a gripe with Presbyterians, for instance, don't even mention it in a one-on-one conversation with somebody who you know for a fact is not a Presbyterian.

Remember the discussion a bit earlier about how information about your personal life will get passed around? Well, John, with whom you shared that bit of information about Presbyterians, just might delight in passing it along to Rich, who happens to be a councilman of the First Presbyterian Church.

Backfire

Let such words as, "I'd appreciate it if you wouldn't mention this to anyone else," serve as a big, big red flag when you're talking to employees about personal information. There's no place for personal secrets in your workplace, least of all if they're coming from you.

211

Politics is another potentially rocky area, so be careful. Don't mention your political party or criticize any other political party, unless you're absolutely certain that everyone belongs to the same party. That's highly unlikely, so it's probably best to stay away from political discussions altogether. It's best if you don't support any fringe political groups. Of course, it's a free country, but if you do, don't talk about it.

If your interests or hobbies are controversial, it might be better not to talk about them. If you love to hunt, for example, but half of your staff are animal rights activists and oppose hunting on any grounds, it's best not to talk about your interest, much less include your best venison recipe with your holiday cards.

Defining Moments

The degree of **sensitivity** in this country has reached an all-time high, and you need to be extremely careful about what you say, what you infer, and how you respond. If somebody tells an ethnic joke, you laugh at it, and somebody else is offended by it, you'll be considered just about as insensitive as the person who told the joke. Be very careful!

Be sensitive to, and respectful of, people's likes and dislikes.

Be extremely sensitive to issues concerning race or ethnicity—and that includes ethnic jokes. In fact, you should refuse to even listen to ethnic jokes, and make it clear that there's no place for them within your department. Don't lump people together because they happen to be of the same race or ethnic group. People are individuals and should be treated accordingly. It's best to avoid making any reference to the racial or ethnic background of any individual.

Obviously, there are plenty more topics and issues that you shouldn't discuss with your employees. Use good judgment and common sense when deciding what to talk about and what should remain unsaid. Whenever possible, stay near the center of the bell curve with whatever it is you're discussing.

Sssshhhhh!

Secrets in the workplace are dangerous, and some workplaces breed secrets like rabbits breed bunnies. They run rampant and cause all kinds of havoc.

I don't think secrets can be completely eliminated or avoided, but leaders must recognize that secrets can cause divisiveness, alienation, and resentment. Secrets can threaten a team's cohesiveness and motivation.

Listening to Secrets

Keep your ears open and you'll be surprised at how many secrets you'll hear. Listen all the time, because it's really important that you have a handle on what's going on in your workplace.

When you do hear secrets, be selective about which ones you respond to. You'll no doubt hear some things that you don't like, but it's usually better to not respond directly. If you do, workers will start being much more careful about letting you hear what's going on. And it's dangerous for a leader to be in the dark about what's happening among his team.

If you hear something that bugs you, make a rather vague reference to it at a later meeting. The employees involved with whatever's going on will get your point, but other employees won't see you as a busybody or as overly controlling.

If your memory is like mine, it's probably a good idea to jot down bits of information or secrets that you hear around the workplace. That way, you can remember them and work your response to them into future training sessions or department discussions on policy and procedure.

Defining Moments

Webster's definition of **secret** is "something known only to a certain person or persons and purposely kept from the knowledge of others." Even the definition sounds sinister, doesn't it? No wonder secrets often turn out to be hurtful and destructive.

If an employee wants to share a secret with you, listen. If it's work-related, you should be able to deal with it, or to develop the resources necessary to deal with it.

Don't try to solve serious problems workers might be experiencing by yourself. Your role should be to listen and get the person some help, when necessary. You might refer him to a counselor with whom your company is affiliated.

Sharing Secrets

If an employee shares a secret that's personal and private, listen to what he has to say. However, don't assume the role of a psychologist or counselor, and don't share her secret with anyone—not even your boss. A shared secret is no longer a secret.

Just be sure that you know in what direction to refer someone who has serious problems.

There might be instances, however, in which you want your team to know about something, but you don't want to have to call a meeting and discuss the details. In cases like that, you might employ some selective sharing of secrets.

Let's say that Jim had to fire Dick for just cause. Dick was a good guy, well liked, and generally very competent. He'd really screwed up, though, and, as much as Jim hated to do it, he had no choice but to get rid of him.

The problem is, Jim's the only one who knows why Dick had to be fired, and the other employees are blaming him for getting rid of their buddy. Public opinion was quickly rising against him, and Jim had to do something to relieve the rising tension.

Backfire

Be careful if you choose to share a secret by selectively informing an office gossip. It can backfire if you do it too often, or if your attempt is too obvious. Selective leaking can be risky, and it's not a tactic you should use often.

He couldn't very well call a staff meeting to discuss Dick's firing, so he did the next best thing. Very discreetly, Jim pulled aside the big office gossip and told him why Dick had been shown the door. A few carefully chosen words, delivered while pouring a cup of coffee, were all it took. By the same afternoon, everyone knew why Dick had been fired, and Jim was off the hook.

Everyone knew that Jim was as sorry as the rest of the staff to see Dick leave, and that he recognized what a valuable worker Dick had been.

Jim did this so effectively that his workers actually felt bad that he'd been forced to do something so unpleasant.

Something you should never do as a leader is to share personal secrets with an employee. To do so would put a great deal of pressure on the person you told, and that's unfair—not to mention unwise on your part.

Learning to Be a Sounding Board

The dictionary definition of a sounding board is a canopy that's hung over a pulpit or platform for the purpose of reflecting a speaker's voice toward the audience.

For our purposes, however, a sounding board is a person who listens and absorbs what somebody tells him, then reflects ideas and observances back to the speaker. Being a sounding board can be difficult because it requires a lot of listening, and not necessarily much talking.

As you know, most of us find talking easier than listening. If someone wants you to be his sounding board, however, there are some guidelines to remember.

➤ Don't speak until the person is finished talking or you're asked for input.

➤ Don't evaluate.

➤ Don't challenge.

➤ Don't tell the speaker what he should do.

➤ Don't offer opinions on what you would do.

➤ Never take notes when the conversation is personal.

Positive guidelines to keep in mind are:

➤ Do take notes when the conversation is about business.

➤ Do listen actively, saying things like "uh-huh," and "I see."

➤ Do reflect by saying things like, "have you thought of trying?"

➤ Do paraphrase by saying something like, "I think what I heard you say is this…is that correct?"

Being a good sounding board often requires little more than some patient listening. Everyone should work to develop their listening skills and be ready to serve as sounding boards, when necessary.

It's difficult to say, but I wonder if these severely troubled kids, who shoot up their schools and do other horrible things, had good, reliable sounding boards, they'd be less likely to act so violently. Who knows, but it's something to think about.

Mentors or Confidants

A mentor is someone who you emulate. A confidant is someone in whom you confide. The same person can be both a mentor and a confidant, but that's not always the case.

Here's How It Works

If you're so inclined, jump on the Internet sometime and check out all the sites that offer or are looking for mentors. There are mentors for women, mentors for writers, mentors for nurses, students, teachers—nearly any group you can think of.

If you're lucky enough to have, or to have had, a good mentor, you know how valuable such as person can be. A mentor is someone you look up to, whose example you follow, and who you can count on to do everything possible to help you.

A trusted confidant is no less valuable than a mentor, nor is it any less important to use great care when choosing one. Anyone who's ever confided in the wrong person can attest to the potential seriousness of the error.

While mentors and confidants are great to have, as a leader, it's important that you know how to be these things to others.

As a leader, you should strive to be someone who others will want to emulate. You should be a role model for your workers, your kids, your kids' friends, and everyone else, for that matter.

Does this put a certain amount of pressure on you? You bet it does. Is being a mentor and/or a confidant a big responsibility? Absolutely. Good leaders, however, don't shy away from pressure or responsibility.

To be a great mentor, you've got to be an excellent listener and have a genuine interest in the person you're mentoring. You've got to be willing to make yourself available and to give of your time.

To be a trusted confidant, you must be sure to never share the information that someone offers you with the understanding that it will go no further. Make it well known that you don't break confidences. If you make that clear, most people will respect that and not ask you to.

Leaders should find their mentors and confidants outside of work. While you must be a good confidant for others, don't use anyone in your workplace as a confidant yourself. You can emulate others, but don't let it appear that they're mentoring you.

The Least You Need to Know

➤ There's a very obvious connection between leadership and motivation, and it works both positively and negatively.

➤ It's important that your workers have a sense of who you are, but you shouldn't share your deepest personal secrets.

➤ Some things, such as politics and religion, can put you on shaky conversational grounds, so be careful.

➤ Secrets can be destructive and divisive, so keep an ear to the ground and stay up on what's going on in your workplace.

➤ A carefully placed secret can be a useful tool for spreading information.

➤ You can be of great service to others by being a sounding board, mentor, or confidant.

Chapter 16

Inspiration

In This Chapter

➤ Inspiring your team with your thoughts and beliefs

➤ Using personalization as a tool to motivate

➤ Making the little things relevant to the cause

➤ Knowing what's close, and what's too close

➤ Being friendly, but not a friend

"And I've seen the promised land. I may not get there with you. But I want you to know tonight, that we, as a people will get to the promised land."

—*Martin Luther King Jr.*

With those words, uttered before a group of people in Memphis, Tennessee on April 3, 1968, Martin Luther King Jr. inspired people all across the United States and the world.

King, like all people who inspire and are powerful motivators, didn't hide behind others, but stood out in front and said what he had to say.

The great motivators, people like King, share their visions of the future and define their roles within those futures. They're willing to recognize, and talk about, their vulnerabilities and uncertainties. And they excite people, arousing emotion and passion.

Great leaders who inspire and motivate cause events to unfold. They make things happen. King inspired people to march, to protest, to fight for what they deserved. He made people believe that their task was noble and their cause just.

Mohandas Gandhi, the spiritual founding father of modern India, inspired other leaders such as King, the Dalai Lama, and Nelson Mandela by the nonviolent campaign he led in his home country for decades.

People who inspire others have a gift that they recognize and use. Sometimes, people can inspire others to do things that are negative, hurtful, or hateful. Hitler inspired an entire group of people to carry out his evil work of genocide. Unfortunately, at the turn of the century, it's still the case that some leaders globally are inspiring racism and a twisted sense of ethnicity. Not all people who inspire do so for worthy causes, but all of them cause things to happen.

Effective Communicators—The Common Trait

All effective leaders, whether or not you agree with their philosophies, have the power to communicate ideas through the effective use of words. Effective communication, like any other skill, requires practice. Fortunately (or in some cases, unfortunately), practicing is easy.

If you want to be a marathon runner, you've got to run and run and run. You've got to build up your ability and endurance through endless practice. Every time you hit a goal, you've got to increase your goal and run a little farther—a little faster.

In many ways, practicing to use words more effectively is the same kind of training. You've got to do it often, and you've got to set and increase goals. Fortunately, it's easier for most people to talk than to run a marathon, and there are plenty of people around on whom to practice.

Volunteer work is an excellent way to practice improving your communication skills. I know a teacher, for example, who is an excellent communicator with her students, but was always a bit uncomfortable around adults.

In an effort to overcome this, she volunteered to be a neighborhood collector for the American Cancer Society. This required her to go out and sell the Cancer Society's goals to the other people in her neighborhood. She was forced to overcome her inhibitions when she knocked on her neighbors' doors and asked to collect money. It didn't happen overnight, but this woman eventually got to the point where she was comfortable talking with anyone—adults or students. She became an effective communicator.

To inspire and motivate people, you'll need to be able to speak well in front of groups of people.

This is a constant topic of discussion in the leadership, sales, and customer service workshops I present. Nearly everyone recognizes the importance of effective communicating, and many people want to know how to improve their skills. Many of those who do take steps to become better communicators do so through Toastmasters.

Here's How It Works

If you're interested in improving your communication skills by using Toastmasters, you can get more information by contacting the national organization at 800-993-7732. Or check out its website at www.toastmasters.org.

Toastmasters International, with chapters globally, is an association dedicated to helping people enhance their leadership and communication capabilities. Members meet, practice presentations, and support each other in their efforts to improve their presentations.

The Power of Personalization

Your job, as a leader, is to inspire your team to move beyond the ordinary. You want your workers to be exceptional and to achieve exceptional things within the workplace. You want them to be at least ten percent better than their competitors. To do so, you need to inspire and motivate them.

We've already discussed many things that serve as motivators, and some things that cause people to lose motivation, as well. But here, we want to learn about how you can be the motivating factor by yourself. No money, no perks, no special projects, or privileges to use as carrots. Just yourself, and your inner resources. How do *you* motivate your team?

You should speak about, and share, your personal beliefs. This has the potential of stimulating the minds and emotions of the people you're trying to motivate and bringing their minds and emotions to high levels of activity.

Make sure, however, that your beliefs are of such a nature that they'll be acceptable to everyone. That's not to say that they've got to be accepted by everyone, but if they're so far out or wild that they appear unacceptable, they sure won't inspire or motivate.

The thoughts you share about your beliefs should be inclusive, focused on the greater good, and linked to the activities of the day. Try to model them after some of the great statements that have served to inspire people over a period of years, such as the following:

➤ "Some people see things as they are and say why. I dream things that never were and say why not?"—Robert F. Kennedy

➤ "I am not concerned that you have fallen—I am concerned that you arise." —Abraham Lincoln

➤ "Risk more than others think is safe.
Care more than others think is wise.
Dream more than others think is practical.
Expect more than others think is possible."
—Cadet Maxim, USMA, West Point, NY

➤ "Energy and persistence conquer all things."—Ben Franklin

➤ "Be sure you put your feet in the right place, then stand firm."—Abraham Lincoln

➤ "Business is the business of finding and keeping customers."—Peter Drucker

➤ "Advice after injury is like medicine after death."—Danish proverb

➤ "Borrow trouble for yourself, if that's your nature, but don't lend it to your neighbors."—Rudyard Kipling

➤ "Advice is what we ask for when we already know the answer, but wish we didn't."—Erica Jong

These are just a few of the powerful inspirational quotes that have been uttered and passed down through the years, and they're thoughts to consider when building leadership. Your team will expect you to be forward-looking—to describe the "where" that we talked about earlier in this book.

Once you've shared your thoughts and beliefs, modeled after concepts that have proven to be inspirational to many, personalize them. You do that by telling your team how those thoughts relate to them and how they'll be affected by the consequences they generate.

Rally the Troops

If you enjoy reading inspirational quotes such as those listed, check out the following books: "Great Quotes from Great Leaders," edited by Peggy Anderson, and "Motivating Quotes for Motivated People," by John Eggers.

Let's say, for example, that you're trying to inspire your team to increase its productivity. You'd first share with them your thoughts and beliefs. You might say something like you believe that people can achieve great things by setting goals and working as a unit to reach them. You'd also tell them why it's important to increase productivity. Have markets shifted? Is there an application for a new technology? A new competitive threat? Are you trying to recover from some error? Is there a short-lived opportunity that must be seized?

Next, you can personalize those thoughts by telling your workers that you believe *they* can achieve great things in the area of their productivity by setting goals and working together to reach them. You can tell them what specifically they can do to meet the challenge of increased productivity. The more specific you can be, the better.

You inspire your team with your thoughts and beliefs, and then you make those thoughts relevant to your team by personalizing them for the team. Personalization is a powerful tool, and you should use it whenever applicable to inspire. Consider the greats. Martin Luther King Jr., for example, never spoke about an individual march. He always spoke of the goal, the prize. The march, the challenge of the day, was only one part of the goal. King was already out in front, however, leading the march, making the challenge of the day the current reality.

Making Seemingly Irrelevant Things Important and Relevant

First of all, I want to go on record as saying that nothing in the workplace should be irrelevant. If there are jobs and responsibilities in the workplace that have become irrelevant, your challenge should be to get rid of them and stop wasting money on them.

Your workers, undoubtedly, will consider some tasks and jobs to be irrelevant, and may try to push them aside, or onto somebody else. When this happens, it's up to you to convince them that all jobs, no matter how insignificant they may seem, are important.

If there's a job that has to be done, it must be relevant to something. You need to show your workers that all jobs relate in some way to the cause. Always relate to the big picture. If a job is undesirable, make your workers understand how it contributes to the overall good of the team.

If an employee refuses to do a job, then you have to deal with a larger issue. Does the person really understand what it means to be a part of a team, or is he going to work within the team framework only as it pleases him?

Remember the story about Hot-Shot Jeff in Chapter 13, "Fair Discipline—Or How to Spank Nicely"? Jeff didn't want to clean his equipment, remember? He thought that doing so was an insignificant and irrelevant task that was best left to somebody else.

Because Jeff perceived his role within the organization to be something other than what it really was, he wasn't able to see the relevance of working toward a goal and doing whatever was necessary to get there.

Jeff was unable to see that cleaning his equipment would help move his team toward the goal they were striving for. He either had to change his perception or leave the team, and he wasn't

Rally the Troops

Workers who resist doing the small tasks that contribute to the greater good will soon be noticed by their co-workers. You often can get away with waiting out these situations and letting things take their course. Don't ignore these kinds of situations for very long. Use coaching, counseling, or disciplinary means as necessary.

about to do the former. As leaders, we must recognize that our teams are better off without the contributions of certain people.

Always focus on the long view and the ultimate goal as the ultimate prize. This helps your employees see that seemingly irrelevant tasks are, indeed, important.

That's exactly what Leonard J. Roberts is trying to do at the Tandy Corporation, owner of the Radio Shack chain.

Roberts took over as CEO of Tandy in January 1999, saying he wants Radio Shack to be buyers' one-stop shop for "home connectivity," whatever that means. But the purpose of defining the ultimate goal to the troops is to start something happening now that will result in a better future for the company.

Roberts explains the goal and how all the small tasks tie into his larger view.

Roberts' goal is for even the least technologically savvy household to be able to integrate its Internet, cable, or satellite TV with its local and long-distance calling services. Technology is increasing rapidly, and it's Roberts' goal that Radio Shack build the tracks to tie all the latest technology together in American households.

This is pretty heady stuff for Radio Shack and its thousands of employees, but it looks like Roberts is on track to make it happen. The 7,000-store Radio Shack chain is on the upswing. Earnings and sales are nosing upward, which of course, means that stock prices can't be far behind. In December 1998, the stock traded at 38. Six months later it was at 53.

You may have to hold up the goal like a prize in order to help your employees see that seemingly irrelevant tasks are indeed important. If you can keep their sights on the goal, like Roberts has, doing the seemingly unimportant things will make more sense, and you'll have willing, motivated workers.

Keeping Some Distance Between You and Them

If you're going to be an inspirational leader, you've got to keep some distance between you and the members of your team.

Your workers can play favorites, but you can't. It's a tricky balance to maintain. You've got to look out for the best interests of each member of your team, but primarily as to how those interests relate to the total group.

Let's say that Beth, who's been a valuable member of your team for a long time, asks if she can have her work hours shifted by an hour. She'll start an hour earlier than everyone else if she can leave an hour ahead of the regular quitting time.

Beth has young children, and it would help her child care situation tremendously if she was able to work out this change of hours. It obviously would be in her best interests—and those of her family—to do so.

If your company policy permits flex time, and it works out for the team, then there's probably no reason why you shouldn't let Beth make the change. You'd be looking

out for her best interests, and being her advocate and leader.

If it's not in the best interests of your team,
however, to have Beth's hours changed, or you
can't make comparable arrangements available
to the rest of the team, then you shouldn't let
her take the early start and quit times.

As a leader, it's your job to look out for the
group first and individuals second. If you let
only Beth shift her hours, or it's not in the best
interests of the group, you're setting yourself up
for big, big problems.

You'll certainly be accused of playing favorites at
the very least, and probably much, much more.

As a leader, it's not your responsibility to solve
Beth's child care problems. You're a manager,
not a parent. Don't let your workers become
dependent on you for things that aren't your
responsibility.

Backfire

Remember that if you act in the
best interests of a particular employee, you've got to do the same
for another if a like situation arises.
Be sure you do, and that other
workers know you acted fairly.
Acting unfairly, or even being
perceived as acting unfairly, will
severely threaten your ability to
lead, much less to motivate.

How Close Is Too Close?

There's nothing wrong with being close to your employees. There's everything wrong
with being too close.

Some bosses and supervisors tend to get too involved with their employees—too
close—and that's not good. I knew a guy who invited one of his employees to live in
his house when the employee was in the midst of a divorce situation. God only
knows what they talked about over breakfast.

You can imagine how the other employees felt when they found out—and they did
find out—that Charlie was bunking in with the boss. It was great fodder for office
gossip and caused a lot of resentment and bad feelings.

I've known supervisors who have loaned money to workers. And some that have
taken it upon themselves to counsel employees who were experiencing problems. I've
known bosses who have invited one employee out for drinks or dinner after work.
I've even known supposed leaders who have tried to get members of their teams set
up on dates with people the leaders knew.

That kind of behavior is a huge mistake. It's getting way too close to employees, and
it's inviting big problems.

Initiating one-on-one contact with an employee, particularly one of the opposite sex,
is a particularly bad idea. Even if it's for valid reasons, you're asking for a lot of

speculation from other employees. It's terribly unwise to put yourself in that situation, and very unfair to the employee.

Here's How It Works

Parents are leaders, and any parent can tell you how difficult it is sometimes to step back from your kids and let them go through something on their own. Wise parents know, however, that you do your kids no favors by getting involved and solving all their problems for them. Wise parents, like all wise leaders, know that you've got to know when close is too close, and be ready to back away.

It's hard sometimes to keep yourself apart from your team, but to be an effective leader, you can't let yourself get too close. You've got to stay one step removed, and you can't get too caught up with individual problems and concerns.

On the eve of D-Day, then-General Eisenhower paid a visit to the troops. He went from man to man, shaking hands with what he knew would be the "first wave" of American troops to hit the beaches of Normandy.

The visit was recorded, and you can see Eisenhower on the recording, shaking hands and asking troops about their families and personal interests. At one point, a soldier assured Eisenhower that the troops would complete their mission and not disappoint their general.

On the film that's been made, you can see Eisenhower turn away from the soldier who tried to reassure him, blinking rapidly and putting his hand up to his eye.

It appears that the general was wiping away a tear, although nobody can know for sure. If he was, it was obvious that he knew he couldn't let anyone see that tear. To do so would have been detrimental to his leadership and weakened his position of great strength. At that point in time, Eisenhower had to be strong, not only for the soldiers that were going into Normandy the next day, but for their families, friends, and all the people of America.

He knew that there were sure to be many lives lost the following day, and that some of these soldiers he was greeting would be among those killed. Can you imagine what it would have done to the morale of the troops, however, if Eisenhower would have broken down and cried?

As a leader, he knew he had to remain apart from the troops in order to be effective.

When Being Close Will Help

It's good to be close to your employees. Now that we've discussed the pitfalls of being too close, we have to take a look at how being close to your employees can be a great benefit.

Remember, we're talking about being close—but not too close. You're going to have to use your good judgment and draw the line as to which is which.

Staying close to your employees practically guarantees that they'll help you out. They'll tell you who the slackers are, and they'll make sure you know who's been going above and beyond the call of duty, too.

Rally the Troops

If you're unsure about whether you're close or too close to your employees, follow your gut. If you even suspect you're getting too close, back off. If you're certain that you're not too close, then don't worry about it.

They'll be willing to come to you to talk about mistakes they've made because they'll feel that they can trust you.

And they'll help you cover your backside when things get rough, and stand by you when you come under pressure.

Being Friendly vs. Being Friends

You can, and should be, friendly with the members of your team. You shouldn't, however, be friends with them.

A listing of the top 20 characteristics of effective leaders, gathered during a leadership survey I conducted, did not include being a friend to employees. Just in case you're interested, though, the top five characteristics as cited on this listing were as follows:

➤ Honest

➤ Competent

➤ Forward-looking

➤ Inspiring

➤ Intelligent

Yes, you can go to the after-work party at the corner bar, as long as everyone on the team is invited.

You can go to a party at a worker's home, as long as everyone on the team was invited. If you run into a worker at a football game, you can sit with him. But you shouldn't ask one employee to go to the game with you.

You can invite team members over to your house for a cookout, as long as everyone's invited. You can give a holiday gift, as long as equivalent gifts are given to everyone.

Defining Moments

A **friend** is defined by Webster's as "a person whom one knows well and is fond of; intimate associate; close acquaintance." These definitions should not apply to you and your workers. One of the definitions of **friendly**, however, is "in the manner of friends, or amicably." There's a big difference in the meanings of those two words, don't you agree?

Feel free to socialize with workers you run into when you're out, but if there's more than one, make sure you spend about equal time with each.

If you feel that you have to turn down an invitation from one of your team members, be careful about how you do it. You don't have to give a detailed explanation of why you're refusing, but make sure you're gracious.

Let's say that Sandy invites you over to her place for a drink after work. You should say something like, "Hey, great! Who all is coming?"

If she continues with, "Well, I invited about half the staff," warning bells should be going off in your head. You don't need to make a big deal about it, but you can't attend if not everyone was invited.

Instead of embarrassing Sandy because she didn't invite everyone, simply tell her you checked your calendar and found you have another engagement. Sorry, Sandy.

The Least You Need to Know

➤ Your thoughts and beliefs can be sources of motivation to your team members.

➤ Personalizing your thoughts and beliefs to make them more applicable to team members will increase your ability to motivate and inspire.

➤ Nothing is irrelevant if you demonstrate how it applies to the cause.

➤ It's good to be close to your workers, but a big mistake to get too close.

➤ Effective leaders must be able to keep some distance between themselves and their workers.

➤ Being friendly is different than being a friend to your team members.

Chapter 17

What You Should Know About the People Who Work for You

In This Chapter

➤ Recognizing work capabilities and preferences

➤ Learning about your workers' personal interests

➤ Relating personal interests back to the job

➤ How background and circumstance affect job performance

➤ Keeping a close watch on behavior patterns

➤ Dealing with destructive behavior

Some supervisors and bosses view the people who work for them as little more than machines—necessary to get the job done, but not very interesting.

They're no more likely to take time to get to know their workers than they are to be elected President. It just doesn't occur to them that the people who show up every day are anything more than workers.

Workers are assigned a job, and are expected to complete it. They're a little piece of the whole, and nothing else. This kind of leader perceives workers as cogs, not as people.

Smart supervisors and bosses, the ones capable of creating a motivated staff, view their workers as important individuals, without whom their businesses wouldn't be able to operate, much less succeed. They want to get to know their workers. They understand that satisfied employees are the most productive employees, and people are more satisfied if they're made to feel important, valued, and part of the total organization.

Smart bosses invest in their workers, build them as part of the team, and include them in as many aspects of the organization as possible.

So, exactly what should you know about the people who work for you?

You need to know what's important to them, and have a sense of how they feel about issues and situations. You need to be able to anticipate how they'll respond to events and problems. This is important because their reaction to events control how you should present those events.

You also need to understand their strengths and weaknesses, and something about their views on life.

While it's important to know enough about the people who work for you so that you understand where they're coming from, it's equally important that you do not become a psychologist or marriage counselor.

So, let's see how you strike this balance between being a leader who knows what's going on, but doesn't know too much or become too intimate.

Knowing Their Work Capabilities

That it's important to understand the capabilities of those who work for you seems so obvious that I wondered if I should even include the topic in this book.

And then I started thinking of all the people I've known who didn't acknowledge the importance of understanding the work capabilities of their employees. And of the people who refused to even provide proper training for their employees in an effort to save money, or time, or whatever.

I remember being reprimanded once by an important executive vice president who was ticked off that we had included significant dollars for training in a big budget.

When we explained that it was important for employees to get the proper training so that they could do their jobs effectively (duh), the guy said, "But we expect all of our people to have those skills when we hire them."

Yeah, right.

It's people like that guy who made me decide to include these topics.

Bob, the president of a small insurance company, is another guy who gave me cause for this discussion. I was doing some contract work for Bob's firm, so I

Backfire

Some bosses get a kick out of jerking around employees. They move them from one area to another, change their hours, take away coffee breaks, impose dress codes, and do all sorts of things, just for the sake of doing them. There's no better way to alienate employees and to demotivate workers. If you ever get an urge to do these things, think long and hard about the results you're likely to get.

had occasion to see firsthand what was going on there. Despite my efforts to save him, Bob was intent on running his company into the ground through terrible management. Eventually, he did.

Bob was one of those guys who couldn't leave well enough alone. He was always switching people around from one position to another, or doing other things that kept his staff in a constant state of turmoil.

Bob thought nothing about pulling somebody out of the customer service department and having him try his hand at sales, or anything else. He found it perfectly acceptable to put the receptionist in charge of complicated marketing projects that were way beyond her scope and abilities. And he never understood why the employees resented him and his actions.

His neglectful attitude toward his workers, of course, eventually came back to haunt him. It happened when Bob insisted that Carrie, the receptionist, supervise a survey the company was doing of its customers.

Carrie was a good receptionist, but she had no business trying to manage a survey, plus handle all the details associated with the mailing, the software for coding responses, interpretation of responses, and so forth. To make a long story short, the great survey project got incredibly screwed up. Bob tried to point the finger at Carrie, but, of course, the blame ultimately rested on him.

If Bob had taken the least bit of time to consider Carrie's capabilities, he wouldn't have given her the survey to manage in the first place. He just didn't get it.

Neither did he ever figure out why our invoices were so high, or why my firm eventually withdrew its services (to save our reputation). And finally, I guess he never understood why he ultimately went bankrupt, a fact I read about in the local press about two years after we withdrew from the account.

Bob was messing up on a lot more than just surveys.

To put someone in a job that is too difficult for her capabilities, or too easy, is to invite discouragement and bad morale. Nobody wants to be set up to fail, and that's exactly what you do if you assign something that's too hard.

On the other hand, nobody wants to feel like he's wasting his time doing work that a six-year-old could handle. Putting a worker in that position is asking for resentment and great dissatisfaction.

Learn about your workers' capabilities, and assign their duties accordingly.

Rally the Troops

Matching your workers and their best capabilities not only keeps them happy and motivated, but is good for business. Why make somebody do something they don't like or aren't good at, when there are other jobs at which he or she will excel? Don't hurt your business just to prove a point with your workers.

Check out their job applications or résumés, and find out what their experiences have been. Maybe they have capabilities that you don't know about. Talk to them.

Ask what they like to do. A worker will be happier doing something that he or she enjoys rather than something that's drudgery.

And watch as your employees work. Gauge their capabilities, and reassign duties if necessary. Rearrange the work layout. Provide more coaching. Pay attention to what they say and how they look while they're working. It's not difficult to distinguish between somebody who likes what he's doing and somebody who's miserable.

Understanding work capabilities isn't difficult, and it's one of the most important things you can do to assure that your part of the operation will run smoothly.

Their Personal Interests

You should take time to learn about the personal interests of your workers. Obviously, those interests are important to them. They're part of what your workers are. You can't understand what somebody's all about if the only things you know about them pertain directly to work.

In addition, their personal interests could be in conflict with yours. I used the example in Chapter 15 of the avid hunter whose interests were in direct conflict with those of some of his team members who happened to be animal rights activists.

If you're aware of the personal interests of the people who work for you, you'll be able to anticipate possible conflicts and avoid them. If you know that some of your team members are animal rights activists, for instance, you simply avoid talking about your hunting exploits.

Here's How It Works

If you're not sensitive to your workers' personal interests, you risk alienating them. I remember an ugly situation in which a supervisor was very active in the National Rifle Association (NRA), and talked about it all the time. He was a huge NRA fan. The brother of one of his workers had been killed in an accident involving a gun several years earlier, and she was vehemently against guns of any sort. The supervisor didn't know this, and the worker felt terribly harassed by his constant pro-NRA rhetoric. The boss never resolved the matter, and she eventually left the job. Be careful!

If you know that somebody is a strict vegetarian, you don't talk about the great rack of lamb you whipped up for your dinner party Friday night.

Avoid talking about things that are offensive or upsetting to your workers. That's not to say you've got to tiptoe around, walking on eggshells in fear that you're going to offend somebody. But you should be sensitive to these kinds of issues.

Know What Makes Them Tick

When you get to know about the personal interests of your team members, you'll begin to know what makes them tick, what's important to them.

If you look at each worker as a complete package, and make it a point to know what he's made of, you'll begin to get an understanding of how each person can be motivated. While you're looking at personal information, be careful not to overlook work-related issues.

Learn what kind of training each worker has. Is everyone adequately trained so as to be comfortable in his job? If not, you're going to be looking at problems down the road.

Get to know about the family heritages of your employees. This, after all, is a huge part of who they are. How do you find out this kind of information? Just ask. Most people are happy to talk about themselves and their backgrounds—if they trust you enough to know the information they reveal won't come back at them later as some sort of discrimination or other repercussion.

The Really Important Stuff

The really important stuff, as far as your workers are concerned, is probably the same stuff that's most important in your own life.

Families, friends, the places where they live, and the things they do (including work) are the most significant factors in nearly all of our lives.

Get a handle on all those things, and then relate it to how your team members work. When you've gotten a good feeling for who a person is, you'll be able to see more clearly what he can do on the job, and how personal interests relate to those abilities.

You'll get a sense of whether a worker is going to be willing to back you up by accepting more job responsibility, and in which areas the worker will be of most value to your team and their overall goals.

Rally the Troops

People everywhere personalize their workspaces with photos and other personal items. You can get a pretty good idea of what's important to someone by observing their workspace and asking some questions about what you see. Don't worry about being too nosy. Most people are more than willing to talk about their personal lives if they perceive that you care.

You'll better understand a person's capacity to withstand frustration and failure, enabling you to relate those factors to his work capacities. Knowing how your worker thinks will help you to know how to treat him, how to motivate him, and how to keep him happy.

Learn the strengths and weaknesses of your workers so you can anticipate in which situations they'll do fine and in which situations they'll need backup.

Getting to know about the really important stuff will make the work situation a lot easier for you and for the members of your team.

What About Their Backgrounds?

I like to know quite a bit about people who work for me. We all have different backgrounds and come from different circumstances. I think it's important for you, as a supervisor, to have at least an idea of those circumstances in order to better understand where your workers are coming from.

Here's How It Works

It's easy to forget that background plays a huge role in a person's personality and attitudes. A person's work ethic, disposition, level of cooperation, and knowledge of his environment are all things that can be drastically affected by his background.

I remember a worker named Jackie. Jackie was a middle-aged woman—a very good employee. She was well-organized and diligent, pleasant to be around, cooperative, and did a good job at her work. The only thing with Jackie was that she rushed out the door every afternoon at 5:00. I never once saw her stay a minute longer than she absolutely needed to.

I finally commented on her behavior one day, saying in a very casual and low-key manner that she must have big plans after work every day because she's always in a hurry to leave.

Jackie explained to me that her elderly, ailing parents lived with her, and a caretaker came each day to stay with them while Jackie worked.

Jackie's problem was that the caretaker left at 5:30 sharp, whether Jackie was home from work or not. Because Jackie's mother had Alzheimer's disease and her father was physically disabled, it was a terrible worry for Jackie if they were left alone, even for a few minutes. She didn't live very far from work, but if the traffic was bad, it was conceivable that she'd get home after the caregiver had left.

So, Jackie got out the door as quickly as she could in order to minimize the possibility of her parents being left alone. Once I understood that, I never again thought twice about Jackie's prompt exits from the building. In fact, I often would tell her to get going about five minutes early.

If I hadn't understood Jackie's personal circumstances, I would have viewed her in a completely different manner. As it was, I developed great respect for her patience and perseverance in working all day, then going home to care for elderly parents.

Here's How It Works

Knowing and understanding circumstances like the ones Jackie had was advantageous in another way, too. Jackie eventually took a leave of absence in order to care full-time for her parents. While I was sorry to see her leave, I wasn't surprised, and had already made tentative plans as to how we'd handle her workload while she was gone.

Admittedly, being up on your workers' backgrounds and personal circumstances sometimes puts you in the middle of situations you wouldn't otherwise be involved with.

I worked with a man once who was named Gunter. Gunter was a very interesting man, with a very interesting background. He'd been educated as a Hitler Youth in Nazi Germany, escaping the country at the end of World War II.

While he had adapted reasonably well to American life, he was still a product of his upbringing and background, and often would express opinions that made most of us cringe. Gunter was pretty much of a racist, and he just didn't understand that some things are far, far better left unsaid.

We all chalked up Gunter's outspoken opinions to the way he'd been raised. I had advised him to keep his opinions to himself, but Gunter still felt that he needed to share his thoughts.

The Gunter problem came to a head during a meeting one day, when he shared his view that babies born with handicaps—either physical or mental—should be "put to sleep" for the greater good of society.

Gunter didn't know that one of his subordinates sitting at the meeting had a daughter who'd been born with some physical disadvantages. The girl had overcome most of the physical problems and was maturing just fine, thanks to her very loving family, and the family's ability and willingness to get her every bit of help possible.

As you can imagine, we all were extremely upset about Gunter's remark, yet Gunter had no idea of what was going on. I suspect that Gunter never did fully understand the gravity of what he'd done. In fact, he continued to make these kinds of outrageous comments throughout his career, losing him a lot of respect that he might have had.

Behavior Patterns

If you're observant, you can learn a lot about your workers by watching their behavior patterns and habits. All of us are creatures of habit. Generally, we dress in a certain manner and talk about particular things. We go to dinner at the usual places and see the same kinds of movies—over and over. Once you get an idea of what your employee's normal patterns are, you can be watchful for changes which might indicate changes in their attitudes or lifestyles.

Someone who's a huge fan of the arts and has had season tickets to the symphony for ten years straight is highly unlikely to suddenly develop an interest in illegal cockfighting.

Backfire

It's a common tendency to judge someone by his behavior. After all, it's what you see. Don't forget, however, that behavior is the outward manifestation of what's going on inside. Don't be too quick to judge your workers on the basis of behavior, because you can't know what's going on inside the person until you take some time to find out. You could be making a serious misjudgment.

What Behavior Reveals About a Person

A person's behavior reveals many things about his or her personality. The danger, however, is making assumptions that may not be true.

I told you a couple of pages back about Jackie and her behavior patterns. Once I knew about Jackie's circumstances, her behavior made perfect sense. Until I understood the circumstances, however, I confess I thought that Jackie was just somebody who didn't want to put in any extra time at work.

It's really easy to jump to conclusions about people, and we do it far too often.

I once supervised a young guy named Mark. Mark was a pretty good worker, except for now and then he'd disappear for 20 or 30 minutes with no explanation except to say he'd be right back.

This happened five or six times in Mark's first three months on the job, and his co-workers were getting a little disturbed about it. Somebody told me what was going on, and I asked to be kept posted.

One day, one of Mark's co-workers came to my office to say Mark had just left for one of his mystery breaks. It was freezing cold outside, and he hadn't taken his coat, so I assumed he was still in the building. Not knowing what to expect, I went off to try to find him.

It didn't take long. Mark was sitting alone in the coffee room, doubled over in pain and holding his head in both hands. I sat down with him, and when he was able to talk, he told me he'd suffered a serious head injury about a year earlier. He was recovering and expected to be all right, but every now and then he'd get very dizzy and then experience horrible pain in his head.

Rally the Troops

Be open to hearing about, and helping with, your workers' problems. If you're known as someone who is sympathetic and willing to help, your employees will be much more open about sharing their concerns.

He had learned to recognize the symptoms of these attacks, and when he felt one coming on, he simply had to leave whatever he was doing and find someplace quiet to sit and wait it out. The pain only lasted for 20 minutes or so and then he'd be okay.

Mark hadn't wanted anyone to know, fearing it would affect the insurance he had with the company and our perception of his work abilities.

So, Mark's mysterious behavior was explained, and we worked with him as the attacks became fewer and farther between, then eventually stopped.

The point is, though, it's easy to make assumptions about somebody's behavior, but it's a dangerous thing to do.

Try to be nonjudgmental about the behavior of your employees, and not assume you know why it's occurring. Of course, if there is destructive or dangerous behavior, it's your responsibility to deal with it.

Recognizing Destructive Behavior

Basically, there are two kinds of destructive behavior. That which is self-destructive, and that which is destructive toward others. Both, as you can imagine, can create big problems in the workplace, and both can threaten the morale and motivation of your entire team.

I don't know which is easier to recognize—I guess it depends on how the behavior is manifested. If one of your employees flips out one day and starts breaking up furniture, damaging equipment, and slamming holes into the walls, that's about as clear an indication of destructive behavior as you'll get.

Defining Moments

Destructive behavior is directed outwardly, toward other people or objects. **Self-destructive behavior**, either intentional or unintentional, is directed inward and harms the person who displays the behavior.

If, on the other hand, somebody has been systematically and intentionally damaging machinery in ways that are practically unnoticeable, that kind of destructive behavior is much harder to recognize.

Self-destructive behavior can be, but isn't necessarily, even more difficult to recognize.

Some psychologists claim that excessive body piercing or tattooing is a sign of self-destructive behavior in some people. Well, depending on where the tattoos or pierces are placed, you might see no evidence at all. Someone could be using illegal drugs at home, but until the problem becomes evident at work, you'd have no idea. This is why many companies have imposed mandatory drug testing for employees. If somebody is on drugs and working around machinery, I don't need to tell you what could happen.

Sometimes you find out quite by accident about destructive behavior, as I did with Bill.

Bill was an okay guy whom I didn't know all that well because he worked for another manager. I was interested in doing some fieldwork to evaluate some technology, and Bill's manager suggested I travel with Bill for a while to get the information I needed.

He picked me up at the hotel, and the first thing that struck me was the condition of his car. It was filthy. It was missing a hubcap and had the look of a car that wasn't looked after. Inside, the ashtray was overflowing and it reeked of cigarette smoke.

Rally the Troops

We're often tempted to overlook small, subtle changes in behavior because we don't want to butt into something we feel is none of our business. Even subtle changes, however, should be closely monitored. You don't have to act at the first little sign of a behavior change, but let it serve as notice to keep an eye on the situation.

Well, okay, I thought. I hadn't realized that Bill was such a heavy smoker, but that's his business. I was a little disturbed about how he maintained his company car because it sure wasn't going to impress potential customers.

Things went from bad to worse, however, when we stopped later for lunch at one of those pubs that has a bar on one side and a small dining area on the other.

We walked in and sat down at the bar to wait for a table. Bill didn't say a word, but the bartender greeted him by name. Without asking, he set a drink in front of Bill, and then asked me what I wanted.

The bartender hovered around, ready to fill Bill's glass, but Bill obviously was taking it easy that day, no doubt on account of me. We sat down and had lunch, and Bill had another drink or two. I definitely was concerned about this drinking at lunch. Bill confirmed my suspicions that he had a problem when I went to make a phone call before we left. I came back quickly because the person I was calling wasn't in, only to find Bill sneaking a quick drink at the bar before we left. He'd had four or five drinks by now, and he expected to drive the car and continue making sales calls.

I was very disturbed by the situation. Not only had I learned of what appeared to be a serious problem on Bill's part, but I also learned that Bill's boss obviously had not been doing his job. He and Bill supposedly traveled together frequently, yet nobody had ever heard a whisper about Bill's self-destructive behavior. Either the boss wasn't traveling with Bill the way he should have been or he was covering up for Bill. Both Bill and his boss ultimately ended up losing their jobs.

Be on the lookout for destructive behavior. The faster it's recognized and confronted, the better the chances that it can be fixed.

Changing Destructive Behavior

If you see destructive behavior among your team, confront it immediately. Don't wait for it to become a Bill story.

Don't be confrontational about the problem, but let the person involved know that you're aware of what's going on and that the behavior is unacceptable. Focus the discussion on the poor job performance that's resulting from the behavior, not the behavior itself. Your problem is the performance. The behavior belongs to the employee.

Make sure the person involved understands the consequences of such behavior, and offer suggestions for improving the behavior, if possible.

For instance, I had another employee, Dan, whose work performance had dropped very noticeably over a period of months. From observing his behavior and understanding a bit about Dan's history, I suspected a serious drinking problem.

I called Dan aside and told him he was not performing to the levels I expected. "I don't know if you are drinking too much or not, and its none of my business," I said. "However, I want you to talk to some professional counselors."

I referred him to the professional counseling service the company had available, then laid out his options. If Dan agreed to counseling, attended faithfully, and I got reports of improvement, he could stay on the job. If he refused to go or didn't take the counseling seriously, he would be fired for poor performance. It was up to him.

Dan went to counseling, quit drinking, and stayed with the company. I always felt good that the problem had been recognized early and dealt with effectively. It certainly saved Dan's job, and may have saved his life.

The Least You Need to Know

➤ Understanding your workers' capabilities and job preferences will make it easier to keep them motivated and happy.

➤ It will be very helpful to you to learn about the personal interests of those on your team.

➤ Once you understand their personal interests, you should relate them back to what your workers do on the job.

➤ Understanding a worker's background and circumstances makes it easier to deal with particular behaviors.

➤ It's important to keep a close watch on behavior, but don't assume you understand why someone acts the way he does.

➤ Destructive behavior should be confronted and dealt with as soon as it's recognized.

Chapter 18

Finding Out What Really Makes Your Workers Tick

> ### In This Chapter
>
> ➤ Blending personal and work-related concerns
>
> ➤ Getting the information you want
>
> ➤ Snooping is dangerous business
>
> ➤ Trolling for information nets good results
>
> ➤ Knowing the kinds of things to look for

Every employee is like a book, with the different areas of their lives as chapters. As a supervisor, you get to know the work chapter pretty well. It's easy to find out job preferences and capabilities if you're paying attention, and observing the people as they work will give you most of the information you need.

The other chapters, however, are harder to read. They remain closed within the book unless you figure out how to open them.

Smart bosses and supervisors will try to get a handle on the whole book, not just the chapter that deals with work. Unless it's a very unusual plot, one chapter isn't a true indication of the whole story.

There are many important aspects of every person's life. Normally, if you ask someone what's important to her, she'll rattle off a list of half a dozen or more things. My family, friends, home, work, traveling, volunteer work, hobbies—all of these things are of high importance in this woman's life. Most of us would have similar lists.

It's very hard for someone to be motivated at work if there are serious problems or dissatisfactions in other areas of her life. Smart bosses look out for these other areas and try to accommodate the person's needs. This isn't just because bosses want to be nice people; it's because it's better for their companies.

Susan works for a company that's ranked among the top 100 in the world. She's very bright, educated at one of the country's best business schools, and a real asset to her company. She's also extremely well paid.

Well, a few years ago, Susan was engaged and planning her wedding. While she was very happy, it was a stressful time because her fiancé had been sent on an assignment in another country.

Intercontinental wedding planning isn't what it's cracked up to be, Susan will tell you. She was under enormous strain, with trying to keep her wedding plans organized while handling a major consulting job for her company. The job required her to work off-site, at the client's offices, and Susan felt like she was barely keeping her head above water.

Susan's supervisor noticed the strain Susan was under, and decided to take action. She reported it to her boss, and the boss was sympathetic, saying she'd see what she could work out for Susan.

When Susan's fiancé returned home for a month-long project review, Susan's company pulled her off her assignment and gave her an in-house assignment for the time that her fiancé was home. This allowed Susan and her fiancé to spend a month in the same city and complete their wedding plans.

Susan created maximum revenue for the firm when she worked at a client's site on billable projects, and her company lost money by pulling her off the project and bringing her back to the office. So, why did Susan's boss do this?

Here's How It Works

As more managers become sensitive to the needs of their workers and attuned to the fact that happy employees are motivated, hardworking employees, we're seeing more and more ways in which workers' needs are being accommodated. A few that come to mind are on-site child-care centers and schools, flexible hours, job sharing opportunities, and family-leave time.

Because her boss knew it was a smart move for the company, that's why. Susan is a very valuable employee. She's also just the kind of person another company would love to have, and be willing to pay premium dollars to get.

Her boss understood all this and was smart enough to blend Susan's personal goals with the goals of the firm. This caused Susan to see up close that her company was flexible and willing to accommodate her personal needs. It caused her to bond with the firm, and she's still there, making big bucks for the company.

It's no coincidence that the employees who work where Susan does love the place and rank it so high. They appreciate their employer's thoughtfulness and willingness to work with them. As a result, they give back 110 percent.

Discovering What You Want to Know

In order to be able to fix a problem the way Susan's company did, you've got to know that the problem exists. Being an interested and caring supervisor, you're anxious to know what's going on with your team members so that you can help out as Susan's boss did.

But how do you go about finding out what's really going on with your workers? I suppose you could listen in on their personal calls or intercept e-mails. You could ask their friends for personal information, or call them on the carpet and demand to know what's going on.

You realize, however, I'm sure, that there's a fine line between being interested and caring and sticking your nose into somebody else's business. If you come off as being interested and caring, you'll do just fine with your workers. If you come off as being a snoop, however, look out!

Pretty much all you need to do is be attentive and available. Walk around, chat informally with the members of your team, and maintain an open-door policy. That means that you're willing and available to discuss any subject your employees want to talk about.

Should You Ask?

Often, it seems that the easiest and most acceptable way of getting information about your workers is simply to come right out and ask. Good idea? In most cases, yes. This doesn't mean that you pry and press somebody for information they don't want to give. But if you walk around and ask casually, "How's your husband doing?" or "Is your son feeling better?" you're opening the door for your employees to give you information if they want to.

Of course, you might find out a lot more than you care to. By asking what's going on, you've opened the door. You've heard the old saying "Be careful what you wish for, it might come true"? Well, in this case, be careful what you ask to find out, you might just be told.

Backfire

When someone confides in us, it's a natural tendency to want to help in any way we can. This often involves offering advice or suggestions concerning whatever the situation might be. Unless you're trained as a counselor or psychologist, however, you certainly don't have the expertise to advise someone on serious matters. And you risk getting yourself in big trouble by doing so.

If somebody does want to talk, are you required to sit and listen to her talk about the intimate details of her marital problems? Her domestic abuse situation? Her child's drug problem? As an effective leader, I think you are. It's not an easy part of the job, that's for sure.

Some people have an awful lot of baggage, and once it's handed to you, it's hard not to carry it around yourself. While you have to listen, you don't have to counsel the person through the problem. Most of the time, the worker is already dealing with the issue and doesn't really need your help, just your reassurance. If they really do need help, you might want to get an idea of the situation, then refer the person to the appropriate source of help.

If you ask for information, and you're doing your job effectively, most people will be willing—even happy—to share it. Think about this for a minute. Your team members aren't strangers. You already know, or should know, something about their personal lives. It's not like you're approaching a complete stranger and asking personal questions.

Most of the time, I think you'll find that your employees will approach you. Someone will tell you it's possible she'll need some time off. When you ask why, she fills you in on her mother's illness and tells you that an operation is scheduled for the following week.

Listening is a better tactic than asking if you're trying to find out information about your workers. By being open and offering some personal information of your own, you might get people to open up a bit about their own situations.

Should You Snoop?

Workplace snooping has risen to new levels with the advent of e-mail and Internet access, and it's become a controversial, sometimes almost frightening issue.

A survey conducted a few years ago by an organization called the Society for Human Resource Management found that 36 percent of organizations that provide e-mail check their employees' e-mail records. Eight percent conducted random reviews of e-mail. And 75 percent of those organizations felt they had a right to read company-provided e-mail.

Court rulings, so far, are supporting the organizations. E-mail, voice mail, and the Internet generally are considered company equipment, and the information stored within it belongs to the company.

Other technologies allow supervisors to do things like monitor their workers' Internet use to find out if it's being used for work purposes or to check out sports scores or stock reports. They also can monitor the length of employees' phone calls, record the number of keystrokes made within a specific amount of time, and monitor the amount of time employees are away from their computers. There's even a device called an "active badge," developed by Olivetti and Xerox, that can track employees' locations within a building via sensors placed throughout the company property.

Here's How It Works

This issue of privacy within the workplace is going to be a hot topic as we enter the 21st century. Watch for clashes between workers who claim their rights are being violated and employers pleading security concerns.

Some employers feel they're perfectly justified in monitoring employees, due to concerns about security issues, productivity issues, and legal issues.

They say that e-mail makes it very easy for an employee who's so inclined to easily transmit confidential information to competitors or whoever else might want it. To prevent that, they must monitor employee e-mail.

Some employers also say they check e-mail to make sure there's no harassment occurring within the system, and check Internet connections to make sure no employee is involved with anything illegal. The justification for this is that employers say they could be held liable for anything illegal that occurs in their office.

And the other big reason given for computer monitoring has to do with productivity. If you've ever used the Internet, you know how tempting some of the sites look that show up on the screen when you're looking for something else. Who could resist taking a quick peek at the "ten easy ways to a fabulous love life—guaranteed" site that pops up when you're looking for statistics concerning the volume of air versus water, or something like that?

Employers are aware of these temptations, and are taking steps to keep the situation under control.

Whether or not you agree with these modern workplace snooping efforts, you should understand that using these tactics will not endear you to your workers. If you're lucky, you'll have a team that might understand why some employers feel these measures are necessary. Then again, you might not.

In the old days, snooping employers would simply rifle through desks after all workers had left for the day. I'm not sure what they were looking for, but this type of snooping is definitely fourth-class.

Here's How It Works

A friend of mine is a school guidance counselor and runs a personal counseling service on the side. The father of three children, now ranging in age from senior high to out of college, he's a firm advocate of parents snooping to find out what their kids are up to. As long as his kids lived in his home, he felt justified in scoping out their rooms to see what was going on. He felt it was his responsibility to know what was going on within his house.

While I'm not endorsing snooping—electronic or otherwise—I do think a supervisor needs to be aware of what's going on within his area. Being observant as to what's left lying around doesn't hurt.

Trolling

Trolling for information, just as you would for fish, is a good way to gather information.

This doesn't mean you walk from desk to desk, gawking at whatever items might be lying on top of it. It doesn't mean that you hide behind partitions, hoping to catch stray bits of interesting discussion. And it doesn't mean that you engage in electronic monitoring. All trolling means is paying close attention to what you see and hear as you move around your department and the company, and processing the information that you get.

While trolling, pay close attention to what you hear concerning the reputation of your department. Be alert to what other people are saying about your team and the people on your team. If something's going on, and you're alert, you'll hear about it.

If you hear that one of your team members—Joe, for instance—is earning himself quite a reputation as a pest to women from other departments, your antenna should go up. It's a fine line these days between somebody being a pest and somebody harassing co-workers. The last thing you need in your department is *that* kind of trouble.

You and other managers within the company can help each other by passing along pertinent information that you hear about each other's workers or departments. Make it clear that you'll welcome getting heads up on any information that might affect your team. Make a point to do the same for them.

After you've gotten used to trolling, it gets to be a habit. You'll find yourself doing it all the time. Your ears will perk up at the mention of one of your team members' names, and you'll become attuned to what's going on around you.

This ability makes it easier for you to stay on top of what's going on, and helps you to discover what you want to know. It's really just a matter of being extra observant.

Knowing What to Look For

All the trolling in the world won't do any good if you don't know what you're looking for.

As you troll for fish, you look for signs. You keep your eyes open for fast-moving schools of small fish that probably are being chased by big fish. Some fish like to hang out in the shadow of sea turtles floating on top of the water, so if you see a sea turtle, it's worth a closer look. It's the same with pieces of board floating on the water's surface. You look for the flash of a fin or tail, and listen for the splash of a jumping fish. These signs help you to find the fish.

Trolling for information also entails careful watching and listening. But what sorts of things should you look and listen for?

You don't want to get paranoid, thinking that everything you hear or see is important to you and your department. On the other hand, you don't want to ignore significant conversation or other signs that could let you know that something's going on.

Rally the Troops

If you're noticing changes and wondering what's going on, be extra sure to keep your ear to the ground. Co-workers generally have at least an idea of what's going on among their group, and, if you listen carefully, you'll probably hear what's happening as you pass the watercooler or coffee room.

Looking for Evidence

Any kind of change can be evidence that something's happening with a member or members of your department. For that reason, it's very important to be alert to changes that occur.

If someone's appearance has changed drastically during a short period of time, it should trip a warning flag in your mind.

If Jack has lost 30 pounds in the past month, something's going on. He's either on a big weight-loss program, he's sick, or there's something else going on in his life. Any other employee should be able to tell you if he's dieting, or you can figure it out by yourself by taking a stroll past the lunchroom.

If Robert, who's always kept to himself and never socialized at all with anyone from work, suddenly starts throwing parties for his co-workers and inviting people out for happy hours, something's going on.

If Sharon, who was always a stickler for neatness and fashion, suddenly starts coming to work in clothes that appear to have been slept in for the past three nights, something's going on.

If Henry starts making and getting personal calls about every 15 minutes for two weeks straight, something's going on.

If Jennifer, who's been the department's ray of sunshine since she started two years ago, suddenly starts snapping at people, resenting suggestions from you and her co-workers, and ignoring people when they talk to her, something's going on.

If Charlie starts wearing T-shirts that say "Join the Local Union," when he's never expressed a word of dissatisfaction with shop leadership, something's going on. Maybe Charlie feels disenfranchised with you or others in leadership, and is visiting the local union hall looking for support.

If Ellie, who was always the first one to work in the morning and the last one to leave at night, starts showing up late three days a week and trying to sneak out before the end of the shift, something's going on.

Changes don't always imply that something bad is happening. Robert's personality has changed, but it's certainly been for the better. Maybe Ellie has just met the guy of her dreams and can't bear to tear herself away from him to come to work. Maybe Jack has taken up running, eliminated his nightly carton of Ben & Jerry's, and become a strict vegetarian. If so, you don't have to worry about Ellie and Jack (other than Ellie's tardiness), but it's still important to know what's going on in their lives.

Backfire

If you notice changes in one of your team members, don't immediately assume that it means something negative is occurring. Many managers have alienated workers by trying to get overly involved in their personal lives. Stand back a little and give the worker some space, but keep your eyes and ears open.

Remember the discussion at the beginning of this chapter about every person being a book, and how each chapter of the book affects the other chapters? Well, if something big is happening in Ellie's personal life, chances are it's going to affect her work life. Same goes for Jack, Robert, Sharon, and Henry.

An observant and informed manager usually can spot the evidence if there's something going on with one or more of his team members. And a smart manager will confront the evidence and figure out how it relates back to the workplace.

Change among your team isn't necessarily bad, but it needs to be evaluated and watched. If team members work well together and have a high level of motivation, you don't want anything to rock the boat.

Watching for Clues

Your workers leave many clues around as to what's important to them—what makes them tick. Anyone who's at all observant can see them.

The workspaces of many people are like miniature versions of their homes, and for good reason. How many hours each day do you spend at work? Eight? Ten? Twelve? It's a natural tendency to want the place where you spend all that time to be comfortable and welcoming.

To that end, most people personalize their workspaces with photographs and other items that tell something about who they are and what they like.

Rally the Troops

It's perfectly natural to ask a worker a personal question when it's prompted by something you see in his or her workspace. It can be awkward to ask a personal question without the benefit of these props, so take advantage when the opportunity arises.

You'll know that Tom is a linkster when you see the golf ball-shaped paperweight on his desk. You'll know that Mary is a bowler when you see the winner's certificate tacked onto her bulletin board, and you'll know that Jack's a fisherman when you see the photo of him proudly holding up the 25-pound cobia he caught during his last trip to Florida.

These are all good indicators of your workers' personalities and interests, and they also open the door to personal conversation. It's perfectly acceptable to walk into Jack's workspace and say something like, "That's quite a fish, Jack. Do you get one like that very often?" Or, "Wow! Did you catch that fish around here?" That opens the door for Jack to tell you about his hobby and his recent trip to Florida.

Workers who post family photos in their workplaces also open the door to personal questions. A picture of a little girl in a dance outfit, or of a boy with a dog, invites all kinds of questions and responses. Listen carefully to the information you'll get as people talk about their families, and think about follow-up questions you can use to get more.

Say that in the course of talking about the photo of Johnny and his dog, for instance, Johnny's mom mentions that Johnny was home from school that day because of an asthma attack. That should be your cue to ask whether Johnny gets frequent attacks. In addition to wanting to know about Johnny, you're gaining information that could be valuable about Johnny's mom.

Asthma can be a serious condition in kids, and if Johnny is prone to frequent attacks, it could be that Johnny's mom is going to have to miss some workdays to take care of him. It would be within your rights, now that the door is open, to ask whether Johnny's under a doctor's care, what happens when the attacks occur, and so forth.

Photos can tell you all kinds of interesting things. If Roger's three kids are pictured wearing the uniforms of the area Catholic school, you can assume that's where they attend. If another picture shows them in soccer uniforms, you can assume they're on a team.

Obviously, your workers are extremely attached to their families, and very interested in their hobbies and outside-work activities. You can build relationships by inquiring about their interests and affirming their attachments to their families.

If you and your workers can maintain a healthy balance between work and personal concerns, chances are good that you'll have a happy, motivated team.

Investigations Are Us

When problems crop up in the workplace, which they inevitably will, prudent leaders recognize the value of a well-planned and thought out fact-finding procedure. Especially in the case of serious problems such as charges of corporate wrongdoing or misconduct, fact-finding is necessary and the smart thing to do.

What is fact-finding? It's just what it says. It's finding out all the facts pertinent to a particular situation. You've got to be a boss, detective, and lawyer all rolled into one to conduct a really effective fact-finding session.

Defining Moments

Fact-finding is the process of gathering all the facts that pertain to a certain situation. It's used in various instances, including investigations into charges of wrongdoing.

If you receive a complaint that wrongdoing has occurred, you'll need to conduct an investigation in a timely manner. Your response to the complaint should be immediate but tempered. Avoid knee-jerk reactions, in which you act before fully understanding what has occurred. If you don't, you could find yourself in big trouble.

The old adage "Look before you leap" applies here.

Take for example, the case of a company executive who was fired after discussing a risqué TV sitcom episode with a female co-worker. His co-worker had accused him of harassment, leading to his termination.

The executive took his employer to court and won a $26 million jury verdict for wrongful discharge and defamation.

In another case, an employee was fired when an investigator accused him of stealing a company telephone. It turned out that the employee owned the phone. His claim of wrongful discharge and defamation netted him a $15 million jury verdict. So you see, "look before you leap" is good advice.

Who Should Investigate?

When someone brings a complaint to your door, who should conduct the investigation? In a potentially serious matter, you probably will need to bring in qualified legal counsel to work with others on the investigative team.

Who else will be needed is somewhat dependent upon the circumstances. If a female employee complains of sexual harassment, for example, then you need to have a mixed-gender team. Hopefully, you've got procedures in place that dictate what you'd do in a case like this. If not, you should.

Be sensitive to the issue at hand when you assign people to conduct interviews. In this case, a woman might be a better choice to do at least the initial interviews with the complainant.

In other cases, technical expertise may be crucial in your choice of an investigator. If there's an environmental problem creating a work hazard, for instance, you'll need a knowledgeable engineer on the team.

Don't neglect to get legal advice when you're looking at a potentially serious situation. If you're not sure, ask. And select an impartial investigator, either from inside or outside the company, who is suitable to handle the subject matter.

How to Investigate

Interviews with employees should be conducted in private settings that are conducive to confidentiality and discretion. Interviews may have to take place outside of your offices.

When somebody brings a complaint, charging another person with wrongdoing, you'll need to get the complaint in writing. This can be a written statement or some form of incident report. Ask the person making the complaint, and the one accused of the wrongdoing, if there are any witnesses to the alleged incident.

Keep all investigations confidential. This is particularly important when they involve complaints of employee misconduct such as dishonesty or sexual harassment.

Be aware that these types of situations can put a manager between the complainant and the accused and their conflicting rights.

Ask them both, as well as all others involved, to sign confidentiality agreements before they're interviewed.

Separate the investigating function from the decision-making function. Your impartial investigator should issue a report of findings, and maybe even make recommendations to the decision-maker. This normally would be an executive, who then decides what to do. All steps should be recorded in writing.

The Least You Need to Know

➤ Smart managers and bosses will work to accommodate valuable workers' personal needs, with the intent to keep them happy, motivated, and invested in the company.

➤ If you ask one of your team members about a personal problem or issue, be prepared to hear more than you might want to.

➤ Thanks to technology, office snooping has risen to new levels; but it still won't endear you to your workers.

➤ Gathering information is primarily a matter of keeping your eyes and ears open all the time.

➤ Workers give you all kinds of signs when something's going on in their lives; all you have to do is be observant.

Chapter 19

100 Percent Guaranteed Turnoffs

In This Chapter

➤ Universal morale busters

➤ Characteristics that really bug employees

➤ Breaking confidences: one of the biggest turnoffs

➤ Responding to workers' concerns and needs

➤ Giving credit where credit is due, and accepting blame all the time

➤ Finding out what your workers really want

While certain things have practically universal appeal—great works of art, beautiful spring days, and single malt scotches, for instance, other things are just about guaranteed to be turnoffs.

Among the category of "things that nobody likes" would be poison ivy, toothaches, repair bills, and you add your own least favorite things. In the workplace, there is another set of guaranteed turnoffs.

Ranking high on that list are creepy, arrogant bosses; insensitive, uncaring bosses; insincerity and phoniness; bosses who pass the buck or take credit for their teams' successes; and being blamed for something you didn't do.

Workers also hate poor communication, nonresponsive bosses, inadequate training, lousy pay, bosses who don't bother to find out what their workers want, bully bosses, and bosses who break confidences.

In this chapter, we'll look at some of these things that nearly all workers agree they don't like. These things are detrimental to the workplace because they can cause your team to lose their motivation and incentive.

Smart managers understand this, and they try to stay far away from the things that their workers hate. Apparently, however, many bosses are not so enlightened, or they don't succeed in their efforts to not alienate the members of their teams.

And workers are getting louder in their protests of what they perceive as unfair or just unenlightened treatment from their bosses.

In fact, there is a blossoming self-help movement among such workers. There are books, such as Bob Rosner's "*Working Wounded,*" in which the author addresses the biggest complaints of employees. There are websites, such as the Gripe Garage at www.os.co.za/gripe.htm and Is Your Company the Worst at www.bizblues.com, where workers can complain about their work situations and get advice and support from others with similar problems.

While workers are uniting to air their grievances and taking steps to improve their work situations, managers had better listen up and do everything they can to get their workers motivated and happy.

Let's have a look at some of the biggest complaints of workers, and what managers can do to work with them to improve the situation.

You Do the Work, and I'll Take the Money

The attitude of "you do the work, and I'll take the money" is one of the worst offenses a company can commit, and one of the biggest complaints of employees. Nothing builds resentment and major cynicism more quickly than the attitude that workers are nothing more than tools for building profit for company leaders.

We looked at the issue of the burgeoning pay gap between workers and top management in Chapter 14, and discussed how it demotivates workers. While many companies are getting more in tune with workers' wants by offering gain sharing, others are lagging behind.

I knew a guy who ran a small company with about 16 employees. This guy was never going to win a boss-of-the-year award, but he had one habit that was particularly obnoxious. He'd hire somebody at a decent salary, leave it in place for six months or so, and then cut it substantially—sometimes by a third or more. He'd tell people before he slashed their pay that the way they were doing their jobs didn't meet his expectations, or they weren't doing what their job descriptions called for, or that the business had taken a downward turn, or something like that.

Basically, though, the guy just wanted a bigger share of the pot for himself.

Here's How It Works

The same boss who habitually cut his employees' salaries had the nerve to buy a $1.2 million home, then ask some of his workers to help him move his belongings into it. While he was greatly resented, the employees who needed their jobs felt compelled to do what he asked them to. It was an ugly situation all around. If there was a list of the world's worst bosses, I'm pretty sure this guy would be on it.

He had a knack for hiring people who'd just been laid off, or were in some kind of financial trouble, or had pretty serious personal problems, or were in some way needy. He'd give them a job, only to kick them in the seat of the pants a few months later by taking away a big chunk of their salary.

Needless to say, the guy had tremendous turnover, the morale of his workers was the worst, and everybody hated him. It was a totally unmotivated workplace, and the business suffered terribly because of it.

Any employer who doesn't realize how important employees are to a company shouldn't be an employer. And any employer who isn't willing to give his employees decent pay for the work they perform is shortsighted and arrogant.

Consider the story of Ray Kroc, the inspiration behind the McDonald's hamburger chain. During the heavy growth years, Kroc made sure that many of the people working with him, particularly the franchisees who were helping to build his empire, got rich. Many of his helpers became millionaires before Kroc did.

Hey, You're Being Paid to Do Your Job

Even when workers are paid fairly to do their jobs, managers shouldn't assume that salary alone is enough to keep them motivated and happy. Too many bosses don't positively reinforce the good behavior they see. They have the attitude of "why should I give 'attaboys' to people for doing what they are paid to do?"

I've seen and heard this attitude among leaders far too often. Yeah, workers are being paid to do their jobs. But consider those who do more than they're asked to, try harder than their peers, and display positive, uplifting attitudes. If they're at the same level as their co-workers, they'll be making the same pay, even though they put more into the job than others do. You might not be able to give them more money, but you can let them know that you've noticed what they're doing with praise and encouragement.

253

Money alone might satisfy employees. But money by itself won't motivate them the way that money combined with positive reinforcement can.

Positive reinforcement assures that you'll get more of the behavior that you want. Knowing that, it makes no sense at all to me that many managers don't use it.

Backfire

If, for some reason, you don't believe in using positive reinforcement, then don't. If you don't like it, but you grudgingly use it because you think you should, your workers will see through you and your half-hearted attempts in a flash. Your efforts will lack authenticity, and you'll come off as a phony (more on that later in the chapter).

You've Gotta Lose the Attitude, Man

There are as many personalities as there are people to own them. The longer you're managing people, the more personalities you'll see.

You'll have folks who will do anything they can to please you, and you'll have those who couldn't care less whether you like what they do or not. There will be workers who are ambitious and hardworking, and others who will do the least amount of work possible. You'll get people who are smart, creative, and always looking for ways to do their jobs better. You'll get others who are dull and not interested in much of anything.

As a manager, you've got to figure out how to get along with and work with all of these people. That'll be a lot easier to do with some than with others. Let's face it: Some people are just more likable than others are.

As a leader, though, you can't degrade people for their personalities, or treat them differently than you might others.

Rally the Troops

Remember that attitudes aren't applicable to the work situation unless they are exhibited as behavior and causing work-related performance problems. If someone's attitudes remain separate from their job performance, they're of no relevance to the job situation.

If you find you just don't like Susie because of the annoying habit she has of whining when she speaks, that's your business. But if Susie is a good worker who never causes any trouble and does everything she's supposed to do, then your feelings about her are completely irrelevant as they pertain to her as an employee.

You don't have to invite her over for dinner (unless you invite everyone else) or schedule Sunday morning tennis matches with her (unless it's a team tournament or something). You do have to treat her just like you treat everyone else. And you need to work hard at getting over your problem with her personality.

Your concern should be with your workers' behaviors, not their personalities. Even if you know somebody's attitude is rotten, if it doesn't affect his job performance, it's not pertinent and you should ignore it.

If, on the other hand, the guy has a crummy attitude and doesn't do a thing to keep it under control while he's at work and has caused the team to perform poorly, then it could cause a problem. Remember though, that your employees are allowed to think whatever they want. It's only what they say or do that is relevant to your team.

Now that we've covered attitudes of employees, let's take just a minute to think about attitudes and personality traits of managers, and how they can serve to motivate, or demotivate, a team.

Cool, Aloof, and Arrogant

These three little characteristics are the absolute main reasons that seemingly effective leaders are nearly always eventually derailed.

These are the characteristics of leaders who completely separate themselves from their workers, making it perfectly clear that they share little in common with subordinates. They see their workers as useful tools for getting the job done, but want little to do with them beyond that.

This kind of manager would never ask a worker if his son is feeling better, or if he got things straightened out after the fender bender he had on his way home from work. He'll never notice that an employee has been looking really down for a few days and take a few minutes to find out why. He'd never comment on a new hairstyle, a significant weight loss, or a snazzy new winter coat.

Here's How It Works

Leaders who are cool, aloof, and arrogant often spend much of their time in their offices, where they can remain removed from the rest of the operation. When they do come out, or if you approach them, they'll often act disinterested in what's going on or in a hurry to get someplace else.

He keeps to himself, tending only to what directly concerns him and his chances of looking good to the big bosses.

Adolph Hitler is a perfect example of a leader who was cool, aloof, and arrogant, and completely detached from the society around him. Records suggest that while wreaking unbelievable evil and havoc throughout Europe, Hitler never once asked about German casualties of the war for which he was largely responsible. Records also show that when Germany was in final defeat, with its armies rapidly retreating toward Berlin, Hitler gave instructions that the retreating German armies were to kill all Germans left in the countryside. They were to burn all the homes and cities, and destroy all the crops and animals. In short, after being responsible for so much devastation in Europe, his final orders were to lay waste to his own country.

You can't build a team by being above the team. Like a good coach, you've got to get down in the mud with them. They've got to see you doing the same jobs you'll ask them to do. Some managers think this degrades them in the eyes of their workers, but that's not the case. They'll respect you a lot more for being genuine and not condescending than they would for being aloof and arrogant.

A Phony

If you pretend to be just one of the gang but secretly think that you've got everything over the people you're managing, your secret won't be one for very long.

Workers see through phony leaders in a heartbeat. Did you ever meet somebody who comes off at first as being really interested in you, only to find out later that he really couldn't care less?

These are the people who ask how you're doing, if everything is okay, or if there's anything you need. If you respond, however, you quickly notice that they're not listening. If forced to acknowledge your response, they'll do so very quickly and shallowly because they don't care. They ask you questions, hoping to establish some kind of rapport, or maybe just to show you what good leaders they are. But they don't care what your answers are.

If your people can't trust you as being genuine, you're going to have an extremely difficult time earning their respect and cooperation. It's hard to believe anything that a phony says or does because you can't be sure that his intentions are what he's trying to make you think they are.

Rally the Troops

Just as the playground bully's outward behavior often is an attempt to cover up some inward insecurity, bully bosses might act mean and tough to compensate for some lack. Many people who have no business being there somehow get themselves into positions of authority. They may employ bully tactics to cover up the fact that they're scared to death to be in a position they know they can't handle.

A Bully

Let's face it. As unfortunate as it is, there are some bosses who act like they're still the biggest, meanest kids on the playground. They love to tell everyone what to do, and make it perfectly clear that they're the head honchos. They lead by intimidation.

I know a guy who runs a gas station. He's perfectly charming to his customers, but he's an absolute jerk to his employees. He treats them like they're stupid kids (which he really feels that they are), yells at them, and orders them around just to let them know he's in charge.

Needless to say, this guy has a lot of trouble keeping employees—especially good ones. When he gets a good worker, he'll try to tone down for a while, but eventually, his bully personality reveals itself. It's too bad, because he's basically a very nice guy. He just doesn't have the necessary skills to handle his workers the way he should, so the best ones are always leaving to work someplace else. He's severely damaging his business with his attitude.

Insensitive

Sensitivity seems to be so easy for some people and so difficult for others. If you find yourself in the latter camp, this might be something you want to work on.

This doesn't mean that you need to sit around in a circle with the members of your team, getting in touch with your inner selves and revealing your deepest fears and aspirations.

It just means that you should try to be aware of, and in touch with, what's going on with your people. If somebody's spouse is very sick and requires constant care during the last weeks of life, it would be completely insensitive to ask that person to put in extra hours during the week and work half a day on Saturday.

It's difficult to believe that any boss would be *that* insensitive, but someone who doesn't know anything about the people who work for him might run the risk.

Being Nonresponsive

Some leaders expect the members of their team to jump through hoops for them but are reluctant to respond when asked to do something in return.

If you demand a lot from your team, be willing and prepared to give the equivalent of what you ask for in return. If you make it clear that employee reports are due every Friday, then do something with the report by Monday. Don't let it sit in your in basket forever. If it's not important enough for you to deal with quickly, then don't bother asking for it.

When your employees ask something from you, be sure that you respond quickly to their requests. If you can't give complete answers right away, give at least partial answers to let them know you've received, and are considering their requests.

Backfire

Expecting a lot from your team is different than taking advantage of your team. If you expect a lot and are willing to do yourself what you ask from your workers, that's okay. But if you demand that your team does its work, and covers your tail by doing most of yours as well, that's taking advantage, and you're setting yourself up for big trouble.

If you demand that your team members clean up the work area every night before they leave to go home, then don't neglect their requests for extra tools to help them. And make sure your own office is clean as well.

Employees who feel they're doing all of the giving and none of the taking won't be happy and motivated workers. Good managers understand that their relationships with team members aren't any different than the relationships they have with other people in their lives. All relationships require give and take. A one-way relationship is an unhealthy one, and it can't last.

Those are some of the attitudes and personality traits that are guaranteed to turn off employees, big time. If you think one or more of them might apply to you, give the situation a good look, and plan for improvement.

But You Said You Wouldn't Tell Anyone!

Breaking confidences is one of the worst offenses a leader can commit. Never, never break a confidence. To do so is to risk ruining any degree of trust between you and your employees. It also just about guarantees that you'll get no more information.

We spent considerable time on secrets in Chapter 15, so we won't get too involved with it again now. If somebody comes to you with a confidence, make sure it remains a confidence.

Backfire

If you do mess up and betray a confidence, and you're found out, you'll have to work hard over a period of time to rebuild the trust you've broken. Be careful that you don't make the situation worse by getting defensive or trying to make excuses for what you've done. That kind of behavior will only further alienate the person whose trust you've betrayed.

There's a danger in not realizing that what somebody tells you is considered a confidence. If you're not sure—ask. In fact, I'd say that if you have any doubt at all whether or not a piece of information is confidential, make sure you find out. If you're not sure, assume it's confidential until you learn otherwise.

If you think it would be beneficial for someone else to hear the information, ask permission first from the person who gave it to you.

For instance, if Sue tells you in confidence that Jack has been very persistent in asking her out and seems to be getting annoyed that she refuses to go, it's natural that you'd want to do something to resolve the situation and help Sue.

Before you charge down the hall to the human resources director, however, make sure you pull Sue aside and ask her permission to do so.

Explain to her that you'd never reveal what she told you in confidence, except that you think that by doing so, you can get the situation taken care of. If she absolutely refuses to have you do so, you're in a tough spot. You still can take action if you want to, but it would be more difficult and create a sticky situation between you and Sue.

You could make a point of being more observant of Jack and Sue, and citing incidents when Jack isn't doing his job. Jump on him for job-related issues, not for bothering Sue. Don't worry, he'll get the point.

Chances are, however, that Sue is somewhat worried about the situation or she wouldn't have come to you in the first place. She'll probably be glad to have it resolved.

Just be sure you do the right thing, and ask her first.

Passing the Buck

A big gripe among workers is managers who don't take responsibility for what goes wrong, doesn't get done, or doesn't get done properly.

It's an unfortunate fact sometimes that the responsibility for what happens among your team is on you. You might not be directly responsible, but ultimately, it's all on your shoulders. If something goes wrong, you've got to be willing to stand up, acknowledge the problem, and take the blame for it.

If you can't do this, then you haven't got what it takes to be a leader. Just as parents have to bear responsibility for what their young children do, good leaders must be responsible for their workers. If a four-year-old comes into a department store with her parents, takes off at top speed for the fine china department, and breaks a $500 serving platter while her parents chat with some acquaintances in the center aisle, who should pay for the broken piece? The store? The child? The parents?

Most people would agree that the parents bear responsibility for the damage. And as a manager, you've got to bear responsibility for what goes wrong, even if someone else directly caused the problem or the damage. You can't pass the buck off on someone else.

Conversely, if something exceptional happens within your department, you've got to be willing to pass along the credit. Leaders take the blame, but they give the credit to their teams. Good leadership speaks for itself. Everyone knows who coaches the teams who win the Super Bowls and World Series.

Rally the Troops

Happily giving credit to your team when it does something particularly well is a great way to demonstrate that you're a caring and enlightened leader. An insecure person will try to grab credit for himself, but an effective manager understands that giving it to his workers will further encourage and motivate them to perform.

If there's a company-wide luncheon to honor your department for meeting every shipping date for six months, for instance, you certainly can smile and accept the certificate. You've got to immediately point out, however, that credit for the achievement goes completely to the members of your team.

You were the facilitator, but your team made it happen.

Lousy Communication

Only a very tiny percentage of people in the workplace are psychics who can know what their managers want them to do without being told.

The rest need clear instruction. Bosses too often expect their teams to fall into place and do their jobs without ever making it clear what those jobs are and how they're to be done.

Backfire

Be sure that you communicate the same information and expectations to all workers. Team meetings are the preferred setting for sharing common information because you can be sure that everyone is getting the same word. If you pass out information in bits and pieces to one or two people at a time, you risk mix-ups and confusion.

If you're willing to give your team time to figure it out and to do their jobs the way team members think they should be done, okay. Stand back and let them work. If you're like most managers, however, and you have a vision of how the job should be performed and what the results should be, then by all means, share it with the members of your team. You'll get the most motivated team when you focus on the vision and let them focus on the process. If, on the other hand, you have a certain way that things have to be done, let your workers know that up front, and explain your reasons for needing it done that way.

Workers who aren't adequately informed of your expectations become extremely frustrated when you tell them they're not living up to what you want from them. Recognize the importance of communication, and make sure you keep them informed.

Not Bothering to Find Out What Your Team Wants

You can think you're offering the best working conditions in your whole state, but if they're not what your workers want, then what's the point?

I know a boss who owned a company with clients nationwide. The firm was located in Pennsylvania, which meant it ran on Eastern Standard Time (EST).

It wasn't a bad idea to have employees in the office until 8 p.m. to take calls from clients in western states who were operating two or three hours behind. Most of what happened between 5 and 8 p.m. EST was troubleshooting and taking messages. The person assigned to stay was pretty much there to assure clients that the applicable person would return their call the next day, or to notify the applicable person if necessary.

The boss insisted that everyone, from the top manager to the receptionist, take a turn in the late-night rotation. There were three or four people who loved the later hours, but most of the workers hated having to stay. It was a huge issue, and morale was being badly undermined by it.

Rally the Troops

When trying to motivate your team, take some time to find out what motivates it. Find out what kind of things matter to team members, and use them as tools to motivate. You'll get much better results and won't end up spinning your wheels wondering why your motivating strategies aren't working.

Worker representatives suggested all kinds of options—a phone system that would forward the calls to their homes, a more sophisticated voice mail system, temporary workers to fill in on the night hours, and so forth. The people who enjoyed working the later hours volunteered to shift their work schedules and work late every night. The boss refused all of the suggestions, saying it would cost too much or wouldn't be effective.

In order to appease his staff, he tried to make the late hours more appealing. Those who worked the 5-to-8 shift got an extra hour off during the day. They weren't required to show up until 1 p.m. The boss provided dinner from one of the nearby restaurants for those staying late and allowed workers to do whatever they wanted to between phone calls.

While trying to give his workers what he thought they wanted, this boss undermined himself and his company without doing a thing for the morale of the workers. All those extra hours added up. Clients couldn't reach the people they needed to talk to. It cost the company a lot of money in lost time—not to mention all those dinners. And the employees still resented having to stay until 8 p.m.

If this boss had been smart, he would have taken all the money he spent on this wayward project and either given incentive pay to workers willing to work late or hired someone to work that specific shift. He tried hard, and he wasted a lot of resources trying to mollify his staff, but he failed because he didn't listen to what the workers really wanted. If he had listened, and had let his team help get a system set up, he could have saved a lot of time and money, and made his workers and customers happy.

The Least You Need to Know

➤ There are some things we do as managers that are practically guaranteed to be morale busters.

➤ Money by itself might keep workers quiet, but it may take more than money to motivate them.

➤ The attitudes of your team members aren't relevant to the workplace, but their behavior is.

➤ Take a look at your own attitude, and assess whether there are areas in which you could use some improvement.

➤ There are certain characteristics in bosses that employees absolutely hate.

➤ Breaking confidences is arguably the worst offense a boss can commit.

➤ You've got to be responsive to the needs and concerns of your workers.

➤ Be ready and willing to take the blame for your team's shortcomings, and to hand all the credit over to team members.

➤ Make an effort to find out what your team really wants in order to avoid wasting time and resources on things that won't help to motivate.

Part 5

Putting It All into Motion

Once you've learned what motivation is, and how to create it and keep it among your workers, you should be aware of some motivational challenges you might run into along the way.

Layoffs, pay cuts, and closings are major roadblocks to keeping your team motivated, and this section will tell you how to deal with those kinds of situations. You'll also learn how to cope with motivational threats created by—believe it or not—prosperity. And how to keep the status quo—another motivation buster—at bay.

You'll also learn about handling high performers and difficult employees, each of which will require different motivational methods.

And you'll discover that the best leaders often are more like coaches than bosses.

Getting the Team Going

As a leader, it's up to you to get your team going. It's your job to help your workers develop skills, and to make them want to do their jobs the very best they can.

How do you achieve these goals? With motivation, of course. When your team is motivated, they will want to perform to their greatest capacity. They will want to do the job well, and they will be inspired to come up with ways to improve how the job is done. You've got to cause your team to transcend the expected and reach beyond what's normally expected.

Some leaders don't encourage motivation among the members of their teams. In fact, some leaders discourage motivation, even to the point of not allowing it. They don't give their workers the capacity for motivation.

To those of us who are enlightened (and you wouldn't be reading this book if you weren't), this seems completely ridiculous. What in the world would a boss stand to gain by keeping her team uninspired and unmotivated?

Well, you'll get the answer if you reread a couple of paragraphs up. An inspired and motivated team will want to perform to their greatest capacity. They will want to do the job well and come up with ways to improve it.

You've probably known leaders who would be very threatened by this type of behavior from their teams. Some bosses don't like change, and they're threatened by individuals on the team who suggest changes. If the boss lacks the inspiration and motivation to grow and improve along with his team, she may try to keep her team down so it won't rise above her level.

Of course, this ultimately brings everyone down. This type of leader usually doesn't last very long. That kind of leadership is unfair to the team that wants to find better ways of doing the job and it's unfair to the company because it impedes its progress.

An inspired and motivated leader serves as a coach to inspire and motivate her team. There are a lot of similarities between the leadership of business and sports.

A good leader is a superior coach who incites her team to rise to the contest at hand. Like any superior sports coach, the inspired leader challenges and motivates her team to compete. In many ways, she operates just like the sports coach, but because she's in business, she has more flexibility. The good business leader defines the game and many of the rules. He defines the competitive challenge and sells the challenge to his team.

In this chapter, we'll look at how you can be an effective coach to motivate and get your team going. We'll talk about some of the potential pitfalls of coaching a team, and how you can skirt them or deal with them head-on to overcome them. Okay, coach. Let's get started.

Being a Good Coach

If you're going to coach a team, you'll want to do it well. What I'd like you to do is take a few minutes and think about the personality of your company, and, more specifically, the personality of your team.

I'm not talking about the personalities of the individual employees—we already learned that only behavior, not individual personality, is relevant to the workplace. I'm talking about the overall personality of your team. Every team has one. In the business world, it's known as company culture. It's the attitudes and beliefs that form the basis on which your company, or team, is run. It's the way that you do things.

You usually get a feeling of the culture of a particular company or team almost immediately. Some are happy places, and it's obvious from the time you walk in the door. Employees are pleasant, and obviously enjoying what they're doing. The place is relaxed, and, while everyone is working hard, nobody is frantic and stressed out.

Other companies, though, aren't happy, and it's obvious. You'll see miserable, bored-looking people sitting in cubicles or working on the floor. You'll hear people whispering about other employees—or their bosses. These are not happy places; they're just places where work occurs. The work is focused around so-called "correct" procedures, and there's little room for any kind of creativity. Management is from the top down, and there's no room for suggestions or ideas from the bottom up. While these places aren't happy, they're usually not too productive or profitable, either.

Your goal as a coach is to make sure your team has the right personality. You, as the coach, will set the tone for the personality. Some characteristics to work toward include:

➤ A happy team in a happy place

➤ A team that's loyal to its purpose and its members

➤ A positive team with a can-do attitude

➤ An optimistic team

➤ A creative team that's always finding a better way

➤ A satisfied team

➤ A forward-looking team that understands its mission and vision

➤ A cooperative team that supports its members, above all else

Defining Moments

Company culture is the collective set of attitudes and beliefs that influence and direct the way your team operates. It's the force that powers your team to work. Every company and team has a culture, but not every one is as positive as it should be.

When you combine all these characteristics, you get a productive team. And, that should be your ultimate goal.

If you can instill you team with these characteristics, you and your team will enjoy the benefits of a positive business personality. If you have those things, your team will run more smoothly, you'll enjoy it more, and, as its coach, you'll have infinitely more satisfaction.

A Good Coach Is a Leader

Being an effective leader certainly is one of the most important characteristics of a coach. In fact, it's practically inconceivable that someone who's not a strong leader would ever be a coach. But believe me, it happens.

A coach who's not a leader is like a parent who gives his children free reign to do whatever they want. He declines to set ground rules because he wants his kids to be happy with him. He doesn't punish, because there are no rules, and, as a result, no infractions. He doesn't instill values, because he finds it difficult to identify any within himself that are worth passing along. The parent may do things differently if he realized that kids want rules. It's been proven again and again that kids are more likely to thrive when they have clear guidelines and rules. As it is, the parent simply doesn't have it within him to take charge and do the job of parenting.

Here's How It Works

Just as every team has a personality, so does every coach. If you've ever played on a sports team, think about different coaches you had and how they handled the job. A coach's personality isn't necessarily his personality as an individual. As with a corporate personality, a coach's personality is the result of his ideals, values, and attitudes concerning the job.

Well, you get the idea, and you certainly could predict the results. All you'd get from that kind of situation is a mixed-up kid, and a parent with a whole lot of problems on his hands.

A good coach is a leader who's not afraid to set and enforce ground rules, discipline when necessary, and make everyone understand the reasons behind the rules and punishments.

Consider the following characteristics of a good coach:

➤ A good coach is a teacher.

➤ A good coach has and can communicate wisdom.

➤ A good coach is equally proficient at working with the entire team, and at giving individual, personalized instruction where needed.

➤ A good coach understands how all the parts fit together to make a whole. She knows how the efforts of each person on her team affect the overall outcome. She knows the strengths and weaknesses of her team members, and works to minimize the weaknesses while cultivating the strengths.

➤ A good coach is available to team members whenever they need her.

➤ A good coach is not afraid to give advice and offer guidance.

➤ A good coach has learned from her own experience, and uses that experience to direct the team.

A coach who has and displays these characteristics will be a good leader, one who has the ability and confidence to direct and guide her team. She won't be afraid to call the necessary plays and to enforce the rules of the game.

A Good Coach is a Motivator

Being an effective motivator is essential for a coach. If a coach can't motivate, how does he ever get his team pumped up for a game, or even get the members to show up for practice?

Motivation is the name of the game. All leaders—coaches and managers included— have different styles of leadership. Some are laid back, while others are intense. There are as many styles of leadership as there are leaders. No two people will do it quite the same way.

Workers will respond differently to various styles of leadership. Some people enjoy being around those who are outgoing and vivacious, while others are more comfortable with a calm, quiet person. If you're an effective leader, your troops will adjust to and work well within your style of leadership.

Let's review a few of the characteristics a person must have in order to be an effective motivator.

Backfire

Remember that as a leader or coach, you must earn the right to lead—don't assume that it's yours automatically. If you're not recognized and acknowledged as the leader, your team won't look to you for guidance and direction. You've got to prove to your team that you're worthy of leadership before members will let you lead. If you try to take control without earning it first, you'll generate resentment and disrespect among your team.

➤ **Accepted.** If the boss is not accepted as a leader, he won't have the power to motivate.

➤ **Authentic.** Phonies can't motivate.

➤ **Respected.** This is different than being liked.

➤ **Fair.** Motivation can't occur in unfair conditions.

➤ **Empathetic.** A boss who motivates is one who understands and appreciates the concerns of her employees.

➤ **Motivated.** An unmotivated leader will never motivate a team.

Take a look at yourself, and see if you need to improve in any of these areas. See how these characteristics, or lack of them, affect your style of leadership and your ability to motivate.

Motivators assume that their teams will do the job. They focus on the positive side, and build into the goals. They convince team members to strive forward, and they display great confidence in their teams. They trust their teams to do their parts, and allow them to fail when necessary.

A Good Coach Is a Big Brother or Sister

Anyone who has a big brother or sister recognizes the polarity of the big brother/little brother or big sister/little sister relationship.

On the one hand, you can't stand to be around the big brother or sister just because that's who he or she is. The very quality of being older gives a big brother or sister license to boss you around, tell you you're dumb, make fun of you, and constantly remind you of his or her superiority.

Rally the Troops

Encourage big brother/big sister relationships, not only between you and the members of your team, but among the members of your team as well. You'll nearly always have situations where one worker will take another under his or her wing, and become a sort of mentor, or act in a big brother or big sister role. While you'll be the ultimate big brother or sister, these supporting relationships can be very helpful and useful.

On the other hand, if some kid from the neighborhood starts picking on you or giving you a hard time, who's going to be there to tell the kid to take a hike and leave you alone? Right. Big bro or sis. If you fall and cut your knee and Mom's not around, who are you going to go to for help with patching up the wound? Right again. And, as you get older and you're wrestling with the tribulations of life, who's you going to look to for advice and encouragement? Big brother or sister.

As a leader and coach, you're called upon to display the latter set of big brother/big sister characteristics. You've got to be an advocate for your workers if they're not getting a fair shake.

You've got to help patch up the wounds and make them feel better when something goes wrong. And you've got to be there to offer advice and encouragement when you're asked.

What you can't do is indiscriminately boss people around. You can tell your workers what to do, but you've got to do it in a way that won't alienate them.

You absolutely cannot tell your workers, or even imply in any way, that they're dumb or inferior. And, you never, never make fun of a worker, either in front of him or behind his back. You surely can imagine how that would undermine the morale of your team and make your coaching ineffective. Remember, the most important factor in motivating people is to constantly focus on the positive and the best things that people do.

A good coach has all the desirable qualities of a big brother or sister, but none of the negative ones. As you establish this kind of relationship with your workers, you'll find that they'll gain respect for you, and look up to you. They'll come to you for guidance, and they'll want to please you.

You'll be important to them, as they are to you. When you establish this kind of bond, your workers will become motivated to do their best for you and each other.

The Importance of Leadership When Working with a Team

We already talked about how important it is for a coach to be a leader, but why is leadership so important to a team?

Think about what happens on a team that doesn't have strong, clear-cut leadership. Because there's not one person who's clearly recognized as the leader, you often get different factions competing for the role.

In simple terms, this is known as a power struggle.

In order to establish clear leadership, you must have the characteristics of a leader that were mentioned earlier in this chapter. And you've got to make it clear, both through communicating your position and leading by example, that you're in charge. This will establish your role and eliminate the possibility of any kind of power struggle.

As a coach who understands the importance of leadership, you've got to keep an eye on the relationships between members of your team.

There will always be strains in the seams of relationships. It's your job to make sure they don't tear and come apart. When you hear sniping among your team about one member or another, avoid getting involved. If it's becoming a morale problem, you'll have to deal with it by making it's clear that such talk won't be tolerated.

Whatever you do, never, never join in. Never talk negatively to any member of your team about any other team member. You can talk about what other workers do, but you can't make who they are an issue.

As a leader or coach, you've got to remain above or in front of your team. You're part of the team; there's no question about it. You must, however, remain on a different level.

Your job as a coach is to help your team put together the pieces that will result in the whole picture. You've got to make team members understand how their parts play into the overall

Defining Moments

Whenever there's control to be had, there will be people who want to get it. If there's not a clear leader in place, there will be people who compete for the position. This will result in a **power struggle.**

Rally the Troops

With people being people, you'll almost never get 100 percent cooperation and camaraderie among the members of your team. There's bound to be some sniping and backstabbing that occurs. Don't expect the members of your team to be angels and get along perfectly all the time. Deal with it if it becomes a morale problem, but stay above it whenever you can.

scheme of things. You've been in their situation, and your job is to help them deal with it and do the best job possible.

When somebody needs extra help, you've got to make sure he or she gets it. If not, it will drag down the collective performance of the team. In order to help, you've first got to recognize when somebody's having a problem. Keeping your ears and eyes open will allow you to do that.

If everybody's working together and doing fine except the catcher, you've got to take some extra time to work with the catcher. He'll need personal attention and instruction until he's back on par with the rest of the team.

It's extremely important to make sure that everyone's strong. A baseball team without a good catcher can't be a really good team.

Creating Plans That You'll Really Use

As the coach of your team, it's your job to plan for it. You'll need plans to move ahead for the future, plans to complete tasks, plans for how to most effectively use your people, plans for how to realize goals, and so on.

You've got to plan which players will play the different positions, and how they'll be trained.

Rally the Troops

A type of plan that many people find to be effective is backdating. Backdating is particularly useful when planning for long-range goals or events. To backdate, you start at where you want to be at a certain point in time. Then, working backward from that date, you plot all intermediate goals and the dates at which they must be met. When you finish, you've got a roadmap to that big goal farther down the road.

While plans can be valuable and necessary tools, they can bog you down if you let them. It's important to know the best kinds of plans to use, and to be able to implement them so they become meaningful. The best plan in the world is useless if it's never put into place.

If your plans are overly complicated or too simplistic, they'll soon be abandoned. If they aren't relevant to what's going on, your workers will ignore them.

If plans are well thought out and prepared, however, they can be indispensable roadmaps that guide you and your team to your destinations.

Making Plans for the Sake of Plans

Plans that are made just for the sake of planning will be of little use to anyone. If a boss insists that you come up with a plan for your team, you have a couple of choices.

You can sit down and carefully and deliberately come up with a useable plan that your team will be able to follow in order to reach its goals.

Or, if you think your boss is looking for a plan just for the sake of having it, you can give her what she's asking for—a plan that's made just for the sake of having it.

There must be millions of these plans sitting on shelves all around the world. They're of little value to the companies for which they were made, and of no value at all to the workers around whom the plans were designed.

If you're forced to make a plan that you know is just for the sake of having a plan, don't spend a lot of time or energy on it. You won't be using it, and it won't benefit your team. There's no point in planning elaborate, complicated running and passing plays if they're never going to be put into action.

Making a Plan That Works

A valuable and living plan is public and visible. It's not one that gets stuck on the shelf and forgotten, but instead is a plan that everyone has access to and understands. It's the game plan that hangs on the bulletin board in the locker room for everybody to read before they suit up.

It's also a plan that works in real time. It establishes goals, and spells out the means for reaching those goals. A good plan is a measuring system that prescribes what and how much of certain ingredients are needed to come up with a finished product. It really is a recipe for success.

A plan—even a good plan—on its own will not produce an organization or a team that's more customer responsive, more competitive or productive, or better run. A plan by itself can't improve the value of your balance sheet.

A living, results-oriented planning system, however, that's built around the involvement of your team, will largely contribute to all those things. A plan that's well implemented, generally understood, easy to use and follow, and faithfully tracked, can be a powerful tool for your team and your company.

Keep the following suggestions in mind concerning the design, implementation, and carrying out of plans for your team.

> **Defining Moments**
>
> Think of all the instances in which we use **plans**. We write business plans, five-year-plans, and expansion plans. We enroll in retirement plans and savings plans, and make travel plans. Plans are an integral part of what we accomplish in many areas.

> ➤ Use time lines that are long enough so that everyone involved can see the overall direction, goals, and purpose of the department, division, or entire company. Activities to be accomplished should reflect the overall goals, as well as demonstrate how individual performance relates to the total plan.

273

➤ Be sure to clearly identify responsibility for various parts of the plan. All key, customer-focused activities that are to be accomplished should be clearly listed. These activities should reflect the overall corporate goals over a period of time. Activities should be adjusted as necessary and team members should be assigned responsibility to particular activities—not activities assigned to team members.

➤ As a good coach, you need to make sure that everyone on your team is invested in the plan and understands that they share responsibility for it. For planning to be meaningful, it must change and grow along with the organization.

➤ Useful planning must be adjusted to reflect daily events. What happens from day to day must be factored in and accounted for when designing and reviewing a plan.

➤ Short-range plans are much more predictable than long-range ones. Keep that in mind as your make your plans, and remember that long-range ones tend to change as circumstances do. Meetings can serve as a unifying concept defining a team as a collective unit.

➤ Remember that the competitive world of business is not always predictable, and it's very difficult to chart clear paths. Don't become so dependent on a plan that you can't cope with changes as they occur.

Putting Your Workers in the Driver's Seat

Sporting events lose much of their appeal without the presence of a centrally located, always-visible scoreboard.

You can have players making spectacular shots all over the basketball court, but it's not as much fun if you don't have a means of keeping track of what's going on and who's winning. The scoreboard keeps us involved in the game by telling us how our team is doing.

It's the same idea with the corporate plan. It has little meaning if those who must implement it aren't involved with its development, coordination, and modification. Watching a corporate plan that you've had no say in play out is like watching a team play ball, but not understanding what's going on, the rules of the game, or who's winning.

While you need to be involved with the design and implementation of the plan, your workers also need to have a say.

We can never forget, as coaches and leaders, how important our workers are to the success or failure of the company. Everyone who will be affected by a plan should be aware of how the plan is made and how it will be carried out. Input should be encouraged.

People usually can produce better ideas, plans, solutions, and decisions when working in groups than when working separately. Give team members the opportunity to do their best work by allowing them to work together.

Team meetings are useful because they serve to help members create commitment to decisions reached, and better identify the objectives that are being pursued. A good meeting will assure that everyone is on the same page, because everyone will be getting the same information at the same time.

You can alternate leaders for your team meetings, giving various members opportunity to set an agenda, run the meeting, and compile results afterward.

As coach, you should focus your management attention on the goals and objectives, and let your team handle the process-related issues. Focus on direction, and let the team decide the steps to take to get there. Once you've made sure your team understands the overall picture, and knows where you're going, then stand back and let team members implement the plan, to a large extent.

Rally the Troops

Within a team of workers, or a team of players, or any team, informal group leaders eventually evolve. This is something of which you should be aware, and that you need to watch. You shouldn't, however, acknowledge the leaders publicly. It's one thing for the members of your team to recognize an informal leader, but it's something else entirely for the manager to do the same thing. Your role as manager is to be a coach and counselor to the total team, and to treat all the members as individuals.

When the team is involved in plan implementation and decision making, there is greater support for the final decisions.

All of these things empower the members of your team, make them more invested in their work, and keep them motivated.

Handling Disputes and Conflicts

Generally, you'll have to deal with two types of conflict: inter-group and intra-group.

Inter-group conflict occurs when different teams begin to compete with each other for scarce resources.

Intra-group conflict occurs when members of the same team encounter difficulty with one another.

Your role as a coach is to observe, gather information, help group members formulate concepts, and support your team. Remember that you're a coach—not a referee. Don't get in the middle of either type of these conflicts. Once you do, you'll find it's difficult to get out.

It's important that everyone on your team understands the importance of having good conflict resolution skills. In other words, team members won't always get along, but they have to be able to work it out when they don't.

Don't panic when you encounter conflicts and disputes. Remember that most people get over arguments fairly easily. If your team is motivated, members will figure out how to put aside their differences in view of the overall goal.

The Least You Need to Know

➤ A coach must have the confidence to build up and improve his team, even if it threatens to surpass him.

➤ As a coach, you need to be a leader, a motivator, and a big brother or big sister.

➤ Effective planning is a vital component to being a good coach, but the plans must be useable and useful.

➤ Get everyone involved with making and carrying out plans.

➤ There are some rules to keep in mind and follow when making and using plans.

➤ Understanding how and why conflict occurs will help you to deal with it more effectively.

Motivating the High Performer

Every team should be fortunate enough to include at least one high performer among its ranks. High performers tend to be high-energy go-getters who can help you to get and keep your team motivated.

They're the ones who are always looking for, and often finding, better ways of doing things. They'll get the job done faster and better than everyone else. They're always busy, they don't complain, and they never say "no" to new assignments and responsibilities.

High performers are the workers who move quickly through the ranks, bypassing managers and supervisors on their way to the top. Many high performers are regarded with suspicion and distrust because they threaten those who sit complacently in their job positions. High performers are easily recognizable and well worth watching and cultivating.

Nearly all successful businesspeople—for that matter, nearly all successful people—are high performers. Regardless of whether they were handed a business on a silver platter or worked their way from the bottom up, it takes a high performer to succeed at running a business.

High performers are confident, and they're not afraid to take risks. If they fail, they're not afraid to try again because they believe in themselves. They're often the workers who will go out on their own to start and grow their own businesses. If you're lucky enough to have one on your team, consider yourself fortunate.

Normally, high performers are pretty self-motivated. It's your job to channel their motivation, and make sure it's maintained and harnessed.

Why You Want Them on Your Team

There are many reasons for seeking out high performers for your team. One of the most important pertains directly to you.

One of the best leadership lessons I ever learned, years ago, is this: "Hire a threat." That means that you should hire someone who can replace you at any time. You definitely should go after the high performers.

Obviously, this is an extremely frightening thought for many leaders. Why hire someone who could, and may, take your job from you? It requires a lot of confidence to do that, but there's a very good reason why you should.

Having a high performer on your team who's able to take over your job makes you available for other promotions within the company. If a member of your team takes over your job, then presumably, someone will come up with something new for you to do.

Assuming you've been doing your job effectively as a leader, the logical solution is to advance you into another position when the high performer takes over yours. Of course, if you've been sitting in your office for the last six months reading Louis L'Amour novels and pretty much ignoring what's happening with your team, then yeah—I'd say you have something to worry about.

Because you're an enlightened and motivated leader, however, it's safe to assume that you'll advance within the company, along with the high performer who'll take your job.

High performers keep things within a company moving, and keep their leaders motivated and on top of what's going on. They provide an impetus for the whole team.

Some other reasons to seek out high performers for your team include the following:

➤ High performers will serve as informal leaders when you're not around. Again, this can be a daunting thought for a leader who's not secure in his position. If a member of your team can step in and take over for you at any given time, who's to say he can't step in and take over permanently? As you learned in the previous paragraphs, however, having someone on your team with that ability isn't necessarily a bad thing.

278

Here's How It Works

Two of the best reasons to have a high performer on your team are because he'll motivate the other members and will set an example for excellence. He can be of great value to you, working almost as a sort of unofficial partner in keeping the team inspired and working to its best ability.

➤ High performers will serve as your best sources of information. Because a high performer makes it his business to stay on top of things and know what's going on, he can be a great source of information. It's your job, as the leader of the team, to encourage him to share pertinent information with you.

➤ High performers will inspire the group and help to reduce discipline problems. Other members of the team tend to look up to and emulate high performers because they see them moving up and they want to do the same. Their energy, discipline, and motivation tend to be contagious.

➤ High performers can serve as mentors for other members of the team. Because they are confident and self-assured, high performers generally are willing to help others on the team. They are influential and willing to share what they've learned. This makes them extremely effective as mentors.

➤ High performers are great at finding new and better ways to do things. Because they're not afraid to go out on limbs and encounter some risks, high performers will come up with creative ideas for doing things better. If their ideas don't work out, they'll go back to work, undaunted, waiting to try again the next time.

Rally the Troops

Psychologists say that part of the reason high achievers excel at their jobs and in other areas of their lives is because they possess a high level of confidence. They believe they will be good at what they do. Keep an eye on the confidence levels of prospective employees when you're interviewing.

There are other reasons to seek out high performers, but these are some of the major ones. The hardest thing for a leader is to get over the notion that a high performer on your team is a threat. Try to look at these people as blessings, not curses. And be willing to let them move on.

A high performer who happens to be on your team isn't your property. Give him room to grow, and wish him luck when he moves onward and upward.

Understanding What Drives a High Performer

There are many factors that drive high performers, and of course, they vary from person to person. Some high performers are driven by personal needs, such as having to prove they can be successful. Perhaps they've lived in the shadows of older siblings or famous parents, and need to prove they can make it on their own. There are lots of individual reasons why people are driven to become high performers.

Some, however, including the ones listed below, are nearly universal.

➤ High performers feel a need to grow and develop, usually both personally and professionally. They aren't content to sit back and accept the status quo, but need to try new things and explore ideas. High performers tend to be creative. They see outside the lines, so to speak, and aren't afraid to be different from the others on their teams. This tends to set high performers apart from the rest of the team pretty quickly, and makes them easy to identify.

➤ High performers desire immediate recognition for jobs well done. While they're driven to stretch themselves and grow, they like the recognition that comes with their successes. They enjoy getting awards and being cited for the work they do.

➤ High performers have high confidence levels. Because they are confident about themselves, they're not afraid to try new ventures. They assume they'll succeed. This is a great benefit to high performers, because it keeps them motivated. These high confidence levels also serve as a form of self-fulfilling prophecies. High performers believe they'll succeed, and, more often than not, they do.

➤ High performers have high energy levels. They run at a faster speed than most people do, and they can go for long stretches at a time. This is a beneficial characteristic because it allows them to accomplish things that others wouldn't.

Rally the Troops

If you want to keep a high per-former in the company, be sure to keep an eye on her. Word spreads about this kind of employee, and she may find opportunities else-where.

➤ High performers enjoy taking risks. They're not afraid of failing, so they're willing to go out on a limb. If they do fail, they don't tend to dwell on their failures. They acknowledge it, then move ahead and come up with a better way for the next time around. High performers realize that to fail at something doesn't make them a failure. It merely means that some thing they tried to do hasn't worked, and they'll have to try another way.

How to Keep High Performers Excited About the Job

Because high performers tend to be creative types who need to keep growing and trying new things, keeping them excited about the job can be a challenge to their leaders.

So, how do you keep your high performers from taking their résumé over to the XYZ Company, your biggest competitor? Or leaving to start their own businesses?

Depending on the level of motivation, it could be difficult to keep a high achiever in one spot for very long. But, there are some things you can do to encourage them to stay, and to keep them excited and motivated about their work.

Basically, there are three ways to motivate high performers and keep them happy on the job. You need to challenge them, recognize them, and reward them. Let's look at how you can do those things, and the benefits of each method. Remember, though, that the three things normally work best in combination with one another.

Challenge Them

There are many ways to challenge workers. The challenge to you is to recognize those methods, and to take time to present the challenges to your high performers.

This sometimes is difficult to do because you need to pay attention to all your workers, not just the outstanding ones. It's similar to a teacher, who must find a way to keep students of different abilities moving ahead. Working at the level of the lowest group certainly will hold back the more advanced students. But, working everyone at the top level is sure to leave some of the class behind.

A good teacher, however, like a good leader, will find a way to accommodate different needs and abilities. A good teacher can organize different levels to work simultaneously on different projects and lessons, with each group working at its own level.

Backfire

When you have a high performer on your team, it can be tempting to try to elevate everyone else to her level. To do that would be a serious mistake. You need to recognize the abilities of each worker, and tailor jobs and tasks to those abilities. Just as kids in schools move along at different reading levels, the members of your team move along at different work levels.

A good leader can do the same thing with the members of his or her team. You don't want to discourage anyone by moving ahead too fast, but to hold workers back is a sure-fire way to wreck your team's motivation.

Fortunately, high performers are self-motivated, and they're able to take the ball and run with it without too much direction or watching. Once you get them moving on a project, you're likely to be able to stand back and let them go with it.

Be sure to provide your high performers with lots of opportunities for growth. They're always looking for ways to grow and develop, so anything you can do to accommodate that need will be beneficial.

Defining Moments

Moderate risk generally means there's about a 15 percent chance that the venture will be a failure.

Be creative along with your high performers, and let their interests guide you. If somebody has an idea of how to get your product shipped out faster, then by all means, make the idea into a project, let him explore it, and come up with some suggestions for implementation.

There are always a thousand ideas for improvement. Don't be afraid to let the high performers explore any number of ideas, create implementation strategies, and perform detailed cost analyses. When the cost-to-benefit ratio is right, let the high performers develop implementation teams and execute some of these projects.

Because high performers tend to be risk takers, give yours chances to take modest risks. These workers generally are pretty dependable, and you can trust them not to take silly or outrageous risks.

Risk taking, however, often leads to advances, and your high performers are just the ones to lead your team toward such advances.

Recognize Them

To get recognition for your high performers, assign special projects that are both challenging and high profile. Assign special projects that temporarily set the worker apart from the rest of the team. Remember that high achievers thrive on recognition and they like others to know about their successes.

Give lots of positive recognition, and be sure to keep it all public. Such things might include:

➤ Representing the company at an important trade show or special industry conference. These are great ways to challenge and recognize, and it puts your best people out in the field to be seen. It's a win-win situation for both the company and the employee.

➤ Conducting new research for the company. There are many reasons a company may need research conducted, and many potential benefits from such research. Every company can benefit from new and ever-changing technology, but it takes research to find out what's available, and what would work best for your company and your team. A motivated, high-performance worker may thrive on the challenge of researching a new issue.

➤ Job switching with other departments. This exposes your high performer to different areas of the company, and earns her recognition from other departments at the same time. You increase her value to the company by giving her additional experience, and you create a challenging situation at the same time.

Rally the Troops

For lots more ideas on how to recognize and reward employees, check out these books: *Managing with a Heart: 100+ Ways To Make Your Employees Feel Appreciated*, by Sharon Good, and *Recognizing and Rewarding Employees: Ideas for Individuals, Teams, and Managers*, by Joan P. Klubnik.

➤ Community work. Many companies make it part of their mission to get involved with community work. If yours does, who better to recognize than your high performer? Make sure that the work is interesting, and that she'll be recognized for her participation. Some possible examples of community work include: representing the company at Chamber of Commerce events; working on a high-profile campaign, such as the United Way or March of Dimes; representing your company in area schools as part of a cooperative work/school campaign; and so forth. Most responsible organizations encourage these activities, and are willing to give employees time off during the normal workday to pursue them.

➤ Special customer projects. If you're having a problem with a particular customer, and you can afford the time to do it, your high performer probably will be the perfect, specialized tough-customer service representative. If you make the problem a project to be figured out and solved, chances are your worker will rally to the cause and fix things up with the customer. This gives the employee recognition, while solving a problem for you and the customer.

➤ Special assignments within the industry. Do you have a trade association that needs a representative from your company? How about a lobbying person to represent your industry? These types of assignments serve to gain recognition for your high performer, while keeping him motivated and challenged. Many of these groups operate with volunteer labor, and working on special projects that benefit the entire industry can be broadening experiences for your best performers.

➤ High-profile positions within the company. Make sure that all the key committees within your company have some of your team members on them, especially your high performers. Coming up with new ways of improving quality, reducing the need for rework, or eliminating scrap are superior ways to showcase your people and their capabilities.

Reward Them

We already talked about the value of making your high performers prime targets for advancement within the company. But, what if your company is small and there aren't many promotions available?

Backfire

Some companies create rewards for high performers. While this can be a nice gesture, it's not without risk. Remember our earlier discussions about authenticity? If the reward is genuine, and it has meaning, then it's okay. But, if the reward is clearly invented just for the sake of giving a reward, it will be regarded as unauthentic, and could actually serve to demotivate.

If you're looking to reward your high performers by getting them promoted, and it doesn't look like you're going to be able to make it happen within your company, don't think that it can't be done. This is your chance to be creative, and think outside of the box.

Consider your best customers and key suppliers. Would there be a job for your high performers within any of their companies? I know that it's a leap to think about promoting your best employees to other companies. At first glance, it doesn't seem to make any sense. Why would you hand over someone of value to another firm?

I'll tell you why. There's nothing better than getting some of your people promoted into key positions with key customers and suppliers. When you think about it for a few minutes, it makes perfect sense.

Getting some of your people properly positioned within these companies can make these strategic relationships even more important. You're likely to create greater synergy and business opportunities between and within your organizations, while making sure your high performers are rewarded.

That idea takes some getting used to, but it's worth consideration. If your high performer gets promoted out of your department, you're going to lose him anyway. If he can't get promoted out of your department within the company, but there's a good spot for him with a customer or supplier's firm, in which circumstances would you rather have him? Bored and dissatisfied within your department, or happy and beneficial to your company in an outside position?

Does That High Performer Have His Eye on Your Job?

Is that high performer gunning for your job? Probably. If that scares the heck out of you, then you might have to rethink your attitude. You might have to rethink your perception of leadership, too.

If it's your plan to sit complacently in the same job for the rest of your career, then yeah—I guess you might be worried about somebody grabbing the position from you.

But, I doubt that you're in that position, and I doubt you'd ever want to be. Just by the fact that you're reading this book, you've shown that you're interested in improving your professional capacities and situation. You're obviously moving up, or, at least interested in moving up. In fact, you've probably established yourself as a high performer.

If that's the case, then you certainly can appreciate that somebody in a position beneath yours is counting the days until he can get his hands on your job.

Okay. I want you to be honest. How many times have you thought about taking your boss's job? Come on. Surely there have been times when you've considered what it would be like to sit in her chair and do her job. Well, turnabout is fair play, they say, and that high performer on your team is only doing what you've been doing about your boss's job.

While there's nothing wrong with the high performer gunning for a promotion—whether it's for your job or another—don't get carried away and give your job away.

As strange as it sounds, leaders sometimes do this without meaning to. They let the word out that the high performer is to be "acting boss" when they're not around. They encourage team members to go to the high performer with problems or questions. They give the high performer more responsibility within the team situation than he or she is entitled to have.

When that happens, it skews the dynamics of the team, and creates an artificial situation.

High achievers almost always will evolve as the team leader. That's fine. If the high performer's leadership abilities become evident, and the group accepts the person as its informal leader, that's a genuine situation that should be recognized and respected.

If you force leadership on the high performer, however, and establish him or her as the team leader, you're risking a bad situation within your team.

When you assign a leadership role to someone, you're forcing that person to take on something that he or she may not be ready for, or just might not want. You're also asking your team to accept someone as its leader, even though that person might not be the team's choice. Essentially, you're creating a new organization chart.

Clearly, the better way is to let the leadership role evolve and become evident on its own.

Backfire

When you force someone into a leadership position, even if it's done with the best intentions, you're setting yourself up for trouble from two fronts. One, the high performer may not want the leadership position, for whatever reason, and may resent you for handing it to him. Two, the team may not be ready to accept the high performer as its leader, and may resent you for assigning the role.

When that happens, the leader will have worked into the role, and most likely will be accepting of it. And the team will have a stake in the leader, having encouraged and promoted the position. As you read a page or two back, it's one thing for the group to informally recognize someone as a leader. It's another matter when you do the same thing.

Working with high achievers is not without challenges, but it's sure great to have these people on your team. As a leader, you should do everything you can to encourage, challenge, recognize, and reward high performers. Try to make their jobs fun and exciting, and let them know the possibilities for their futures. Don't try to force these special people into mundane, routine roles. They won't accept it, and it would be a terrible waste of their energy and talent.

The Least You Need to Know

➤ Take time to recognize and appreciate high performers, because they can be tremendous assets to your team.

➤ Use your high performers to your greatest advantage by letting them motivate and serve as examples to the rest of your team.

➤ Encourage high performers by making their jobs as fun, challenging, and exciting as possible.

➤ The three most important things to do for a high performer are to: challenge, recognize, and reward.

➤ High performers are very likely to be looking to take over your job, but you should recognize that as the natural order of things and not think it's threatening or upsetting.

➤ Avoid the temptation to force high performers into leadership roles; instead, let the roles evolve naturally.

➤ Never force high performers into roles that are mundane or routine.

Motivating the Difficult Employee

In a perfect world, all employees would be diligent and hardworking. They'd show up on time, work willingly and happily until quitting time, and then decide they simply couldn't bear to leave until the project they were working on was completely finished.

They'd come up with new ideas and find better ways of doing their jobs. They'd never complain or roll their eyes when you asked them to try something new or take on additional duties. And they'd willingly help each other out in order to make the team productive and able to function at its peak level.

Well, I'm sure I don't need to tell you that it's not a perfect world. We all get our share of good workers, pretty much like the "wishful thinking" ones described above. We also get our share of troublemakers.

Troublemakers—I usually call them jerks or skunks—are the workers that cause you to keep the jar of your pain reliever of choice in the top drawer. They're the ones that cause those gray hairs you see in the mirror and the worry lines around your mouth and eyes. They're the ones that you can't seem to stop thinking about, and the ones that keep you awake at night.

If you're stuck with a skunk, like I was at one point of my career, it's difficult just to think about dealing with her, much less motivating her into becoming a contributing and valuable member of your team. Sometimes that's impossible to do. Other times, however, it can be done without too much trouble.

In this chapter, we'll look at some different types of difficult employees, and how you might go about dealing with them and motivating them.

A Jerk Can Be a Dangerous Guy to Have Around

For the purposes of this chapter, we're going to discuss three kinds of difficult employees. The first kind is the annoying jerk. The second is the blatant behavior problem, and the third kind is the dangerous jerk. You'll see as we go along how these different types of difficult employees pose varying degrees of problems for their managers, and how each kind should be handled differently.

Annoying Jerks

Sometimes jerks are just annoying. They bug the other members of their teams, or they show up late, or they talk about themselves all the time.

Some jerks can't stop talking about how great their kids are, or how much trouble their kids are, or the problems they're having with their cars, or mothers-in-law, or whatever. These workers get downright irritating after a while, and other workers normally get fed up with them pretty quickly.

You can usually bring the annoying jerk under control simply by sitting down with her and discussing the problem. She may not realize how irritating her behavior is, or how she's perceived by other employees. It could be that this kind of worker really wants to fit in, and wants to do a good job, but doesn't have the personal skills necessary to be an effective member of a team.

While working with this person might take some time, the problem usually is fixable.

The Blatant Behavior Problem

The next category of difficult employee is that with the blatant behavior problems. These are the employees that steal, lie, or just don't bother to show up for work. They're the ones that harass people, threaten co-workers, or start fights. They're trouble, all right. But they're obvious trouble.

As you know, it's easier to deal with problems that you can see, than problems that you can't see. I worry a lot more about those tiny deer ticks that are responsible for Lyme disease, for instance, than I do about the old-fashioned kind of tick that

288

occasionally spreads a case of Rocky Mountain spotted fever. It's a lot easier to find the tick that you can see rather than the deer tick, which is roughly the size of a pinhead.

Here's How It Works

As a leader, you might have a tendency to try to help employees with obvious problems. If the worker is willing to be helped, cooperates with your efforts, and is making clear progress, then go ahead and spend some time on the problem. Be really careful, however, that your efforts to work with a difficult employee don't undermine the rest of the department. If the rest of your team perceives that the difficult employee's behavior is being rewarded with your time and attention, you'll end up with resentful and unmotivated employees. Under no circumstances should you work with people who have committed illegal acts such as stealing or falsifying documents. These flagrant violators should be dismissed and prosecuted immediately.

This second kind of difficult employee, the blatant behavior problem, is also fairly easy to deal with. With this guy, all you have to do is follow your company's discipline procedures.

She's clearly breaking rules, and it's your job to deal with the matter swiftly and effectively. If you don't, your other workers are going to wonder why the jerk is getting away with that kind of behavior, and question your judgment and effectiveness as a leader. If she doesn't respond to the first few levels of the discipline policy, then follow through on what you need to do to get rid of her.

It's not your job to rehabilitate a thief or someone who loves to start fights and cause trouble. You can't sacrifice the rest of your team and its productivity to try to save one worker who's done nothing to show that she wants to be saved. Also, your own job could be at stake. If you don't take action against the thief, for example, someone higher up might fire you *and* the thief.

If the jerk doesn't straighten up after the first warning or so, write her off as a bad hire, get rid of her, and move on. Thieves and others involved in illegal activities get no warnings. Just get rid of them. Most companies clearly state in their employment policies that any violation of the law is grounds for immediate dismissal.

The Dangerous Jerk

The third category of difficult employee—the dangerous jerk—is the hardest type to recognize, and the most potentially hazardous to your team.

I'm not referring to physical danger when I talk about the dangerous jerk. It's true that, these days, it's not inconceivable that some poor, mentally ill employee will show up with a gun and start blasting away. That, however, is not what we're talking about here.

When I refer to the dangerous jerk, I mean the kind of employee who can undermine the morale of the entire team, pit workers against each other, or against management (yep, that's you), and generally cause bad feelings among your entire department.

Backfire

While some employees are jerks just for the sake of being jerks, others suffer from psychological or mental problems that prevent them from getting along with or working effectively with other people. People with these kinds of problems should by no means be called jerks because their problems are not within their immediate control. They can, however, pose the same dangers to your team's morale as a true jerk and must be handled carefully.

Dangerous jerks can appear to fit into the team—at least for a while. She'll look like she's doing her job, but really she isn't. This sort of employee tends to camouflage herself. She hides out and can go unnoticed for quite a while.

She knows all the tricks. She says all the right things. She can appear to be really busy while actually doing next to nothing. She can appear to be interacting with other team members while really undermining team unity by being controlling, or making fellow employees feel guilty, helpless, or sorry for her.

Keeping a difficult, dangerous employee around isn't at all fair to the rest of your team, nor is it fair to the skunk.

If she's been around for a while, she very well might be making more money than some of the other, more productive members of your team. Don't kid yourself by thinking that employees don't know where they fall on the salary scale. If John, who hasn't put in a good day's work in 15 years, is making twice as much as Doug and Sharon, who haven't been with the company very long but bust their tails every single day, you can be sure that Doug and Sharon know that.

And you can be even more sure that they're not happy about it.

The flip side is that if a person is allowed to hang out for 15 or 20 years without doing the job she's supposed to do, she's lost a lot of opportunity to contribute and be a valuable member of a team. This happens all too often. Managers put up with difficult employees because they like them personally, or they don't know how to deal with the problem, or they simply don't feel like dealing with it.

The worst is when an employee's allowed to slide by for 20 years or so, and then new management comes in, sees what's going on, and lets the old skunk go. The employee may have been sliding by for so long that she no longer realizes she's not pulling her weight. And then, out of the blue, she's fired. This is when the court battles start. A company that lets somebody sit around for 20 years, gives her a paycheck when it's

due, and then fires her is asking for a discrimination suit—or worse.

Is the Jerk Really a Jerk, or Somebody Who Can't Do the Job?

If your difficult employee is a bona fide jerk—
somebody who really enjoys annoying people,
who goes out of her way to be troublesome, and
who's generally disliked by everybody on your
team because of her behavior—then, that's on her.

If your difficult employee is somebody who
can't do her job because she never received
proper training or was given work that's simply
too difficult for her, then, that's on you.

Be very careful to make sure your difficult
employee has been trained and is qualified to do
her assigned work. If not, get busy providing
some training, right away.

Some employees who appear to be difficult are
fully redeemable. Some simply don't understand
the concept of working as part of the team, or
they've never learned how their contribution
affects the overall operation.

Rally the Troops

Remember that people with certain
problems, like excessive drinking or
drug use, often are really good at
concealing them. We once hired a
woman with excellent credentials
who started out right on track.
Before long, however, she started
coming in late without calling, dis-
appearing for periods of time at
trade shows and conferences, and
ignoring her responsibilities. It
turned out she was an alcoholic
who was quickly heading for rock
bottom. Don't kick yourself for not
seeing these kinds of problems
immediately, but be prepared to
deal with them should they occur.

It's my feeling that some employees, maybe many,
in fact, really want to be helped. They want to be able to perform their work more
effectively and contribute to the good of the team. If you have this type of worker on
your team, you stand a good chance of bringing her around with a little special attention and effort.

People often try to hide feelings of inadequacy by showing off or causing trouble. It's
a natural reaction that you can see exhibited in people of all ages. Kids act out when
they're unsure or scared about something. Teenagers do the same thing. As adults, we
expect that we should be better able to handle our feelings and behavior, but old
insecurities and our means for dealing with them die hard.

Insecure adults may display a lot of bravado, or try to make others feel bad by spreading rumors or saying hurtful things, or they may withdraw. While some of these
behaviors can be hurtful and demoralizing to your team, this kind of employee probably can be helped.

Try these steps when dealing with this kind of difficult employee:

Backfire

You're asking for a lawsuit if you try to fire somebody who was never properly trained for the job she's expected to be doing. Don't even mention termination until you're absolutely sure she was properly trained.

➤ Be lavish with praise. Encourage the worker by praising even small successes. Make sure that you do it in front of other workers, but don't go overboard and create resentment among them.

➤ Assign only appropriate tasks to the employee. Be extra sensitive to what you ask the person to do. Be sure not to assign any jobs that she'll have trouble with, or be unable to complete.

➤ Provide all the necessary training to get the person prepared to be able to do what it takes to remain in the department. She's going to have to be able to pull her own weight.

➤ Be prepared to be patient. Show patience with both the difficult employee, and the other members of your team. Any situation that causes the cogs of your department's machinery to slow down is a nuisance and is disruptive to everyone.

Of course, if your employee is simply unable to do any job well enough to be a contributing member of your department, you'll have to come up with another solution. Every employee who tries, however, is worth some effort. You might be surprised at what a little extra attention, help, and training will produce.

Dealing with a Dangerous Jerk

It's true, I think, that some employees just won't be helped. These are the ones that get extremely resentful at any hint that they could improve their work habits. They balk at any hint of criticism and make no effort to work effectively with others. If you've got one or more of this type, you've got your hands full.

If you get an employee who you think is beyond help, there are certain things you should do. One thing you shouldn't do, however, is get her transferred to a different department. I call this practice "passing the skunk."

Earlier in my career, I took a job with which I inherited a skunk. He'd been a skunk for 40 years, and no one had ever confronted him about it. All management did was lie to each other about the guy and pass him around the company.

Throughout the skunk's career, he'd been given the idea that it was okay to do nothing. Everything would be okay. He'd simply be moved to another department and allowed to do nothing some more. Other employees deeply resented that this guy was allowed to get away with this behavior, particularly because he'd been there a long time, was making big bucks, and got four weeks vacation. He really was dangerous because his role was causing a lot of resentment among the other employees.

Fortunately, I was able to work with this skunk and managed to get him operating at a minimum level of competency. We struggled—don't get me wrong. We went through write-ups and warnings, and he fought the entire process. I'm sure that he resented me terribly, but I was determined to get him to improve his attitude—at least a little.

If you have somebody in your department who fits into the dangerous jerk category, you've got to take action. You just can't risk having your team demoralized and damaged for the sake of one employee.

If you decide you're going to have to get rid of the skunk, then get on with it, but prepare yourself for the worst. People like this generally know all the tricks and might just be watching for you to slip up with dismissal procedures and allege unfair firing practices, or something of that nature.

When you've determined that an employee is beyond help, or won't accept help, then it's time to look at your company's firing procedures.

Backfire

Passing around a difficult employee from department to department might be a well-meaning gesture on the part of management, but it's extremely dangerous. A potentially harmful employee who gets access to different departments when she's transferred around has the perfect opportunity to infect the entire company with her lousy attitude. You don't want this employee exposed to any more people than is absolutely necessary. If she is, you're risking passing along her poison to the whole company

Keep the following tips in mind.

➤ Carefully follow all your company's rules regarding disciplinary matters. Make sure you cross every t and dot every i. Review Chapter 13, "Fair Discipline—Or How to Spank Nicely," for more advice about dealing with discipline problems.

➤ Don't discuss your actions with others in the department, but don't worry, either. Everyone who's been dealing with the jerk will have at least an idea of what's going on.

➤ Document everything in writing. List all reported incidents, complaints from co-workers, work disruptions, and so forth. Record your conversations with the difficult employee, and the steps you've taken to improve the situation. Be very specific with details.

➤ Don't assume that your boss, or others within the company, will support you. If they're not fully aware of what's been going on in your department, they might not realize the need to get rid of the difficult employee. They'll accept your actions because they have to, but supporting it may be another matter.

➤ Stand firm. Your position when you talk to your boss about firing the difficult employee must be that you've decided what must be done, and you want to

Rally the Troops

If you decide your difficult employee is redeemable and you're working to rehab her, start trying to get the rest of the team to accept the difficult employee as one of them. This probably will take a while, so it's good to start as soon as your rehab efforts begin.

review your plans. Don't report that you're having trouble with the worker and then ask for advice on what to do about it. If you take that position, you're just handing over your responsibility to your boss or personnel officer. If you do that, you risk the possibility that the boss might decide to give the skunk another chance. He might urge you to try for six more months—six more months that'll seem like forever when you're working with this employee.

If you really feel that this employee has to go, then stand firm in your decision. You're the one that has to work with her, and it's your department that's suffering because of her. Involve your superiors in your decision, but don't ask for their permission to act.

Making the Jerk an Effective Part of the Team

If you've decided that the jerk might not be such a jerk after all, and she might be redeemable and even pretty good, then you'll have to work hard to make her an effective member of the team.

You're going to have to set some guidelines and establish some ground rules. And, you'll need to be very specific. Remember, skunks, even redeemable skunks, know all the tricks.

So, how do you go about making this person, who's been disruptive and unproductive, fit in as a useful member of your team?

Use everything that we've discussed so far in this book. Focus on coaching, goal setting, and other means of motivation. Offer incentives and rewards for meeting goals. Remember that turning a difficult employee into a productive and effective member of the team is going to require time and effort. It won't happen overnight. Be prepared to follow through if you decide to make the commitment.

Establish Goals and Time Frames

Set up specific goals with specific time frames. You're going to have to make it exactly clear what you expect from the difficult employee and when you expect it.

To make sure that you're both on the same page, put everything in writing. Avoid general instructions such as "production must improve" or "quality must improve."

Instead, specifically state that "unit output per hour must be maintained at (pick your own number) level." Or try "the reject rate must be reduced to (pick your own number, again) and maintained at that level."

Spell out all your expectations and provide clear examples of what kind of behavior you're looking for. For example, instead of telling the difficult employee that she has to cut down on absences, make it clear that you expect absences only when she's ill or has a family emergency, and state specifically what the average absence rate is among the company or your group.

Instead of telling her to keep her mind on her work, tell her that any personal discussion must be limited to break times. Instead of saying that you want to see improvement in her behavior, tell her that she's expected to remain calm with co-workers, regardless of how heated their side of the discussion becomes. Tell her that she is not to be involved in any arguments whatsoever.

Rally the Troops

While you're working out an agreement with your difficult employee, make sure you keep those who should know involved. That probably means your company's personnel lawyer or somebody from the personnel office, as well as your boss.

And make sure she understands your expectations. Have her read the written expectations, and go over them to make sure she understands them. Don't assume anything.

Once the expectations are established, work together to figure out how you'll measure her progress. A customer service representative, for instance, might be judged on her retention of customers. A factory worker might be judged on productivity and quality.

When the goals and time frames have been established and recorded, make it clear to the difficult employee what will happen if she doesn't meet, or at least come close to meeting, the goals. I can't stress how important it is to have everything written down.

Be as specific as you can in your explanation of terms. You might want to use the paragraph below as an example.

"This (you'd put the performance levels that you're expecting from the difficult employee here) is the minimal acceptable standard for continuing in this department. We will follow the prescribed program to get to this needed performance level. If we do not achieve this performance level in the prescribed time frame, then you will be released from the payroll on (whatever the agreed-upon date may be)."

That should make the expectations and possible consequences perfectly clear to everyone involved.

I don't know why, but everywhere I travel, people are very reluctant to use that you-will-be-released-from-the-payroll phrase. These, however, are the most important words in your statement.

Specifically stating that if the difficult employee doesn't meet the terms of the agreement, she'll be released on a specific date keeps you on the moral high ground. It lets the employee know several things:

295

➤ Things are serious.

➤ You've taken steps concerning her behavior and/or performance.

➤ If she doesn't intend to live up to your expectations and your agreement, then she should start looking for another job.

Describing specifically the action you intend to take is the most fair thing you can do for a difficult employee.

Make Sure You Keep Control of the Process

Don't let anybody else take charge of your agreement with the difficult employee. You need to establish and maintain control.

And don't get more people involved than you need to. Some well-meaning supervisor could interfere with your plans for your difficult worker.

If you craft a statement of expectations and keep control of it but the employee doesn't live up to its terms, then it's time to say good-bye. Be specific about your expectations, and work with her to help her be productive and accepted. If you can't, then don't beat yourself up. End the relationship and move on.

The Least You Need to Know

➤ There are different levels of difficult employees, but none of them makes your workplace a nicer place to be.

➤ The most dangerous type of employee is the one who appears to be something that she is not.

➤ Different types of difficult employees must handled in different ways; don't treat an annoying employee in the same manner you would a dangerous employee or blatant behavior problem.

➤ Some difficult employees are fully redeemable, while others can't be saved.

➤ It's important that you know when it's appropriate to invest time and money to bring a difficult employee back on board with the team, and when it's appropriate to say good-bye.

➤ Don't risk a lawsuit by confusing a jerk with an inadequately trained and disciplined employee.

➤ Once you decide that a difficult employee is savable, you'll be in for some hard work to get her back on board.

Keeping Motivation High in the Good Times

Knock on wood, but we've been enjoying a really booming economy, haven't we?

Consumer confidence and stock prices are near all-time highs. Unemployment is low. America's share of global trade increased by an average of 9.2 percent between 1985 and 1995, and we enjoy the highest living standards of any major industrialized country in the world.

Our workers are working and making lots of money. We're buying new homes as fast as they can be constructed. We're buying new cars, new computers, and new appliances. We're taking vacations, buying vacation homes, and generally living the good life.

So, what's wrong with that, you ask? Well, there's nothing wrong with it.

But while a booming economy is great, with lots of obvious advantages, it's not without its challenges. I hate to be a wet blanket, but prosperity comes and goes. You know as well as I do that the economy, like most other things, is a continuous, cyclical process, not a series of unrelated events. It goes up, it comes down, and then it starts over. When we're in good times, we tend to think they'll last forever. When they don't, we feel cheated and angry.

In this chapter, we'll look at some of those challenges as they pertain to management, especially when it comes to keeping your workers motivated. Prosperity tends to breed complacency, and we all know how dangerous *that* characteristic can be.

Keeping Up the Momentum

Things are humming along. Orders are up, production is up, and everybody is working hard. They're making lots of overtime, and it seems like every time you turn around somebody's got a brand-new vehicle in the parking lot.

For all the prosperity, though, something seems to be wrong with the members of your team. Everybody seems a little down. A little lethargic. Like they've lost their edge. What's going on? you wonder.

Well, let's have a look at what happened at Jim's foundry during the same kind of circumstances. His workers, too, were making big bucks, working lots of overtime, and trying to keep up with orders. Jim's profits were soaring. It was the kind of business conditions of which most owners only ever dream.

It took a while, but Jim started to notice that things weren't all rosy with his workers. They were tired. They were irritable. Differences weren't being resolved, and arguments were regular occurrences. People were starting to call in sick, something that wasn't factored into the work schedule.

It seems like morale should have been at an all-time high, but it wasn't. In fact, it was sinking fast.

Defining Moments

The Japanese recognize something called **karoshi,** which means "death by overwork." Thousands of Japanese workers succumb to "karoshi" every year.

I was working with Jim at this time, and together we watched conditions deteriorate. Unresolved problems between co-workers were mounting, along with the absentee rate. Workers kept asking for time off, but Jim couldn't give it to them because of the workload. The new cars in the parking lot didn't have much appeal because the workers never had time to take them anyplace to enjoy them. It was to work early, back home late, and work on the weekends, too. We were running seven days a week, 12 hours every day.

Jim and I worried a lot about the very real possibility of accidents. Everybody was tired, and concentration wasn't what it should have been. This heavy, cast iron foundry poured tons of 2,000°F molten iron every day. That's hot! There are all kinds of heavy machines. The heat can be overwhelming. There's grit in the air, and it's noisy. All these things add up to potential disaster for workers who aren't giving adequate attention to safety standards.

We knew we had to do something to improve morale and regain our momentum with the workers. We couldn't give them time off; we needed them to work the long hours in order to keep up with orders. Hiring more staff wasn't a viable option, either. We needed highly skilled, technical workers, very few of which were available in our area. What we could do, we decided, was to try to make the work time more enjoyable.

Once we committed ourselves to addressing the issue and getting things back on track, we found it wasn't all that difficult. All we had to do was relieve some of the tediousness that was threatening Jim's workplace, and regain the momentum of a motivated team.

To do that, we did all sorts of spontaneous things. We implemented random, forced breaks. Every now and then, managers were instructed to tell their teams it was break time, and everyone was included—no questions asked. We'd supply shiny new trash cans packed with ice and filled to the brim with cold lemonade and iced tea on hot summer days.

On some days, we'd announce that picnic lunches would be served for all workers. Other days, we'd extend the lunch break and provide entertainment. We did bonus nights, where we'd hand out gift certificates to area restaurants for workers and their spouses.

Here's How It Works

I was just reading about a company that ran a telephone help line that had to be staffed on weekends. The company was located in a scenic, recreational area, and, of course, employees hated having to work Saturdays and Sundays. The boss strung up volleyball nets between workstations, had beach towels printed up with "Summer Beach Time," and let employees play volleyball when the phones weren't ringing. The morale-booster cost less than $100, and the employees loved it.

It's always the same problem. When you're making lots of money, there's never enough time to enjoy it. When you've got enough time to do stuff, you don't have enough money. *C'est la vie!*

Recent studies have shown that more and more workers are looking to strike a balance between their work and personal time, and that many are willing to make less money in order to have more time off.

A quality-of-life poll conducted jointly by *U.S. News & World Report* and Bozell Worldwide Inc. showed that 51 percent of Americans say they'd prefer more free time, even if it means less money. Sixty-eight percent of those polled ranked family life as one of their top three priorities, while only 23 percent said the same about their jobs.

When times are good, however, and you need your workers to be there for you, you've got to look for ways to keep them happy and motivated. Spontaneity is a great way to stave off complacency. Let's look at some other fun, spontaneous things that I've known bosses and managers to do to ward off the too-busy blues and keep their workers motivated.

➤ First-day-of-spring softball games in the parking lot.

➤ Champagne breaks to celebrate reaching significant milestones (this one doesn't apply if there's machinery in use!).

➤ Dress-down days.

➤ Dress-up days.

➤ Pizza parties for the whole family on nights when the team is working late.

➤ Make-your-own sundae parties during afternoon breaks.

➤ Drawings in which all employees' names are put in a container, names are picked at random at various times during the day, and prizes awarded to the winners.

You can do all sorts of inspirational stuff to keep momentum high and your workers motivated. All it takes is the sensitivity to realize that when your employees are overworked, there'll be problems, and the creativity to find ways to alleviate those problems.

Making the Extra Work Worth Their While

Nobody wants to work for nothing. Regardless of if you're running four-hour shifts, seven-hour shifts, or 12-hour shifts, workers want to be paid for the time they're putting in and the jobs they're performing.

When the work gets tedious and the hours long, workers expect to be compensated over and above their basic pay.

We already discussed the role of money in keeping workers motivated in Chapter 8, "What's in It for Me?" Just to remind you, it works—to a point. And then, workers look for something more.

Given the choice, more and more workers are opting out of overtime—after a while. The trend is that they're happy for it at first, but it quickly becomes old, and their personal lives can suffer because of it.

Here's How It Works

Fifteen corporations, including AT&T, Xerox, Levi Strauss & Co., Johnson & Johnson, DuPont, and American Express, recently participated in a study to determine what makes work worthwhile for employees. They found that things like flexibility and adequate time off ranked higher among many workers than monetary rewards.

If you can't give time off because of production demands, try to think of other ways to make work worthwhile.

Figure out something meaningful that will motivate your workers and keep them satisfied when their work and hours get demanding. They know that all their overtime work results in bigger profits for the company. So you'd better let them share in the gain.

Smart managers and bosses will offer some kind of extra bonus. If you're flush with cash, you might offer to pay for financial planning for your employees. Or buy gifts that the entire family can use. Maybe you could start a fund, and let the workers decide what they wanted to do with it. They could choose to fund a charity or scholarship fund in their names, or provide a gift to the local high school.

You don't, however, always need to give cash. In fact, cash isn't always a good idea. It wouldn't be the first time if one of your workers got a big cash bonus, only to decide he's had enough of working 60 hours a week and he's going to quit altogether.

Stock is a good alternative to cash, as is a better retirement program, or bonuses set up to kick in after workers have been with the company for a certain number of years.

You want to motivate and provide incentives, but they don't have to be immediate.

What Goes Around, Comes Around

At risk of being a wet blanket again, I'll remind you that what goes around, comes around. And, to throw in another cliché, remember that the grass is always greener on the other side of the fence.

When the current economic boom ends—and it will eventually end—many workers will look back on "the good old days" and bemoan the fact that they can't work the long days with all the overtime that they enjoyed in the late 1990s.

For now, as I cited earlier, many workers are looking for more time off, even if it means less pay. Not all, mind you. There are always workers who are looking for all

Rally the Troops

Keep an eye on workers who volunteer to work overtime at every chance they get. Remember that tired employees are employees who have accidents, risk burnout, and suffer from other stress-related ills.

the overtime they can get because they've just bought a new home, or a new car, or have a kid getting close to college age.

Your job, as a leader, is to strike a balance with your workers. Let those who want to, work, but don't let them exhaust themselves. Try to accommodate those who are balking at all the overtime by letting them accept fewer hours. Yeah, you might have to hire people to do their work, but it's better than losing good employees who get too stressed out to do a job properly. If you don't want to hire extra people because of an expected downturn, try working a deal with somebody, and subcontract some of the work. Or you could try to hire a few temporary workers.

Telling Workers That Good Times Don't Last Forever

Convincing your team that the good times won't last forever is not an easy task.

When times are good, we forget about hard times. It's a natural thing. It's like when you're sick, you think you'll never get well. When you do, you quickly forget what it was like to be ill. Good times become the norm—the standard.

You don't want to be a voice of doom, but it's important that your team understand the concept of economic cycles. If they do, they'll be motivated to work while the working's good. And, more importantly, they'll be motivated to save some of what they earn.

Getting Them to Save While the Saving's Good

If we all would have started saving money as soon as we started making any, we'd be in pretty good shape. Unfortunately, saving money doesn't rank as high for most folks as spending it does. When we have it, most of us find something to spend it on.

Many of us are incredibly shortsighted when it comes to saving money. Intellectually, we know that it's better to start saving when you're 20 rather than 30, but there's so damned many things to want when you first start earning.

Show the statistics below to the young members of your team, and maybe you'll be able to get them motivated to start saving their money now.

➤ If you invest $5,000 when you're 25 and let it sit at 8 percent interest until you're 60, you'll have $73,925.

➤ If you invest $5,000 when you're 35, and let it sit at 8 percent interest until you're 60, you'll have only $34,242.

➤ And if you don't invest the $5,000 until you're 45, you'll be looking at only $15,860 when you turn 60.

Clearly, the lesson is to start saving as early as possible.

Another concept many people have trouble understanding is that little savings add up to big savings. Here are some fun facts from Fidelity Investments that demonstrate that important concept. All the amounts are based on saving for 30 years at 9 percent interest:

➤ If you save $300 a year by exercising at home instead of joining a gym, you'll have saved $44,572 in 30 years.

➤ If you save $7 a week by making your daily cappuccino an every other day cappuccino, you'll have $56,092 in 30 years.

Backfire

It's an unfortunate fact, but studies show that 25 percent of American adults between 35 and 54 haven't even started to save for retirement. If you're one of them, get started, and get started fast. If you don't, you'll never have the kind of lifestyle to which you've become accustomed, or even anything close. Get some advice from a good financial advisor.

➤ If you save $12 a month by renting a video instead of going to the movies (with popcorn, please), you'll have $22,134 in 30 years.

➤ If you save $35 a month by collecting all your change, you'll have $64,557 in 30 years.

If you do all those things, you'll have $187,355 in 30 years. Not a bad exchange for some little sacrifices, is it? Most of us though, still go ahead and buy the cappuccinos.

In recent years, the U.S. household savings rate has been among the lowest of the major industrial nations, lagging behind those of France, Germany, Italy, and Japan. There's growing concern about this American tendency, and with good reason.

Government projections estimate that the Social Security system, which is funded by payroll taxes on current workers to pay retirees' benefits, will begin running deficits in about 20 years, and will exhaust its accumulated surpluses by 2032.

Imagine. A country full of people who didn't save enough money for retirement, and no Social Security. Not a pretty thought, is it?

The politicians think this concern is real and very serious. In fact, it was enough to make the likes of Newt Gingrich and Trent Lott share the podium with Bill Clinton in 1998. Clinton, flanked by Republican leaders, took the stage to urge Americans to start saving more. Together, they warned of the dangers of overspending now and living to regret it later.

Here's How It Works

Studies report that if you make it to 50, you stand a good chance of living to be 85. That's a lot of years after retirement, during which you've got to be able to support yourself!

So, what are these political types doing to make it easier for American workers to save for retirement?

As of 1998, employers are permitted to set up 401(k) plans so that workers are automatically enrolled, unless they specify they don't want to be. It's estimated that 90 percent of all workers will get involved in a 401(k) that's set up like this, compared with only 67 percent who participate if they have to make a point to sign up and enroll themselves.

Defining Moments

Introduced in 1982 as a way for employers to save the money they'd been putting in pension plans, **401(k)s** are plans that allow employees to contribute a portion of their paychecks to a company investment plan. Very often, the employer matches a portion of the worker's contribution. 401(k)s were named after the section of the tax code that created them.

You could do your workers a great service by checking out your company's retirement plan. If there's a 401(k) plan, are workers enrolled automatically or must they enroll themselves? If your company offers a 401(k) or other type of retirement plan, by all means encourage your workers to participate. These are some of the easiest and smartest ways to save money and yet a lot of people don't take advantage of them.

Much of this lack of interest in saving money stems from a lack of education about personal finance. Many young people graduate from high school with no knowledge of different kinds of bank accounts, opportunities for retirement saving, or how a credit card account works.

While young people often are in the dark, there's no shortage of institutions that are willing to take advantage of that lack of knowledge. Bank card companies and retail stores make it very easy for young, financially uneducated people to start racking up debt at an early age. Often, the first real financial lesson occurs when somebody realizes he's got too much credit card debt, without the means to pay it off.

If you can make your team understand the importance of saving money while there's money to save, you will have done everyone on it a great service. It's a good idea to bring in financial planners or advisors to talk to your workers about various options for saving.

When and where you can, build incentives for saving. Retirement plans or special savings plans that supplement money put into savings rather than taken out in cash are methods with which you can reward and encourage your workers.

Creating Something Special to Celebrate Good Fortune

When times are good and everyone's working hard, it's extremely important to foster the team attitude within your company. Workers who feel that they're part of a cohesive group will work harder and better than those who feel alienated or unappreciated.

Acknowledge that times are good and the company is doing well. Your employees know it anyway. Then, find ways to celebrate, and make sure your workers are invited to the party.

Showing Recognition

When recognizing the contributions of your team, remember to include their family members. When you overwork your employees, their families feel the strain. It's recognized that overtime can result in family problems, including divorce. Think about it. Working a lot of overtime removes a family member from the family setting. There are all kinds of implications to that.

Here's How It Works

Polls show that Generation Xers, typically defined as the 46 million or so Americans in their 20s and early 30s, are looking more toward family, spirituality, and personal satisfaction as important parts of their lives. Sociologists see this as a generation's backlash to the high divorce rate, obvious consumption, and get-ahead mentality of their baby boomer parents. There will be implications for the workplace, but it sure will be interesting to see.

Some companies make time for family appreciation days, or company-sponsored picnics, or parties to which family members are invited. Of course, there are other ways to recognize employees, as well.

Cisco Systems, a supplier of hardware for the information age, is a super-hot growth operation that's been enjoying the good times for years, thanks to the growth of the Internet and the expansion of the entire information age. It also is a company with a really neat way of recognizing its 13,000 hardworking employees and keeping them inspired to maintain the growth momentum.

John Chambers, the CEO, came up with the idea of birthday meetings for all employees.

Employees are invited to have breakfast with Chambers and other executives on a particular morning of the month in which their birthdays fall. Granted, these are big breakfasts, with somewhere around 1,000 employees having birthdays in any given month. Still, 1,000 employees is a lot more manageable than 13,000.

Chambers and the other executives meet with staff members, mingle, and answer questions in an informal setting.

Cisco workers love these birthday breakfasts, and participation is always high. Employees get access to the top guy of the whole company and are able to share issues that are important to their jobs. Chambers, on the other hand, uses the meetings to gain valuable insights into how his operations are performing. It's a smart move on the part of the company because it pulls employees into the system.

Showing Appreciation

While recognition is nice, appreciation is even better. Don't assume your employees know they're appreciated if you don't tell them. Get out there and publicly tell them how much you appreciate what they're doing, especially if you've been pushing them hard with extra work.

Loudly praise those who come up with innovative ideas for getting the job done better, and cite specific examples of how people have excelled in one area or another.

Here's How It Works

Johnsonville Foods, a sausage manufacturer in Sheboygan, Wisconsin, was asked in 1986 to assume production at a plant that a competitor was closing. CEO Ralph Stayer really wanted to accept the offer, knowing it would be great for the company. He was concerned, though, about the extra work it would create for his employees, and the stress that would result. Being a smart leader, Stayer asked his employees what they thought the company should do. Nearly everyone thought the company should "go for it" and take over business at the other plant. This made it everyone's decision, and productivity increased by 50 percent.

Let your workers know what you're doing for them because this expresses the appreciation you feel. And let them have a say in how to handle the increased workload that's resulted from good economic times. After all, if they're expected to put in extra hours, isn't it reasonable that they should have a say in how they should be worked?

If overtime is necessary, let employees have some input into how it's scheduled. They're much more apt to be receptive to ideas that they've come up with themselves rather than to plans forced upon them.

Good bosses will tell you that employees are the most important resource a business has. Let them know that as often as possible to keep them motivated in good times—and bad.

The Least You Need to Know

➤ Good economic times are great, but there are potential drawbacks.

➤ You've got to find ways to motivate workers and maintain momentum when the days get long and the work hard.

➤ Find out what your workers want in exchange for the extra work they're doing—and help them get it.

➤ It's important that everybody understands that good times come and go, but they never last forever.

➤ You can do a great favor to your team by teaching members the importance of starting to save as early and as much as possible.

➤ Workers know that the company is doing well in good times, so be sure to include them in the celebration.

➤ Your workers won't know they're appreciated unless you tell them, so make sure you do.

Chapter 24

Keeping Motivation High in the Bad Times

In This Chapter

➤ Knowing that sooner or later your company will run into bad times

➤ Dealing with economic bad times

➤ Laying off is hard to do

➤ Shutting down is even harder to do

➤ Making salary cuts less painful

➤ Dealing with bad times caused by other reasons

➤ Knowing how to handle sticky situations effectively

While there are some challenges involved in keeping motivation high during good times, it's much more difficult to do when times are bad.

I'm not trying to paint a bleak picture here, but it's only common sense that it's easier to keep a team motivated when it's got a 12-2 season than a 2-12 season.

Sure, a team that's won 12 and lost two might be a little cocky—a little complacent—a little off the top of its game. But a team that's 2-and-12 most likely has more serious problems.

The same theory applies in business. When times are great, everybody's feeling pretty good. Sure, there can be stresses caused by working too hard to keep up with orders, burnout from too much overtime, and frustration because there's no time to go out and enjoy the money that everybody's making.

When times are bad, however, it's harder to feel motivated and up about coming to work, and about performing well while you're there. Whether the hard times are caused by financial factors, other factors, or a combination of financial and other, keeping your team happy during these periods will definitely be a challenge.

In this chapter, we'll look at some reasons that bad times happen. Financial problems are a major cause of bad times, but other negatives, like a horrible boss, for instance, also can result in problems in the workplace.

We'll come up with some solutions for keeping your team motivated, no matter how bad things get, and how to do dirty work—like firing—without getting too dirty.

So let's get started. This is an important chapter because, as you read in Chapter 23, good times can't last forever, and some bad times are inevitable.

When Economic Times Are Tough

It's perfectly normal to forget about bad times when you're going through good times. After all, who wants to think about problems and concerns when you're having a great time? Why stop and think about tomorrow, when everything is coming up roses today?

The problem is that we've always had bad times. We've always had good times, too, that's true, but we haven't yet figured out a way to eliminate periods of trouble.

Backfire

Remember that being laid off or downsized can be a devastating experience. Whatever you do, don't appear to take layoffs lightly when they occur within your company. Layoffs affect how people feel about who they are, and their role within society. Layoffs affect people's families and their lives, and they're not to be taken lightly. Enlightened companies will do whatever possible to lessen the impact of layoffs for their employees.

Economic downturns occur for many reasons, most of which hardly anyone fully understands, and all of which are too complicated to get into here.

One important thing I do know about bad economic times, however, is that they feed themselves. An economic downturn begins. When people finally notice it, they go into a defensive mode and stop spending money. They put off buying the new cars they were considering or substitute a vacation spot near home for the proposed trip through the French countryside.

This sudden tightening of the purse strings slows things down even more, and the problem escalates.

Nobody likes hard times, but unfortunately, they're inevitable. When times get tough in business, there can be some pretty nasty consequences. Layoffs, wage reductions, plant closings, shortened production shifts—these are just a few of the consequences of economic hard times. As we all know, the effects of these economic hard times can linger for years, long after the economy has rebounded.

There are still people now, for example, who are reeling from the effects of the 1990–91 recession that resulted in massive layoffs across the country. We've all heard the stories of laid-off men and women forced to take jobs in fast-food restaurants or on the check-out lines of grocery stores despite college educations and years of experience in business.

Well, some of them are still out there, having never been able to get back on track.

As difficult as it might be, there are ways to keep your team motivated during bad economic times. Let's look at some of the things that can go wrong and what you can do to boost morale while they're happening.

Motivating During or After Layoffs

Layoffs are real morale busters, there's no question about it. Unfortunately, they are a part of the way business responds to economic pressures, and the way it changes and transforms itself.

Millions of people were laid off between 1991 and 1999, a period during which the economy experienced unprecedented growth. The layoffs weren't caused by poor business conditions; they were caused by business transformation. Business has been employing highly productive technology throughout the 1990s, and thousands of jobs have been outsourced due to that technology. This business transformation has created millions of new jobs, while eliminating millions of old ones.

There's no question about it, the emphasis in business is on increased productivity, flexibility, and better utilization of human resources. That means there will be changes, including layoffs. Change is always difficult for those it affects.

Here's How It Works

Susan Larson, vice president for human resources at VF Corporation, one of the world's largest apparel manufacturers whose brands include Lee, Wrangler, Vanity Fair, Jantzen, Jansport, Healthtex, Joe Boxer Jeans, and Red Kap, says her attitude toward unemployment has changed drastically over the past 10 years, due to the many layoffs during the early 1990s. "Ten years ago, I'd wonder what was wrong with a person who'd been let go from a company after a long period of employment there," she says, "but now, I don't think twice if somebody's been laid off or downsized."

Layoffs are hard to take, regardless of how they occur. Most companies, however, could save some wear and tear on their workers if, when layoffs become necessary, they'd do them fast and get them over with.

Here's what happens. Executives sit by and watch as business declines. Eventually, they decide they need to do something. Nobody likes to lay off employees, but these bosses see no other way out of their economic problems. In an attempt to soften the blow, they lay off absolutely as few people as possible.

In their reluctance to rock the boat, however, they don't cut expenses far enough, and as business continues to decline, more layoffs become necessary.

This is the worst possible way to go about it. Once the first group of layoffs occur, the remaining workers are on edge and stressed out. They can see that business isn't getting any better, and it appears that the writing is on the wall. As a result, employees spend their time waiting for the next cut and wondering whose heads will roll.

That atmosphere certainly isn't conducive to motivated employees, nor is it good for productivity. It's a lousy situation.

The better way to handle a bad situation would be to make all of the layoffs at the same time, and then let employees know that they're over. This eliminates the process of having your workers wonder who's next. You won't lose the employees who are trying to protect themselves by finding new jobs before their old ones disappear. In short, you eliminate a lot of stress and anxiety.

Rally the Troops

Always avoid layoffs if possible by reducing your workforce by attrition or offering "buyout" programs for your senior people. If you do this, you've got to make sure the incentives you provide are strong enough to make enough of them willing to leave.

It's like Vietnam versus the Persian Gulf War. The crisis in Vietnam built up very slowly, and it went on, and on, and on. The Gulf War, on the other hand, was quick.

There's no such thing as a good war, but at least the Gulf War was over quickly. Vietnam, with its agonizing inertia, became engrained in the fabric of our nation and ripped it apart.

And so it is with getting rid of people on your workforce. If you must lay people off, do it all at once. Get it over with so at least the survivors will be able to get back to work.

Your job as a leader, in the aftermath of a round of layoffs, is to focus on the workers who remain. As bad as you might feel about the layoffs, you've got to look past it, and be there to lead those who are left.

Do everything you can to ease the blow that layoffs inevitably will cause. Some things you can do, if they're within your power, include:

➤ Provide generous severance pay to those you have to let go.

➤ Provide job-hunting services.

➤ Find someone to assist them with writing or updating résumés.

➤ Allow those who are laid off to use your company's office space and equipment to contact possible future employers.

➤ Provide counseling services if necessary.

➤ Talk your former employees up to people you know at other companies.

➤ Invite representatives from other companies to come in and interview your workers.

All these are moral acts, and you should do them because they're the right things to do. They also will help you maintain a positive image with those workers still on the job. Also keep in mind that in the future you'll need to hire people again, and prospective employees will consider the reputation of your company when they decide whether they want to join your team.

When the smoke from the layoffs clears, start with a clean slate.

Reorganize your department as a part of the company's overall effort to reduce the workforce. Work with your remaining people to set some new goals, and look in some new, exciting directions. You might form some new teams, with new initiatives. Involve your workers as much as possible, and assure them that they're important to the company and its long-term objectives.

Here's How It Works

I'm sure you can understand how workers feel after watching their colleagues being laid off. Some of these people, no doubt, were friends of some who are left behind. Don't think for a minute that the people remaining aren't on the phone at night, listening to friends and former co-workers bad-mouth the company and its management.

Workers who get laid off might be resentful against the company, and understandably so. Remaining employees can be poisoned by the attitudes of the laid-off workers if you don't combat the negative talk.

It may take several explanations until the remaining workers begin to accept the reasons why their friends and co-workers had to be let go. It's extremely important that they're made to feel valuable and that they're contributing to the success of the company. Encourage them to come up with some ideas for increasing production, finding new customers, or improving customer service. Be sure to recognize and reward them when they do. Very importantly, be sure to share all the information that indicates conditions are improving.

Some big companies lay off hundreds of people but never bother to change the way they do business. As a result, the business doesn't become successful, and the layoffs were in vain.

If layoffs happen at your company, keep the following suggestions in mind:

➤ Make the work experience as positive as possible for the workers who survive layoffs.

➤ Assure workers (if you can) that the layoffs are over and work will continue as usual.

➤ Change the routine and try new things to jump-start momentum and get everybody's minds off what has occurred.

➤ Don't lie. If you know there are more layoffs down the road, don't tell your team that everything's rosy. Don't be a prophet of gloom, but don't lie.

Layoffs are tough, no doubt about it. But by being sensitive to the needs and feelings of your team, you can all get through them.

Motivating When the Place Is Shutting Down

Whew! Layoffs are tough to get through, but shutdowns are even worse.

The stickiest thing about shutdowns is that you need to keep your team motivated to do their best right up until the end. That's because you need their help.

When a business shuts down, there's hardly ever anybody happy. Maybe the owner, if he's finally getting out of it after 40 years to retire to an Italian villa, or just to spend his days fishing from his bass boat. Maybe a few employees, who never really liked their jobs and now have a great excuse to leave and some severance pay to boot.

Generally, though, it's not a happy bunch of campers during the closing weeks of a business.

In some cases, watching a business close down can be like watching a loved one die. People invest a lot of their lives in the companies for which they work. It's not uncommon to feel betrayed or abandoned when the place shuts down.

Here's How It Works

A friend recently lost her job after 16 years with a company that contracts physical therapy services. The entire division she worked for was shut down, with hundreds of layoffs resulting. What angered her the most was management's failure to address the issue at all with employees, either before or after the closing. Rumors were flying everywhere, and everyone knew something was about to happen. Management, however, chose to ignore the situation, as it applied to employees. Its decision to handle the closing that way has created a great deal of bad will and hard feelings among the people who lost their jobs.

To make this painful experience as painless as possible, get your workers to help you plan the transition. Let them be involved with the mechanics of closing down the company, and invest them in the process. And you should get involved with wherever they're heading after their jobs end. Be sure they know that an orderly shutdown and a willingness to stick things out will help them tremendously when they're interviewed for employment elsewhere.

Let your team know that you're going to help them find new jobs after the shutdown is over. And explain to them that it's to their benefit to stay on and help with the work of shutting down the plant.

If they do that, it will demonstrate several things to prospective employers:

➤ They're loyal to the company, even in the worst of times.

➤ They're disciplined and able to stay on a difficult course.

➤ They can be counted on to pitch in when the chips are down.

If your workers understand this, they'll be a lot more willing to stick around and put forth a good effort during the shut down.

Put your money where your mouth is. Bring in people to help your workers prepare résumés, brush up on interview skills, or even get technological or other types of training that might better qualify them for other jobs.

Advise everyone that the effort to place them elsewhere will continue after the shutdown.

Motivating During Salary Cuts

If you're going to cut salaries, make sure that yours is among the casualties.

When Lee Iacocca was working to turn Chrysler around, he worked for a $1 annual salary. His willingness to do that was a smart move because it prevented resentment among workers and made the pay-gap problem nonexistent. Of course, everyone knew Iococca wasn't going to starve to death by not taking a salary—his gesture was largely symbolic. Still, it illustrated that everyone would be involved with the cutbacks, not just the average workers.

Rally the Troops

Be painfully aware of the effect that cutting workers' salaries might have on their lives. Many people live basically from paycheck to paycheck, and a reduction in that paycheck hits real hard. Don't expect them to be happy about it, and don't minimize what they might be feeling and how it impacts their lives.

Explain to your team that sacrificing some salary now will make it possible to avoid layoffs and for them to experience gain sharing in the future. Tell them the salary will be replaced at some future point, although do not specify exactly when unless you're 100 percent sure you'll be able to meet the date.

It's not easy to maintain your credibility, much less their motivation, when you've got to cut people's salaries. Don't apologize for doing what needs to be done. Assure your workers that bad times don't last forever, and that you're doing all you can to save the organization and as many jobs as possible. Let them know that you're all in it together.

Other Factors That Create Tough Times

In most cases, poor economic conditions are responsible for the most serious and potentially devastating problems in the workplace.

There are, however, other problems that can undermine motivation and make your team less-than-willing to do their best. Let's have a look at a few situations that are bound to result in problems and how you can deal with them as a leader.

Motivating When the Boss Is an Idiot

If your boss is an idiot, you've got a big problem to overcome. However, it's not an impossible situation.

I'm currently working with a client company that has an idiot CEO. Executives who are below him in rank are constantly forced to endure his condescending behavior, and to serve as buffers between the big boss and the rest of the management team.

It's a bad situation, but smart managers will learn to work around the idiot.

Let the idiot boss rant and rave, scream and shout, or do whatever else appeals to him. Once he goes away, you can get down to business and do what needs doing.

Tell your team that you intend to stand up for them when necessary. Team members need to be able to count on you to be their advocate and to shield them from an unreasonable person who happens to be at the top of the food chain within your company.

Give the idiot lip service and ear service, but go ahead and do what you need to do to get your work done and keep your department on track. Get close to other managers and run the company around the idiot. My client company, for instance, schedules secret meetings off premises, during which officials figure out how they'll keep things running effectively despite the CEO. These managers also are working to cultivate relationships with the board of directors, and letting board members know what's going on.

Backfire

Be very careful to not be too obvious about your dislike for a boss. Don't for instance, blatantly bad-mouth him in front of your team. You can say something like, "As you know, I don't always see eye-to-eye with John's policies." But you can't say, "John's a big, fat windbag, and his polices are the stupidest things I've ever seen." You get it. Big difference!

Eventually, the idiot will fall, and the company can get back to business without the problems he causes.

Be your team's advocate, but don't forget that you're not one of them. You'll need to maintain some middle ground between your workers and the idiot boss.

Hey! You Just Fired My Best Buddy!

Firing somebody is always tricky, for a lot of reasons.

If the person fired was a popular, one-of-the-gang, good-guy employee, the other workers won't be happy. If he was a real jerk, chances are *he* won't be happy, and you could be looking at legal challenges, or whatever.

Firing is a real test of leadership skills, and you've got to take steps to make it as small a hurdle as possible.

If you have to fire somebody who was popular among co-workers, or who was particularly close to one or a group of co-workers, you'll probably need to address the issue.

You can't fire Suzanne, for instance, and then go on with your business like nothing happened, while Suzanne's lunch crowd is banging on your door, demanding to know why you axed their buddy.

If that happens, you'll need to talk to them. Keep conversations informal, and leak necessary information if you have to. Don't call any meetings or do anything that suggests formal discussion. Tell them during casual dialogue that you liked Suzanne and you were sorry to see her go, but sometimes differences of opinion occur and matters can't be resolved.

Tell them that you liked Suzanne, but you had to fire her because:

➤ She had violated company policy after several warnings.

➤ Her behavior was not in the best interests of the entire team.

➤ She was not willing to conform to the expectations of management.

➤ She wasn't doing the job she was hired to do.

➤ She had broken a law, and so on.

Backfire

Don't tell more than you need to because the information could come back to haunt you. If you confidentially tell some workers that Tom was fired because the big boss couldn't stand his body piercings, for instance, look out. That information could give Tom legal grounds to challenge the firing and get you in serious trouble with the big boss.

Explain in general terms why Suzanne was fired, but don't go into great detail. Don't give employees a chance to misinterpret what you're saying, and don't get into a position where you're defending your actions.

Tell them why their friend was fired and close the conversation. Make sure they understand that the decision to get rid of Suzanne was not a personal one, and don't bad-mouth her.

Hey! You Just Fired a Really Good Guy!

If your team thinks you fired a really good guy, and they don't know the reasons behind it, you might be the target of some resentment and anger.

People tend to view situations as how they appear on the surface without bothering to look deeper. We all know, however, that things are seldom as they appear.

Jim was a good guy with whom I worked back in ancient times, when we both were just starting our careers.

We both were employed as technical trainers, and Jim was good at it. Unfortunately, he made a bad mistake that pretty much derailed his career.

While going through a tough divorce, Jim got way too close to some of his female trainees. Two of the women complained about his behavior to our boss, and Jim soon was transferred to a terrible job in one of the company's Siberias. He left the company soon after.

A lot of employees who'd worked with Jim complained bitterly when he was transferred. They really liked the guy and knew that he was good at what he did. They didn't, however, know the rest of the story (where's Paul Harvey when you need him?), and nobody was willing to tell them.

Management took the brunt of the employees' anger and resentment about Jim, and many of his former co-workers never did find out what had really happened.

If you're forced to fire a really good guy, you'll need to just take the heat. As with firing a friend, don't tell more than necessary, and don't open the subject to debate.

Handling Sticky Situations

Let's face it. Workplaces are full of sticky situations. Personality conflicts. Hirings and firings. Promotions and demotions.

When a sticky situation is threatening your team's motivation, it's usually best to address it, but not always head-on.

Here's How It Works

If there's a sticky situation going on within your team that's disrupting work and/or morale, deal with it quickly. If Mary and John are having an affair, for instance, and everybody is abuzz about it to the point that productivity is down, address only the productivity issue. Don't talk about the affair with anyone, especially John and Mary, and more especially, not with their co-workers. Simply find another job in another department for either John or Mary. Don't make the transfer a choice, just tell them that's the way it will be.

I don't blame Jim's boss for not sitting everybody down and telling them about Jim's inability to control his amorous impulses toward certain female trainees. What he should have done, however, is made sure that word about how Jim had acted inappropriately leaked out. Why? Because management was taking the rap for Jim's screw-up. Employees were angry at management for getting rid of Jim because they didn't know that Jim had acted like a jerk. Had they known the reason he was transferred, they would have been able to understand why it was necessary.

I mentioned earlier that selective leaking of information within a workplace is not difficult to accomplish. All Jim's boss would have had to do was to catch the office gossip in the coffee room and mutter a few sentences about Jim. That's it.

If a sticky situation involves a business matter, like rumors of layoffs, or the plant shutting down, your best bet is to address the issue.

Never try to pretend that everything is okay when it isn't. Your team will find out soon enough, and you'll lose credibility for not leveling with them. Deal with it, and have a plan in place for your team members. Remember, it's your job to take care of them.

Bad times are tough to deal with, there's no question about it. Remember, though, that all companies, and all leaders, go through bad times. If they're weak, and can't deal with the pressures caused by these times, they may fold. If they're strong, however, they'll get through them, and maybe even come out stronger.

The Least You Need to Know

➤ Bad times happen for various reasons, but sooner or later, they always happen.

➤ Many bad times are caused by economic problems, but they can result from other situations as well.

➤ If layoffs are necessary, try to get them over with quickly and all at once.

➤ Be understanding and reassuring to the workers who aren't laid off but are worried about those who were dismissed and about their own job security.

➤ If your company is shutting down, make your team understand that it's to their advantage to hang in to the end.

➤ Try to make your workers understand that the sacrifice of salary cuts will be worthwhile in the long run.

➤ Bad times can result from noneconomic reasons, such as a really terrible boss.

➤ Sticky situations pop up in workplaces, and should be dealt with quickly and effectively.

Chapter 25

Keeping Motivation High When Things Are Just Ho-Hum

> ### In This Chapter
>
> ➤ Watching out for ordinary circumstances that can undercut motivation
>
> ➤ Being on constant lookout for the status quo
>
> ➤ Keeping your operation from being ho-hum
>
> ➤ Encouraging employees to identify and solve problems
>
> ➤ Fixing what's not broken to keep it healthy
>
> ➤ Getting and keeping workers involved with what's going on

You've learned in the past two chapters that good times can threaten motivation, and the bad times threaten it even more.

Well, hang on for one more chapter, because now I'm going to tell you that even middle-of-the-road, ho-hum times can bring down your team.

Yeah, I know. You're probably sitting there right now, shaking your head and wondering just what the heck I'm talking about. How can ordinary working conditions threaten the morale and motivation of your team?

The keyword here is ordinary. Ordinary, as in boring. As in, "Let's just do the job without thinking much about it." As in dangerous.

When times are good, and there's lots of work with lots of pay, your team gets pumped up. Its adrenaline kicks in. Sure, the excitement dies down after while, and that's when you start getting complaints about enforced overtime and that sort of thing.

If you're a smart manager, you'll capitalize on the initial energy and extend it by providing extra incentives for tired, overworked employees.

When times are bad, your team is motivated by its survival instincts. You need to direct the motivation by dealing with layoffs, salary cuts, and other problems, but when done properly, you can harness your team's anxieties and keep it operating effectively.

When everything is just going along, however, you have neither the excitement of the good times nor the anxiety of the bad times to fuel your team. As a result, it tends to slow down, and sometimes even runs out of gas.

It's easy to settle into the ho-hum routine, especially if you've just been through extraordinary times—either good or bad. It's a relief to just coast along for a while instead of riding the roller coaster of ups and downs. What you need to be aware of, though, is how quickly your team can become demotivated during these ho-hum times.

In this chapter, you'll learn how to keep motivation high during these ordinary times.

Smart managers use these times to undertake things you can't do when you're putting out fires during bad times, or trying to keep everybody together during good times. You'll work to improve procedures, increase productivity, and come up with new systems where necessary.

You'll involve your team in all these efforts, keeping them invested in the goals and operating at peak capacity.

Nothing Destroys Motivation Like the Status Quo

The status quo is one of the most dangerous traps of the workplace.

It causes us and our workers to grow lazy and inattentive. It allows us to coast along, ignoring the rocks and rapids along the way. The status quo is bad news.

When we get lazy, we get careless, and that provides the perfect setting for trouble. The trouble can come from within, but more than likely it will come from outside the organization.

While you're not looking, a competitor builds unanticipated strength, or the markets shift and you're left out in the cold, or a new technology pops up and you don't take advantage of it.

Even the mighty Microsoft was caught napping when the Internet hit (remember the discussion from Chapter 1?) and had to scurry like rabbits escaping a hound to catch up. Fortunately for

Defining Moments

The **status quo** is the existing state of affairs at any specified time. Most commonly, it refers to ordinary, ho-hum situations in which there are no extraordinary circumstances.

Microsoft, it had the resources (such as billions in the bank) and know-how to do that. Other companies may not have had the opportunity and means to rebound.

Recognizing When Status Quo Is About to Hit

Generally, we all have pretty short memories. We forget about bad times almost as soon as they're over. Maybe it's a defense mechanism, who knows?

When things are good, we forget that it takes work to maintain good times and we slide into status-quo mode. It's like the captain of a ship guiding his boat through untroubled waters. Nothing is visible on the horizon. No dangers are in sight. Nobody is anticipating any danger and most of the crew has turned in for the night. As far as the captain is concerned, this tranquil journey will last forever. All of a sudden, the wind picks up, the sea gets rough, and the surprised captain knows he's in for one heck of a storm.

The same thing happens with unprepared teams and their leaders. You're going along on cruise control, enjoying the ride, and taking things as they come. All of a sudden you find out that your biggest competitor has wooed away one of your best customers and is planning to enlarge his manufacturing facilities. Yikes!

It's difficult to know exactly when the status quo will hit your team, but it's good to be constantly on the lookout. If you notice that your workers seem a little bored, a little too laid-back, or generally uninterested, look out. You might be heading for a run in with status quo.

Ducking the Status Quo Missile

The best way to avoid the status quo missile is to keep your team active and on the lookout for the always-inevitable change that sooner or later will occur. Moving targets are hard to hit, and a team that's busy and involved isn't likely to be a sitting duck for status quo.

Discourage your team from the idea that status quo is good. As I said earlier, status quo can seem like a good deal after your company has gone through extraordinary times. But watch out. When everybody sits back and breathes a big, collective sigh of relief that things are "back to normal," you can be pretty sure that a status quo missile is heading your way.

Backfire

One of the most obvious signs that status quo has engulfed your team is the cry of "But we've always done it this way." If you hear this among your workers, you'd better do something quick to inspire their creativity and get things moving.

To duck the status quo missile, focus constantly on the idea of continuous improvement. Don't be content, and don't let your team be content to have things remain as they are.

Make sure that the following responsibilities are clearly understood by everyone on your team and that everyone works to fulfill them.

➤ Team members have the responsibility to do the job.

➤ Team members have the responsibility to define what should be done to improve the job.

➤ Team members have the responsibility to come with ways to cause the improvements to occur.

➤ Team members have the responsibility to implement the approved improvements they design.

If everyone understands and buys into these responsibilities as goals, you'll have a motivated team that's seeking continuous improvement.

And that's a team that the status quo missile will never be able to hit.

Avoiding a Ho-Hum Operation

Anything can be improved upon. The minute you start thinking you've got the perfect operation, you're at risk of falling into the ho-hum trap.

As a leader, you need to encourage creativity among the members of your team. And remember, you never can tell from where, or whom, the best ideas will come.

Among my clients is an insurance company that encourages its employees to be creative and come up with new and better ways of doing things. This attitude paid off with a good idea for improvement coming from an unlikely source.

As you probably know, a signed application for a policy, along with the actual policy once it's issued, is a pretty important document to an insurance company. I mean, without applications, you're not going to generate new business, and you know what that means. Along with the actual policies, the signed applications also serve as records, and are used frequently in the course of working on claims, renewals, and so forth. Because these are such important documents, the originals are normally kept secured within designated areas of the company. These areas are commonly called the "app-vault" departments.

In my client company, managers are asked to rank their departments as part of a company-wide "total quality initiative."

A while back, when the reviews were done, managers of the app-vault department gave their team the highest possible rankings in every category. Now, this should have spelled trouble to somebody. Red flags should have been going up all over the place.

But the rankings went unchallenged, except by an 18-year-old clerk who worked in the department.

Abby, let's call her, thought her department had room for improvement. She wasn't afraid to say so, and she did so in a constructive manner that caught the attention of management. She also had ideas to back up her criticisms of the department, which gave her credibility that someone offering criticism without suggestions for improvement wouldn't have.

You see, Abby had a different perspective than the other members of the department. While most people within the department worked only within the department, as the clerk, Abby had contact with people from all over the company. It was her job to provide the signed application forms to people in various departments within the company who needed them for whatever purposes.

Backfire

We sometimes tend to overlook employees who are new, or very young, and that's a big mistake. Often, these workers have fresh outlooks on what's going on and can see things that others have stopped looking at. Don't make the mistake of not being receptive to bright, young employees.

It wasn't an easy process for people who wanted them to get their hands on these forms. A request had to be filed, then processed, then the application pulled from the stack.

After that, the person who'd requested the form was notified that it was available. This sometimes took a day, sometimes even two days. Abby was the only one in the app-vault department who understood how frustrating this delay was to the people who needed the forms to do their work. She heard all the complaints and knew that her department had a terrible reputation among other workers in the company.

Abby was very diligent, and this situation upset her. To her, the people in the other departments were her customers. Every time one of them complained, she felt she was letting down a customer.

The more complaints she heard, the more Abby became convinced that her department needed to improve the way it handled its responsibilities.

She convinced her boss to conduct a study of what the "customers" wanted, and to see how the department was perceived by the rest of the staff.

The results were devastating to the app-vault department, which was abruptly knocked from its seat of complacency.

Results of the study showed everyone what Abby already knew. The app-vault department was held in low regard by almost everyone within the company. People in other departments perceived that the app-vault staff was lazy, slow, arrogant, and unresponsive.

Rally the Troops

If somebody comes up with a suggestion or plan that results in beneficial changes within a department, or even the entire company, make sure he's suitably recognized and rewarded. Some companies recognize "employees of the month," or give awards for the most innovative ideas. Those are good ways to encourage workers to be creative and to keep their motivation high.

So much for app-vault management's highest rankings on the total quality improvement evaluation.

It must have been extremely satisfying for Abby when the department managers called for a complete overview of its procedures. The necessary changes were made, and soon the department was turning around the applications in an average of two hours instead of two days.

It's reputation greatly improved throughout the company, and everyone was able to work more efficiently because of the quicker turnaround of these important documents.

Abby showed herself to be a high-performance employee, and managed to help her department out of its ho-hum situation. She upset the status quo, and, as a result, everyone benefited.

A good leader will make identifying things that need to be changed part of the normal job of every employee. Everyone should always be looking with a critical eye at how the department is organized and run. Remember that there's no such thing as a bad suggestion. There are great suggestions, unusable suggestions, and off-the-wall suggestions, but every suggestion should be considered.

Any employee who does only the routine job without ever giving a thought to how it could be done differently, or better, should be defined as doing less than the minimum job requirements. Employees like Abby, who come up with suggestions that improve conditions, should be recognized, rewarded, and constantly encouraged.

Sometimes You've Gotta Fix What's Not Broken

If you hear a strange noise in your car but it seems to be running okay, what do you do?

Some people will immediately have the noise checked out. They want to see what's causing it and whether it's indicative of a problem.

Others will ignore it. They'll keep driving along like they never heard a thing. Noise? What noise?

Well, you know what happens. The people who get their cars checked out learn either one of two things. One—the noise is meaningless, at which point they go about their business, reassured that nothing is wrong. Or two—the noise means that, yes indeed, the engine is just about to seize up and render the car worthless. In that case, they have the car fixed, thereby saving the engine and their means of transportation.

The other people, those who ignore the noise, might find out by default that the noise is meaningless. Or they'll find out when the engine seizes up that they should have had the noise checked out.

The point of all this is that sometimes you've gotta fix what's not broken. A noise doesn't necessarily indicate a problem, but it might. We do, or should do, all kinds of things that are preventive.

We exercise, eat properly, and take vitamins so we can stay healthy. We don't drink and drive, so that we don't hurt ourselves or anyone else. We wear seat belts. We get vaccinations. We get checkups to detect possible problems early on. We get our cars inspected. We wash fruits and vegetables before we eat them. We pay our taxes on time to prevent IRS agents from knocking on our doors.

We don't, or shouldn't, wait until something happens and then react. We're proactive.

Here's How It Works

If you can motivate your team to anticipate problems and be proactive, you'll be doing its members a great service, and not only as far as their jobs are concerned. Being aware and proactive are desirable characteristics for people in all circumstances—not just the workplace.

We should think about managing our teams in the same way. When Abby persuaded her boss to really find out what was going on, and how the app-vault department was regarded by other employees, she fixed something before it broke.

It was only a matter of time until the situation had exploded and general revolt against the department and its deplorable service broke out. Abby averted a major problem with her creativity and ingenuity. She was proactive.

But Abby's a high-performance employee who didn't need much encouragement to see that something needed to be done, and come up with a way to do it. How do you, as a leader, encourage your team to get involved with fixing things before they break? Let's have a look.

Getting and Keeping the Team Involved

To get and keep your team involved with preventive maintenance and fixing things before they break, start with a list of "doables."

Defining Moments

Doables are all the things that can be done to create improvement within your department. Some will be simple and others will be complicated, but all are possible and can be accomplished.

Every team should have such a list, which is exactly what it says it is. It's a list of things that can or should be done. Not things that are *being* done, but things that *could* be done.

When my kids were small, I encouraged them to be can-do kids. Can-do kids, I told them, are kids who don't complain or give up when they have trouble with something they're trying to do. Can-do kids think the problem through and come up with another way to do whatever they're trying to do.

Say, for instance, that Johnny wants to get his dad a present for his birthday. He really wants to get him a birdhouse, in fact, because his dad loves birds and has been wanting a house. The problem is, the birdhouse Johnny knows his dad would just love costs $50, and Johnny only has $30.

If Johnny's a no-can-do kid, he'll whine and feel sorry for himself, and carry on about not having enough money to buy the birdhouse. If Johnny's a can-do kid, he'll figure out a way to get the birdhouse. Maybe he'll offer to mow a couple of lawns, or pull some weeds, or walk a dog for a few dollars. Or maybe he'll buy a kit for $30 and build a birdhouse for his dad.

Anyway, you get the idea, and the same idea applies to your workers. If they're encouraged to be can-do people, they'll figure out ways that things can be done. Their "doable" lists will be long and challenging.

Ideally, a "doable" list will always contain more items than there's time or resources to do.

A big benefit of such a list is that it allows you to look at what can be done and prioritize what should happen first. Once you've decided what "doable" you want to tackle, follow these steps:

➤ Examine no-cost or low-cost ideas for implementation. What can be done to implement the "doable" with the resources that are already on hand?

➤ Break down the "doable" into small, bite-size pieces, and start by doing one piece.

➤ Examine your progress often, and decide whether or not to continue.

➤ Constantly add more "doables" to the list.

To make sure everyone is involved, keep the "doable" list public and prominent.

Let everyone know what's going on, who's doing it, and how it's getting accomplished. It's a good idea to allow the people working on "doables" to share their progress with the rest of the team. This not only allows other team members to know the techniques and mechanics of a project, but it encourages them to undertake their own projects.

The feeling tends to be, "Well, gee, if Roger can do that, I don't see why I wouldn't be able to do it." And that's good.

If you're assigning "doables," organize a team and then assign a project to the team.

However, don't assign a leader. Allow the team to begin work, and watch who evolves as the leader. Don't worry—somebody will.

Here's How It Works

You'll be able to get a good idea of who the natural leaders of your team are by watching how people work in groups. If you don't assign a leader, somebody will take charge. It may not happen immediately, but eventually someone will emerge as the person in charge. Sometimes, a group will assign a leader. If that happens, it's still indicative of who the natural leaders are because co-workers recognize that quality in each other.

Be sure to reward your team for the progress it makes on its "doables" list. When a project is successfully completed, everyone should share in the gain.

When "doable" is not completed as planned, the team should be held accountable. The more you put your team in charge of its "doable," the more invested individual members will be in making things happen.

To do this, resist the temptation to jump in at the first sign of trouble and tell your workers what they're doing wrong. Just as parents must sometimes let their children make mistakes, you've got to occasionally let the team fall on its face in order to motivate it to try again and find a better way.

If you get and keep your team involved with what's going on within your department, members will get into the habit of being creative and looking for better ways of doing things. You'll avoid getting stuck in the status quo and your operation won't become stale and ho-hum.

As a leader, total team involvement should be a top priority. Workers who are involved are most likely to be happy and motivated. And that's what it's all about.

The Least You Need to Know

➤ Ordinary times can be as threatening to your team's motivation as extraordinary times.

➤ It takes constant vigilance to keep the status quo from invading your operation.

➤ Encourage your team to identify problems and come up with and implement solutions.

➤ Reward employees who come up with creative solutions, and make sure the entire team benefits.

➤ Preventive work can't hurt, and sometimes it saves you a lot of trouble in the long haul.

➤ An involved, proactive team is a happy team; and a happy team is likely to be a motivated team.

Glossary

410(k) plans   Plans that allow employees to contribute a portion of their paychecks to a company investment plan. Very often, the employer matches a portion of the worker's contribution. 401(k)s, introduced in 1982 as a way for employers to save the money they'd been putting in pension plans, were named after the section of the tax code that created them.

Authenticity   The quality of being real. When something is authentic, it conforms to the facts that we believe about it.

Behavior   The outwardly visible result of attitude.

Code of conduct   The framework for behavior within an organization. Rules that establish expected behavior and the results of not adhering to those expectations.

Commission   A certain percentage of the amount of money taken in on sales that's paid to the person who made the sales.

Company culture   The collective set of attitudes and beliefs that influence and direct the way your team operates.

Conflict   An emotional disturbance that results from a clash of opposing goals, and the inability to determine which goals should be pursued.

Corporate character   The makeup, or personality, of a corporation.

Defining resource requirements   The process of figuring out what you need in order to accomplish your goals.

Destructive behavior   Harmful behavior that's directed outwardly, toward other people, objects, departments, or organizations.

Discipline   Correction, chastisement, or punishment inflicted by way of correction and training. Training that develops self-control, character, or orderliness and efficiency.

Doables   All the things that can, or should, be done to create improvement.

Driving force   A powerful feeling that, when used properly, can motivate people to realize their dreams and accomplish goals. On the flip side, a driving force not properly managed can be an unhealthy obsession.

Fact-finding   The process of gathering all the facts that pertain to a certain situation. It's used in various instances, including investigations into charges of wrongdoing.

Goals   The culmination of tasks performed successfully.

Incentive   A specific amount of money, or other item of value, given to someone in return for certain behavior or actions.

Inquisitiveness   The quality that drives a person to learn more about a particular topic, or about everything, and what motivates someone to try to figure out a better way to complete a task.

Karoshi   A Japanese word that means "death by overwork." Thousands of Japanese workers succumb to karoshi every year.

Listening   The accurate perception of what is being communicated.

Matrix management system   A dotted-line, informal reporting structure, designed to give necessary attention to products or projects. The system pulls developments off to the side of the traditional business structure or standard line organization in order to give them special attention.

Model change system   A system that halts project design at an assigned time. Any additional changes and enhancements are worked into a new model of the project, and released at a future time.

Moderate risk   A roughly 15 percent chance that a particular venture will fail.

Motivation   An eternal, internal engine that drives us to do what we do. It is fueled by perception and imagination.

Negative incentives   Tools used to manipulate behavior that result in discomfort or punishment for certain, specific behavior or actions.

Orchestrate   To arrange, or to put something together. To organize a thing, or a group, so as to achieve a desired or effective result.

Participative management   The practice of enlisting the participation of employees or other groups to help define, manage, and solve problems.

Positive confrontations   Confrontations that address the impact of some action on the goals of your operation, without being critical of the person or persons who caused the action.

Positive incentives   Tools used to manipulate behavior by causing people to want to act in a particular manner, or to demonstrate specific behavior. Positive incentives generally involve some kind of award or recognition.

Security   The sense of being safe and cared for. Being able to anticipate what will occur, and what your responses will be. A feeling of being comfortable within your environment, without excessive doubt, anxiety, or fear.

Self-destructive behavior   Harmful behavior, either intentional or unintentional, that's directed inward and harms the person who displays the behavior.

Status quo   The existing state of affairs at any specified time. Generally refers to everyday, routine, and ordinary happenings.

Tasks   The steps necessary to complete in order to reach goals.

Value building   The process of continuously determining, defining, structuring, and creating additional profitability for the customer and yourself.

Additional Resources

Beck, Robert C. *Motivation: Theories and Principles.*

Bowen, Carolyn M., and George R. Perkins. *Energizing Employees.*

Boylan, Bob. *Get Everyone in Your Boat Rowing in the Same Direction: 5 Leadership Principles to Follow So Others Will Follow You.*

Cairo, Jim. *Motivation and Goal Setting: How to Set and Achieve Goals and Inspire Others.*

Campbell, Donald E. *Incentives: Motivation and the Economics of Information.*

Decatanzaro, Denys A. *Motivation and Emotion: Evolutionary, Physiological, Developmental, and Social Perspectives.*

Fazzi, Robert A. *Management Plus: Maximizing Productivity Through Motivation, Performance, and Commitment.*

Gilley, Jerry W., and Nathaniel W. Boughton. *Stop Managing, Start Coaching!: How Performance Coaching Can Enhance Commiment and Improve Productivity.*

Glanz, Barbara A. *Care Packages for the Workplace: Dozens of Little Things You Can Do to Regenerate Spirit at Work.*

Good, Sharon. *Managing with a Heart: 100+ Ways to Make Your Employees Feel Appreciated.*

Heermann, Barry, Ph.D. *Building Team Spirit: Activities for Inspiring and Energizing Teams.*

Heller, Robert, and Tim Hindle. *Motivating People.*

Hume, David A. *Reward Management: Employee Performance, Motivation and Pay.*

Klubnik, Joan P. *Rewarding and Recognizing Employees: Ideas for Individuals, Teams, and Managers.*

Knouse, Stephen B. *The Reward and Recognition Process in Total Quality Management.*

Losoncy, Lewis E. *The Motivating Team Leader.*

McKenzie, Richard B., and Dwight R. Lee. *Managing Through Incentives: How to Develop a More Collaborative, Productive, and Profitable Organization.*

Mendes, Anthony. *Inspiring Commitment: How to Win Employee Loyalty in Chaotic Times.*

Mook, Douglas G. *Motivation: The Organization of Action.*

Nelson, Bob. *1001 Ways to Energize Employees.*

Reeve, John M. *Motivating Others: Nurturing Inner Motivational Resources.*

Rye, David E. *1,001 Ways to Inspire: Your Organization, Your Team and Yourself.*

Scitovsky, Tibor. *The Joyless Economy: The Psychology of Human Satisfaction.*

Wenderlich, Raymond L. *The ABCs of Successful Leadership: Proven, Practical Attitudes, Behaviors & Concepts Based on Core Values That Result in Successful Leadership.*

Whitworth, Laura. *Co-Active Coaching: New Skills for Coaching People Toward Success in Work and Life.*

Internet Resources

BrainwareMedia. At www.brainware.com. A listing of videos, training programs, and other resources relating to motivating your team.

BusinessTown. At www.businesstown.com. Includes tips on getting the most out of your employees, and increasing the efficiency of your business through motivation, good communications, dealing effectively with employees, and more.

Creative Incentives. At www.logohere.com. Offers premium incentives used for increasing sales, motivating employees, introducing new products, and so forth.

Davis & Company. At www.davishays.com. Deals with employee communications, corporate communications, management consulting, and marketing. Also has samples of the Communications Strategy newsletter.

Directory Managing. At www.entamerica.com. A list of books and other publications dealing with motivating employees and workers.

Effectively Managing and Motivating People. At www.gday-mate.com. Sponsored by Townsend International, an Australian company, this site provides tips on motivating employees and effective use of human resources.

Essentially Yours. At www.eyicom.com. Promotes retention of employees and encourages team building.

H.E. Huhn Training Services, Ltd. At www.hhuhntraining.com. Provides listings of workshops for managers, leaders, and supervisors.

Human Resources Management Concentration. At http://bus.utexas.edu. Offered as part of the MBA program at the University of Texas at Austin, the site deals with finding, motivating, and keeping people with appropriate skills.

Leading Others. At www.srg.co.uk/srgmylo3.html. Relates to all aspects of leadership, empowerment, team building, delegation, coaching, influencing skills, motivation, and communication.

Learning Objectives. At www.csie.ncnu.edu. Deals with various aspects of motivating your team and organizational control.

Motivating Customer Service Employees. At www.alexcommgrp.com. A hands-on guide to improving morale, motivation, and productivity in your customer service department.

Motivating Without Money. At www.beam-intl.com. Provides tips on creating a motivated team using positive means.

Motivation Master. At http://motivationmaster.com. Deals with motivating for specific circumstances, such as selling, being a leader, getting out of debt, saving money, and so forth.

Motivational Moments. At www.motivateus.com. Contains inspirational quotes, related to business, grieving, everyday life, and more. Some of it is overly sentimental, but much is good and useable. The site is updated three times a week, and you can add your own quotes if you want to.

MSN Business Community. At http://communities.msn.com. A series of articles about motivating employees and related topics.

On With Learning. At http://videoed.com. Offers various videos that deal with motivating, training, and inspiring employees.

Rainmaker Thinking Inc. At www.rainmakerthinking.com. A site designed to help business leaders gain strategic advantage by recruiting, motivating, and retaining outstanding young talent. Also aimed at young people looking for strategies needed to get and keep jobs.

South Carolina State Library. At www.state.sc.us/scsl/pubs/motivate.html. Provides a list of materials on motivation that are available from this library.

The Training Registry. At www.tregistry.com. Includes information on motivation skills and other management/supervision-related resources.

TRI Performance Improvement Systems. At http://www.reinforce.com. Contains tips for motivating employees through recognition and involvement. Includes a performance handbook that can be downloaded, and free award certificates.

University of North Florida. At www.unf.edu. This site teaches how to make the members in your group want to do things, and to recognize that each one is motivated by different things. Also contains tips on how to criticize members of your team, and other topics.

Index

U-V

W